ECONOMIC AND SOCIAL COMMISSION FOR ASIA AND THE PACIFIC

SUSTAINABLE DEVELOPMENT OF WATER RESOURCES IN ASIA AND THE PACIFIC: AN OVERVIEW

UNITED NATIONS

New York , 1997

ST/ESCAP/1784

UNITED NATIONS PUBLICATION
Sales No. E.98.II.F.39

ISBN 92-1-119826-7

The designations employed and the presentation of the material in this publication do not imply the expression of any opinion whatsoever on the part of the Secretariat of the United Nations concerning the legal status of any country, territory, city or area, or of its authorities, or concerning the delimitation of its frontiers or boundaries.

This publication has been issued without formal editing.

SUSTAINABLE DEVELOPMENT OF WATER RESOURCES IN ASIA AND THE PACIFIC: AN OVERVIEW

Contents

Pages

List of tables

List of figures

Abbreviations

ABS	Alkyl benzene sulfonates
ADB	Asian Development Bank
ADB/N	Agricultural Development Bank of Nepal
AMD	Agriculture Mechanization Department
AMIS	Agency Managed Irrigation System
ASD	Agrarian Services Department
BADC	Bangladesh Agriculture Development Committee, Ministry of Agriculture
BAPPEDAS	Regional Planning Board
BAPPENAS	National Planning Board
bcm	Billion cubic metre
BIWTA	Bangladesh Inland Water Transport Authority
BOD	Biochemical oxygen demand
BWDB	Bangladesh Water Development Board
CBA	Cost-benefit analysis
CCCIM	Central Coordinating Committee on Irrigation Management
CCD	Coast Conservation Department
CEA	Central Environmental Authority
CEB	Ceylon Electricity Board
CGWB	Central Ground Water Board
CHRDU	Central Human Resources Development Unit
CISIR	Ceylon Institute of Scientific and Industrial Research
COAG	Council of Australian Governments
COD	Chemical oxygen demand
CPCB	Central Pollution Control Board
CWC	Central Water Commission
DENR	Department of Environmental and Natural Resources
DGWRD	Directorate General of Water Resources Development
DHM	Department of Hydrology and Meteorology
DID	Department of Irrigation and Drainage
DILG/LGUs	Department of Interior and Local Government/Local Government Units
DMI	Domestic, municipal and industrial
DMWHRW	Department for Management of Water Resources and Hydraulic Works
DO	Dissolved oxygen
DOA	Department of Agriculture
DOE	Department of Environment
DOEF	Department of Environment and Forests
DOI	Department of Irrigation
DOH	Department of Health
DOR	Department of Roads
DPHE	Department of Public Health Engineering
DPWH	Department of Public Works and Highways
DSCWM	Department of Soil Conservation and Watershed Management
DWSS	Department of Water Supply and Sewerage
EAC	Environmental Appraisal Committee
ECE	Economic Commission for Europe

i

EDF	Electricité de France
EIA	Environment Impact Assessment
EIS	Environmental Impact Statement
EMB	Environmental Management Bureau
EMC	Environmental Management Committee
EMP	Environmental Management Plan
EPA	Environmental Protection Agencies
EPC	Environmental Protection Council
EPL	Environmental Protection License
EPWAPDA	East Pakistan Water and Power Development Authority
EQS	Environmental quality standards
EU	European Union
FAO	Food and Agriculture Organization of the United Nations
FCDI	Flood control, drainage and irrigation
FD	Fishery Department
FMB	Forest Management Bureau
FMIS	Farmers' Managed Irrigation System
FO	Field Office
FOs	Farmer organizations
GAP	Ganga Action Plan
GDP	Gross domestic product
GEMS	Global Environmental Monitoring System
GLOFs	Glacier lake outburst floods
GMS	Geostationary Meteorological Satellite
GNP	Gross national product
GOI	Government of India
GW	Gegawatt
GWh (GWH)	Gegawatt hours
HDI	Human Development Index
HRD	Human Resources Development
IAD	Impact Assessment Division
ICPC	Indian Centre for Promotion of Clean Technology
ID	Irrigation Department
IDA	International Development Association
IIMI	International Irrigation Management Institute
ILC	Irrigation Land of Credit
IMD	Irrigation Management Division
IMP	Irrigation Management Project
IQQM	Integrated Quantity/Quality Model
ISF	Irrigation service fee
ISP	Irrigation sector project
ISSP	Irrigation sector support project
IUCN	International Union for the Conservation of Nature and Natural Resources
IWK	Indah Water Konsortium
JICA	Japan International Cooperation Agency

LGED	Local Government Engineering Department
lpcd	Litre per capita per day
LWUA/WDs	Local Water Utilities Administration/Water Districts
MAF	Million acre-feet
MARD	Ministry of Agriculture and Rural Development
MASL	Mahaweli Authority of Sri Lanka
MB	Megabyte
MBAS	Methylene Blue Alkyl Substance
MCM/day	Million cubic metres per day
MDBC	Murray-Darling Basin Commission
MEA	Mahaweli Economic Agency
Mha	Million hectares
MHPP	Ministry of Housing and Physical Planning
MIPE	Ministry of Irrigation, Power and Energy (Sri Lanka)
MLD	Million litres per day
MOC	Ministry of Construction and Urban Development
MOEF	Ministry of Environment and Forests
MOH	Ministry of Health
MOHI	Ministry of Heavy Industry
MPI	Ministry of Planning and Investment
mPN/dl	Maximum probable number per decilitre (or 100 ml)
MRC	Mekong River Commission
MWA	Mahaweli Authority (of Sri Lanka)
MWR	Ministry of Water Resources
MWSS	Metropolitan Water Supply and Sewerage System
NARA	National Aquatic Resources Agency
NBRO	National Building Research Organization
NARESA	National Resources Energy and Science Authority
NCEA	National Committee on Environmental Affairs
NCSS	National Conservation Strategy Secretariat
NCP	North Central Province
NDC	National Development Council
NDP	National Drainage Programme
NEA	Nepal Electricity Authority
NEDA	National Economic and Development Authority
NEM	New Economic Mechanism
NESC	National Environmental Steering Committee
NGOs	Non-governmental organizations
NIA	National Irrigation Administration
NIMI	National Irrigation Management Institute
NIS	National irrigation system
NLP	National Landcare Programme
NPC	National Planning Commission
NPD	National Planning Department
NPI	New or proposed industry
NRAP	National River Action Plan
NRMC	Natural Resources Management Centre
NRMS	Natural Resources Management Strategy
NSCC	National Water Supply Sector Coordination Committee

NSW	New South Wales
NWFP	North West Frontier Province
NWP	National Water Plan
NWRB	National Water Resources Board
NWRDC	National Water Resources Development Council
NWS & DB	National Water Supply and Drainage Board
NWSC	Nepal Water Supply Corporation
O & M	Operation and maintenance
OECF	Overseas Economic Cooperation Fund
OEI	Old or existing industry
PCBs	Polychlorinated biphenyls
PCU	Platinum Cobalt Unit
P.D.	Presidential Decree
PDAMS	Water Supply Regional Companies
PIP	Public Investment Programme
PJP-II	Second 25-year (1994-2019) Development Plan
ppm	Parts per million
PPP	Public-private partnership
PSP	Private sector participation
PSTW	Private sector tubewells
PTWs	Private tubewells
PWD	Public Works Department
R & R	Resettlement and rehabilitation
RBW	Receiving Body of Water
REPELITA VI	Sixth 5-year Development Plan
RVP	River valley projects
RWSD	Rural Water Supply Division
SAZDA	Sindh Arid Zone Development Authority
SCOR	Share Control of Resources
SLR & DC	Sri Lanka Land Reclamation and Development Board
SOB	Survey of Bangladesh
SS	Suspended solids
SWS	Satuan Wilayah Sungai (River Basin Approach)
TA	Technical assistance
TAC	Technical Advisory Committee
TCM	Total Catchment Management
TFAP	Tropical Forestry Action Plan
UNDP	United Nations Development Programme
UNICEF	United Nations Children's Fund
USAID	United States Agency for International Development
UWSD	Urban Water Supply Department
WADCO	Water Resources Development Consultants
WALMI	Water and Land Management Institutes
WAPDA	Water and Power Development Authority

WARPO	Water Resources Planning Organization
WASA	Water and Sewerage Authority
WC	Watercourses
WECS	Water Energy Commission Secretariat
WHO	World Health Organization
WP & P	Water Planning and Projects
WRB	Water Resources Board
WRC	Water Resources Council
WRD	Water Resources Development (Division, Sri Lanka)
WRDM	Water resources development and management
WRM	Water resources management
WUA	Water Users' Association
WUCs	Water Users' Committees
WUGs	Water User Groups

v

I. INTRODUCTION

Fresh water is a renewable but finite resource. The scale of its development and use therefore must not exceed certain limits if ecological balance is to be maintained. These limits are generally determined by the rates of recovery, that is, both the regenerative rate of the hydrological cycle as well as the assimilative capacities of receiving water bodies.

The main principle for the sustainable development of water resources is that the rate of extraction both from ground and surface water sources should not exceed the rate at which the resource is renewed and its extraction must not jeopardize the biodiversity of the ecosystem. For example, the extraction of surface water upstream should not adversely affect the biodiversity of the river downstream.

In almost all countries in Asia and the Pacific there have been growing environmental problems due to unsustainable use and development of water resources. Pollution of fresh water has also become a major environmental problem. Asian rivers are badly polluted and renewable freshwater resources are dwindling as a result. Besides, overuse of groundwater is adversely affecting the availability of safe drinking water in Pacific countries.

Growing scarcity and misuse of fresh water pose a serious threat to sustained socio-economic development in countries of the ESCAP region. At the United Nations Conference on Environment and Development held at Rio de Janeiro in June 1992, a blueprint for action for global sustainable development into the twenty-first century called Agenda 21 was adopted. According to Article 18.2 of this Agenda, "Water is needed in all aspects of life. The general objective is to make certain that adequate supplies of water of good quality are maintained for the entire population of this planet, while preserving the hydrological, biological and chemical functions of ecosystems, adapting human activities within the capacity limits of nature and combating vectors of water-related diseases". Article 18.6 of the Agenda also said, "The holistic management of fresh water as finite and vulnerable resource, and the integration of sectoral water plans and programmes within the framework of national economic and social policy, are of paramount importance for action in the 1990s and beyond".

Recognizing the importance of sustainable development of water resources for the sustained socio-economic growth of countries in the region, the ESCAP secretariat has undertaken a project on the establishment of guidelines on water and sustainable development with the funding assistance from the Government of the Netherlands. Under this project an Ad Hoc Expert Group Meeting on Sustainable Development of Water Resources was held in Bangkok from 10 to 12 July 1996 to assess the status of sustainable development of water resources in countries of the region as well as to discuss and agree on the contents of the guidelines on water and sustainable development. Subsequently, the draft guidelines were prepared by the ESCAP secretariat with the assistance of a consultant. These were reviewed and adopted at a Seminar on the Establishment of Guidelines on Water and Sustainable Development held in Bangkok from 9 to 13 December 1996.

The present publication is a review of the situation of water resources development and use in the region based on the situation in individual countries as presented and discussed by country experts at the above two meetings. It should be found useful for both decision makers and professionals in the field of water development and management in drawing on the experience of some countries which are leaders in certain aspects of water development and management.

II. STATUS OF SUSTAINABLE DEVELOPMENT OF WATER RESOURCES IN THE ESCAP REGION

A. Water resources availability and use in the ESCAP region

A general picture of water resources availability and use in the region is given in table 1. In this connection, the water resources availability refers to the annual internal renewable water resources (ground and surface water) excluding river flow from other countries. The water resources use refers to the annual water withdrawal both from ground and surface water sources.

The water resources availability and use in the region vary widely for different countries depending on their respective physiographic conditions as well as socio-economic development. The region has some of the world's most important river systems. Seven of Asia's largest river systems, namely the Changhua Jiang, Huang He, Mekong, Ayeyarwady, Brahmaputra, Ganges and Indus, have a total drainage area of more than 6 million square kilometres, much of which is heavily populated. Therefore, the economic development and the welfare of people in the region are very dependent on the progress made in the development and management of its water resources.

The most meaningful measure of freshwater resources is the total annual flow of rivers and the recharge to aquifers, that is the annual amount of renewable water resources. The total volume of run-off on earth is estimated to be between 41,000 km^3 and 46,000 km^3 per year. The share of Asia and the Pacific is about 13,260 km^3, comprising between 29 and 32 per cent of the global total.

It should be noted that users can obtain only part of the renewable water resources from water bodies, owing to the high variability of stream flow between low water and flood seasons and the lack of storage sites on many catchments. Since a large part of the run-off, occurring in the form of flood flows of relatively short duration, runs out to sea unarrested, the volume of usable flow is substantially less than the total renewable water resources. Moreover, much of the water resources are available in remote areas where it is difficult and uneconomic to undertake development activities. For example, it is estimated that in Australia

only 100 km^3 out of a total of 398 km^3 of annual renewable water resources can be considered exploitable for use on a sustained basis.

The total amount of annual water withdrawal in Asia and the Pacific region is roughly estimated at 1,677 km^3, accounting for about a quarter of the global total.

In general, the ratio of water use to water availability may be taken as an indicator of the degree of water scarcity in a particular situation. It is estimated that water tends to become a limiting factor in national socio-economic development when water withdrawal exceeds 20 per cent of annual total renewable water resources.

Countries which have the ratio of water use to water availability less than 1 per cent include Lao People's Democratic Republic, Myanmar, New Zealand and Papua New Guinea. Obviously, the water resources in these countries apparently remain largely untapped and therefore have less likelihood to face water crisis in the near future.

Countries which have the ratio of water use to water availability between 1 and 20 per cent may be considered as those which have some potential for water crisis. Countries belonging to this category include Australia, Bangladesh, Bhutan, Cambodia, China, Fiji, Indonesia, Malaysia, Mongolia, Nepal, Solomon Islands, Thailand and Viet Nam.

Countries which have the ratio of water use to water availability exceeding 20 per cent may be considered as those which have the highest potential for water crisis. Countries which belong to this category include Afghanistan, Democratic People's Republic of Korea, India, Islamic Republic of Iran, Japan, Pakistan, Philippines, Republic of Korea and Sri Lanka. These countries need urgent attention with regard to taking necessary actions to avoid a water crisis.

Owing to the uneven spatial distribution of water resources, the development of vast regions of some countries, such as China, India, Pakistan, Thailand, etc. is hampered by shortage of water, although on the

Table 1. Water resources availability and use in selected countries of the ESCAP region

COUNTRY/AREA	POPULATION (Thousands) (1995)	TOTAL LAND AREA (km²)	WATER RESOURCES AVAILABILITY (km³/yr)	WATER RESOURCES USE (km³/yr)	WATER USE AS PERCENTAGE OF WATER AVAILABILITY (%)
Afghanistan	20,141	652,090	60	26	43
Australia	18,040	7,682,640	398	24	6
Bangladesh	120,433	130,170	115	23	20
Bhutan	1,638	47,000	95	<1	1
Cambodia	10,251	176,520	88	1	1
China	1,227,000	9,600,000	2,812	500	18
Democratic People's Republic of Korea	23,917	120,410	67	14	21
Fiji	784	18,270	29	<1	3
India	935,744	3,287,260	1,869	552	30
Indonesia	195,756	1,811,570	2,986	49	2
Iran (Islamic Republic of)	67,283	1,636,000	130	75	58
Japan	125,251	377,800	435	90	21
Lao People's Democratic Republic	4,882	230,800	270	1	<1
Malaysia	19,948	328,550	566	12	2
Mongolia	2,410	1,566,500	25	<1	4
Myanmar	46,527	657,540	606	4	<1
Nepal	20,892	147,181	207	3	2
New Zealand	3,536	270,530	397	2	<1
Pakistan	130,660	770,880	550	126	23
Papua New Guinea	4,302	452,850	801	<1	<1
Philippines	67,581	298,170	356	105	30
Republic of Korea	44,851	99,390	70	29	41
Solomon Islands	378	27,990	45	<1	2
Sri Lanka	18,354	65,610	47	10	21
Thailand	59,401	510,890	210	33	16
Viet Nam	71,000	330,000	324	54	17

Source: Information provided by country experts participating at the ESCAP Ad Hoc Expert Group Meeting on Sustainable Development of Water Resources, Bangkok, 10-12 July 1996, supplemented by information contained in ESCAP, Water Resources Series No. 74.

whole about 15-35 per cent of the renewable water resources are at present exploited in those countries. Taking into consideration the temporal distribution of water, Bangladesh is also affected by a shortage of water.

Water availability may thus become a limiting factor in national development as a whole or in the development of certain regions in a number of countries of Asia and the Pacific region.

B. Summary of water resources management policies in addressing water sector issues in selected countries

Australia is pursuing an approach to water resources management that is based on the integrated management of land and water. There is a wide range of strategies, policies and plans being implemented at all scales of applications from the individual property to the river basin. The country is also implementing a package of reforms in the water industry to address the pressures on water resources and place water resources management and the water industry on a more sustainable and efficient basis. The package includes measures in relation to water pricing, property rights in water quantity and quality and trading of these rights, environmental requirements, institutional reform, public participation and education, and research and development. The integrated approach and the reform package are being supported by new developments in data collection and management, analytical tools and information presentation tools.

In *Bangladesh*, the water resources from the river basins of Ganges, Brahmaputra and Meghna play a key role in the overall development of the country. The ecological balance within the country also depends on the change in the amount and nature of water discharges in these rivers. Some of adverse impacts of hydrological change in the rivers include siltation and rise of river beds, floods, erosion of river banks, changes in the river courses and salinity hazards affecting agriculture, industry and other infrastructure. Consequently, restoration of natural flows in the rivers is considered as a major requirement for sustainable development of water resources in the country.

In *Cambodia*, changing rural and urban population mix and growing affluence in urban areas are bringing about a significant change in its socio-economic conditions that place unprecedented demands upon its water resources. Deforestation, soil erosion and sedimentation in the Great Lake (Tonle Sap Lake), changes in the hydrologic regime caused by water diversion schemes, and sedimentation of water ways have resulted in abnormal floods and droughts. The country has the potential to develop its major streams for hydro-power generation much needed in the overall development of the country.

In *China*, the main mandate and responsibility for water resources development utilization and management is assigned by the Central Government to the Ministry of Water Resources, which is supported by major river basin commissions and local government agencies at the provincial, prefectural and country levels. Major issues at present are over-exploitation of groundwaters and pollution of surface water by industrial waste. Strategies are being developed to combat these problems. Water conservation technologies have been practised since the 1970's to improve irrigation efficiencies. It is planned to increase use of water-saving technologies and water recycling rates across all sectors of water consumption. Water pricing also has a key role to play in managing demand, and ensuring sustainable water resources use.

In *India*, due to the spatial and temporal variation of flows the amount of water that can be put to beneficial use is much less than the total available. The constraint in creating sufficient storages results in non-utilization of all the available water resources. By 2025, all the utilizable water resources is expected to be put to beneficial use. As additional surface water resources will not be available for meeting subsequent increased demand, there is an urgent need for identifying suitable strategies for conservation and management of available resources in the most optimal way.

National water policy places emphasis on preservation of the quality of the environment. The Environment (protection) Act is an umbrella act covering all aspects of the environment including water. Under this Act, it is mandatory to prepare an Environmental Impact Statement for development projects to obtain environmental clearance. The Central Water Commission is monitoring environmental safeguards stipulated by the Ministry of Environment and Forests and it has developed guidelines for sustainable water resources development and management. The current need is to develop trained manpower adequately in terms of both quantity and quality to handle the environmental aspects in the field.

In *Indonesia*, the availability of water resources varies from island to island. Java which has 65 per cent of the country's population has only 4.5 per cent of the water resources available during the dry season. The country's economic development has created a tremendous pressure on its water resources for various purposes both in terms of quantity and quality. To meet its future demand, the country considered it necessary to increase its water supply capacity and establish a sound system of water allocation, as well as a series of legal instruments and water resources institutions. A more holistic and integrative approach towards sustainable development is considered necessary. The country is making efforts towards reducing subsidies, improving cost recovery through the application of appropriate water pricing and water service charges. Promotion of community, public and private participation in projects concerning water resources development and management is also given due consideration in this country. The water resources development and management policy in the country is moving from a sectoral approach to an multi-sectoral approach. For example, it had taken a major step towards water resources development and management based on a holistic and integrative approach to supporting sustainable development for the nation's second twenty-five-year development period (1994-2019). To support the policies on water resources development and management, the Ministry of Public Works, through the Directorate-General of Water Resources Development, had launched a new planning and programming approach in that area, beginning with REPELITA VI in 1994, as part of its effort to support the sustainability concept in development, which included supporting self-sufficiency in food production, raw water supply and management, flood control and water resources conservation. The new programming structure had shifted from the project programming system to a more holistic mission programming system which was expected to facilitate the more efficient use of the country's water and economic resources.

In *Malaysia*, the water resources availability as at 1996 is estimated at 28,000 m^3 per capita per year. The main issue challenging sustainable water resources development in the country is identified as the increasing deterioration of river water quality. About 12 per cent of Malaysian rivers are classified as highly polluted and the trend is worsening as a result of rapid industrial development. There are no problems concerning financial sustainability of projects due to strong support by the Federal Government as well as due to successful cost recovery from the users.

One of the major problems facing Malaysia is the shortage of experienced water resources professionals in the country. With regard to private investments in the water sector, it is expected that investments will increase significantly in the areas of water supply, sewerage and hydropower projects. The irrigation sector is currently heavily subsidized with little incentive to improve its efficiency. With growing awareness of water as a finite resource both Federal and State Governments have recognized the need to adopt a sound national water policy to ensure sustainable development of water resources in the country. There is an urgent need to review the existing legislation related to water use and watershed management as well as to introduce new legislation pertaining to river management.

Malaysia is rich in water resources, with current demand representing less than 3 per cent of the available water supply and 28,000 m^3 per capita available annually. However, increasing water stress had occurred in some of the more developed areas owing to wide variation in rainfall distribution. Water quality deterioration is also becoming a serious issue, affecting sustainable water resources development and use in the country. About 80 per cent of the water is currently used for irrigation, but that is expected to decrease as demand for domestic and industrial uses shifted from 20 per cent in 1995 to about 32 per cent in 2000. Emphasis had shifted from development of new resources to water conservation, water resource allocation and education, so as to ensure sustainable use. The fragmentation of responsibilities amongst the various federal ministries and the 13 state governments in the development and management of water resources, coupled with the non-existence of legislation dealing directly with watershed management and institutional arrangements, have led to constraints on integrated resource planning. The commitment by the Government to protect the environment in order to maintain the long-term sustainability of the country's development, as outlined in the National Development Policy, is expected to remove those constraints.

While *Myanmar*, has relatively abundant water resources, the percentage of its water use is considered very small. Presently, the country is making efforts to develop its water resources through construction of dams and resources as well as through the implementation of pump irrigation projects. The main source of drinking water in rural areas is groundwater, the development of which has yet to make significant progress to meet the increasing demand. A major problem faced by the country in this regard is the lack of adequately trained water resources professionals. Uncontrolled deforestation in the country during the past two or three years has resulted in serious silting and erosion problems in the river basins. The country expressed its urgent need for technical assistance from United Nations and other international organizations for the sustainable development of its water resources.

Nepal is rich in water resources possessing about 2.27 per cent of the world total. These are mainly used for irrigation and drinking purposes. At present, however, the capital city, Kathmandu, is facing an acute problem of shortage of drinking water and to address this problem, His Majesty's Government has started the Melanmchi Water Supply Project which is expected to provide drinking water to the capital city for the next 50 years.

At present, about 51 per cent of the country's population has access to safe drinking water. The Government has a target of providing drinking water to the entire population by the end of the year 2000. The country is implementing a number of large hydro power projects as well as irrigation projects.

In *Pakistan*, agriculture remained the major and most important user of water. However, as the society developed, water for human consumption and sanitation and for industrial development would also make substantial claims on that precious resource. The average annual inflow into the Indus basin of Pakistan had been estimated at 144 million acre-feet, of which 85 per cent occurred during the rainy season. A substantial part of the surface flow in rivers and the canal system found its way into an underground aquifer spread over some 25 million acres, from where it was pumped by tubewells for agricultural use. Groundwater development in the country had begun in the 1960s, first for waterlogging control and then for supplementing irrigation. Currently some 300,000 private and public tubewells pumped 43 million acre-feet of water for irrigation development in the country. Such a large irrigation system, without a matching drainage system, had caused the water table to rise to dangerous levels for the crop root zone, and in turn had

caused some major adverse environmental impacts -- namely, waterlogging, salinity and surface water pollution. Those factors had affected the agricultural health of the country. An ambitious drainage programme had been planned to combat those problems.

Although water resources were nationally abundant, the *Philippines* was confronted with formidable water problems, such as a recurrent water supply shortage; inadequate water infrastructures to keep up with rapidly increasing demand; severe water pollution, particularly near urban centres; and watershed and environmental degradation, which threatened the health of the population (especially the poor) and aquatic life. The problem is not the shortage of water per se, as the current demand for water is far less than the renewable water available nationally. The problem emanated from supply-demand mismatches caused by an inadequate water infrastructure that could not regulate flood flows and store water in the rainy season. The problem is compounded by limited financial resources for source development and expansion of water distribution facilities. Wasteful use of water and weakness of regulatory agencies in enforcement and monitoring activities exist primarily due to inadequate manpower resources and logistic support facilities. Some of the above-mentioned issues were expected to be resolved through: larger public investment for developing a new water infrastructure; economic pricing of water and higher recovery of project costs; greater participation by beneficiaries in the planning and implementation of projects; increased participation by the private sector in water service delivery; and institutional strengthening of concerned water utilities and regulatory agencies to improve efficiency in service delivery and water use. The Government had undertaken an overall action plan for sustainable water resources management covering six key areas, namely: water resources management at the national and regional levels; water resources planning at the national and regional levels; regulatory and coordination system enforcement; investment needs in the sector; watershed management; and water resources sectoral reform.

The total amount of water available for use in *Sri Lanka* is approximately 127 km^3 per year. Surface water is used mainly for agriculture, hydro power and domestic water supplies while groundwater is used for industry and commercial agriculture as well as for domestic consumption. Major constraints for sustainable development of water resources in the country include, *inter alia*, inadequate measures for watershed management, water quality deterioration, lack of regulations for extraction of groundwater, lack of financial sustainability of operations and maintenance for irrigation and water supply projects, unclear policy directions and lack of coordination among various agencies responsible for water resources development and management.

In the *Republic of Korea*, 65 per cent of the national territory is mountainous, and more than 60 per cent of the annual precipitation occur during the wet season. That causes a wide disparity in the available water resources during different seasons, requiring construction of multi-purpose dams to receive the water supply. To prevent water pollution, the Government had established the Water Quality Preservation Act, that adopted 28 parameters for determining water quality standards which should be met in four different regions designated as either clean zones, A zones, B zones, or special zones for wastewater discharge standards.

To achieve freshwater conservation, supply and sustainable development, the Ministry of Environment and seven other ministries had launched a five-year project called the "Comprehensive Plan for Clean Water Supply in 1993". The Government also had plans to implement the following programmes for the promotion of water and sustainable development as part of the action plan of Agenda 21: comprehensive water resources development and establishment of an efficient management system; inspection, development and management of groundwater resources; improvement and restoration of the quality of freshwater resources (to improve the water quality of five major rivers to a level suitable for the use of drinking-water supply resources and to improve the water quality of rivers); and promotion of water conservation policies.

Viet Nam has an abundance of water resources but the resources are unevenly distributed over space and time. At present, the water resources are deteriorating in both quantity and quality, probably as a result of the formation of a multisectoral economy and

the discharge of domestic and industrial wastewater directly into water bodies without treatment. For example, a large number of private industries utilizing hazardous and pollutant technologies had become diversified sources of solid wastes and untreated effluents adversely affecting the quality of water resources. Apart from the high population growth rate, deforestation in the mountainous areas and discharge of untreated wastewater are major reasons for water pollution in the country. For sustainable development of water resources, it is considered that institutional arrangements will be needed to better manage the increasing water demands, coordinate sector investments, and improve the operational and financial performance of water service entities.

In Central Asia, the excessive withdrawal of water for irrigation from the Amu Darya and Syr Darya rivers had led to the drying up of the Aral Sea and an unprecedented disastrous impact on the region's environment such as the degradation of soils and vegetation, changes in flora and fauna, collapse of the fishing industry and reduction in agriculture production. Five countries located in the Aral Sea basin, namely, Kazakhstan, Kyrgyzstan, Tajikistan, Turkmenistan and Uzbekistan, had adopted a sustainable development-oriented approach towards undertaking joint activities for mitigating the adverse impact on environment. The multisectoral Aral Sea Basin Programme, approved in 1994 by the five Heads of State of the Central Asian countries, was funded by the World Bank, UNDP and multilateral and bilateral donors. The implementation of the Programme was being coordinated by the Interstate Council on the Problems of the Aral Sea Basin and the International Aral Sea Rehabilitation Fund. The backbone of the Aral Sea Basin Programme was a Regional Water Resources Management Strategy, aimed at achieving sustainability of water resources in the Aral Sea Basin through increased water use efficiency, especially in agriculture, along with improvement of water quality. To implement this strategy, legal instruments and institutions would be developed, economic instruments including water use charges, which had played a minimal role in the past, would be introduced, and various criteria and procedures for sharing transboundary water resources would be developed.

III. SUSTAINABLE WATER RESOURCES MANAGEMENT IN AUSTRALIA

Dugald Black
New South Wales Department of Land and Water Conservation
P.O. Box 3720, Parramatta, 2124 Australia

Abstract

The basic philosophy of water resources development and management in Australia recognizes that land and water resources are inextricably linked and that an integrated natural resources management approach is needed. There is a wide range of strategies, policies and plans being implemented at all scales of application from the individual property scale to the river basin scale. There is a strong focus on community involvement and ownership, as this is seen as the key to success in natural resources management.

This paper gives some background on the status of water resources in Australia and an overview of the institutional arrangements in place, mainly from the perspective of the state of New South Wales. The paper also describes the key management strategies being implemented and briefly discusses some of the new management tools to assist managers and the community make informed decisions.

A. Status of water resources

Australia is a Federation of six states (Queensland, New South Wales, Victoria, Tasmania, South Australia and Western Australia) and two self-governing territories (Northern Territory and the Australian Capital Territory). The basis of water resources development and management in Australia is that land and water resources are inextricably linked and that an integrated approach is needed, in accordance with the recommendations of Agenda 21. Primary responsibility for natural resources management, including land, water, forests, coasts and estuaries, air and minerals resides with the states and territories. Commonwealth Government involvement occurs where issues are considered to be of national importance or where there is a need to facilitate interstate coordination and cooperation. The Commonwealth Government also has primary responsibility for national economic management.

Australia's water resources are facing a number of significant pressures. Some of these are the legacy of past decisions or actions which were well-intentioned at the time, based on community expectations or scientific knowledged available then.

The issues are diverse and include environmental problems as well as economic and social issues, such as the need to ensure that the infrastructure needs of irrigation farmers can be met in the future and their livelihood (and a significant portion of Australia's food production) can be sustained.

One of the most important resource management decisions was taken in February 1994, when all Australian governments at the federal, State and local level, through the Council of Australian Governments (COAG), agreed to a strategic framework of reform to address the pressures on water resources and to manage them on a more sustainable and efficient basis. Given Australia's political system, where responsibility for resource management resides with the six States and two Territories, the initiative reflected the significance of the issues and the fact that they transcended jurisdictional or political boundaries. The COAG reform framework will play an important part in giving effect to Australia's achievement of Agenda 21 objectives for freshwater resources.

The area of Australia that is perhaps of greatest importance from a natural resources management point of view is the Murray-Darling Basin (Figure 1). The Murray-Darling River system drains an area of approximately 1 million km², and includes 75 per cent of New South Wales (NSW), over 50 per cent of Victoria, 15 per cent of Queensland and 7 per cent of South Australia, as well as almost the entire Australian Capital Territory. It includes half Australia's crop land, half the sheep and one quarter of the national beef and dairy cattle herd. It also includes 75 per cent of the irrigated farmland (1.2 million hectares) which produces about 90 per cent of the nation's irrigated field crops (such as rice, cotton, oil seed), 80 per cent of the pasture and lucerne, 70 per cent of the fruit and 25 per cent of the vegetables. The annual value of this production is about $A10,000 million (about $US7,500 million). There are also 140 parks and reserves totalling about 1.5 million hectares that include internationally significant wetlands such as the 240,000 ha Macquarie Marshes (not all in parks or reserves).

Extensive water resources developments have taken place to support the economic activity in the Basin, starting in the late 19th Century, but mostly occurring since 1945. These developments include major storage dams and irrigation infrastructure. The rivers are used extensively as water delivery conduits. Total storage capacity in major dams in the Basin is now approximately 30,000 million m^3. With the increase in storage availability over the years came increased diversions for irrigation.

Development in the Murray-Darling Basin has come with a price and there are now significant resource degradation issues to be addressed. For example, issues concerning land degradation include, irrigation salinity and waterlogging; wind and water erosion; dryland salinity; soil structure decline; soil acidification and pests that harm plants and animals. Issues pertaining to water include, over commitment of water resources; deterioration of groundwater resources; and deteriorating water quality due to salinity, turbidity, nutrients, pesticides, algae, bacteria, etc.

Similar issues apply to all river systems in Australia, although to different extents. Urbanization pressures are a significant issue in several river basins, most notably the Hawkesbury-Nepean River basin which provides the main source of water for Sydney is coming under increasing pressure as Sydney, the capital city of NSW, expands. Fortunately, the urban areas are all downstream of the water supply storages but since there are extensive rural activities and several country towns in the main water supply catchment, water quality is a major concern.

Large scale new development in water resources by various state governments has largely ceased in Australia, although there are some large developments planned in Queensland and an expansion of the Ord River Scheme planned in Western Australia. The emphasis has now moved to better management of existing infrastructure, taking a more holistic view of water management to give greater consideration to the environment and reducing consumptive water usage in cases where current usage levels are clearly unsustainable. Private developments are continuing and mainly comprise on-farm storage construction by cotton growers. These storages are a significant factor in the management of water resources in river systems where cotton is grown. Total on-farm storage capacity in NSW, where most of these storages are, increased from just over 500 million m^3 in 1988 to almost 900 million m^3 in 1994.

B. Institutional arrangements

The Murray-Darling Basin Commission (MDBC) was established in 1985 under the Murray-Darling Basin Agreement as a successor to the River Murray Commission which was formed in 1917. Signatories to this Agreement are NSW, Victoria, South Australia, the Commonwealth and (since 1991) Queensland. Its charter is to promote and coordinate effective planning and management for the equitable, efficient and sustainable use of the land, water and environmental resources of the Murray-Darling Basin. It also has an operational responsibility in respect of the Murray River downstream of Hume Dam and the Darling River downstream of Menindee Lakes (Figure 1).

Otherwise, the responsibility for management policies, strategies, practices and procedures in respect of land, water and environmental resources resides with State agencies. In NSW the agency responsible for land and water management is the Department of Land and Water Conservation, while primary responsibility for environmental issues resides with the Environment Protection Authority. Similar arrangements operate in the other States.

In the Hawkesbury-Nepean River Basin near Sydney, a Catchment Management Trust has been established with the charter of conserving and improving the health of the river system using an integrated approach to land and water resources management with a strong community focus. Trusts have also been established in the Upper Parramatta River Catchment in the western suburbs of Sydney and for the Hunter River; the role of these two trusts was originally flood mitigation but is widening to include management of water quality and the aquatic environment. Outside the Trust areas, local government has primary responsibility for floodplain management in NSW.

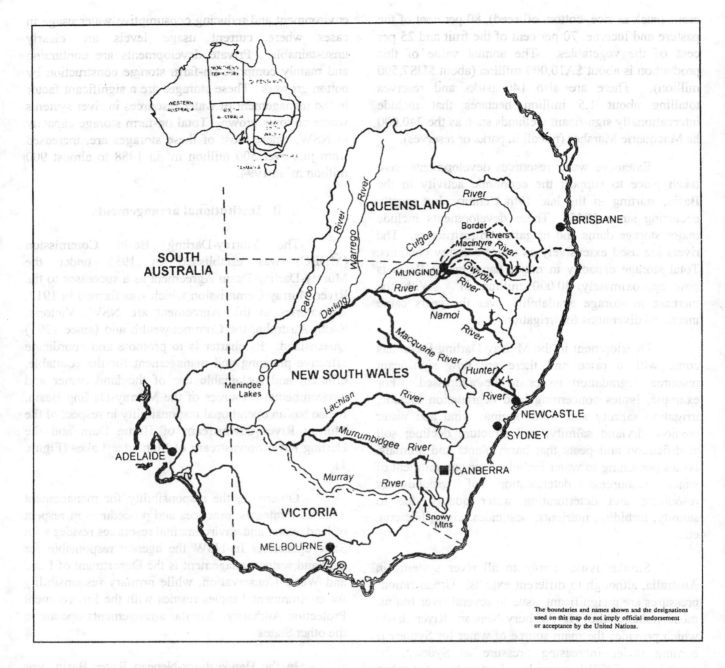

The boundaries and names shown and the designations used on this map do not imply official endorsement or acceptance by the United Nations.

Figure 1. Location map of the Murray-Darling river basin

Also of relevance is the Border Rivers Agreement between Queensland and NSW. This was established in 1947 to formalize arrangements for sharing the waters of the Dumaresq-Barwon River System upstream of Mungindi (Figure 1).

C. National and interstate strategies

National strategies include:

- The National Landcare Program (NLP), which encourages development of an integrated approach to natural resources management, especially at the community level. Its focus is to encourage best natural resource management practices in rural and regional Australia, including improved water management in small country towns. Considerable emphasis is placed on establishing and supporting local Landcare groups, changing practices and promoting partnerships between industry, the community and government. This program is administered by the Commonwealth Department of Primary Industries and Energy.

- The National Nature Conservation Program which has the main objective of conserving, protecting or restoring native flora and fauna and also has a mainly small scale focus. The community components of this strategy are amalgamated into NLP.

- The National Water Quality Management Strategy, for which the overall objective is to achieve sustainable use of the nation's water resources by protecting and enhancing their quality while maintaining economic and social development.

- Council of Australian Governments (COAG) Water Reform Framework, discussed in the companion paper " Achieving Sustainable Water Resource Management: Australia's Approach" prepared by the Commonwealth Department of Primary Industries and Energy.

- National Strategy for Ecologically Sustainable Development.

There are also a number of strategies, policies and plans that operate under the auspices of the MDBC, including:

- The Natural Resources Management Strategy (NRMS) which over-arches a number of resource specific sub-strategies including the Salinity and Drainage Strategy, the Algal Management strategy, the Irrigation Management Strategy, the Dryland Salinity Strategy, the Fish Management Strategy, the Sustainable Rivers Program, the Integrated Catchment Management Program and the Community Education Program. NRMS provides for targeted research and policy developments, technical and financial support to

implement "on the ground" improvements with a focus on the regional or sub-basin scale, and help to communities to merge requirements of the sub-strategies into "action plans".

- Interstate water sharing arrangements which include rules for sharing flows in the River Murray and the Lower Darling River between NSW, Victoria and South Australia.

- Moratorium on growth in diversions for which the interim objective is to hold diversions at 1993/94 levels with due allowance for fluctuations in seasonal climatic conditions.

D. Natural resources management in New South Wales

Natural resources management in NSW is based on the principles of ecologically sustainable development and conservation of biological diversity while maintaining quality of life. There is a strong focus on community involvement and integration across natural resources, using the catchment as the management unit, through the Total Catchment Management (TCM) process.

Total Catchment Management in NSW is defined as the coordinated and sustainable management of land, water, vegetation and other natural resources on a catchment basis so as to balance resource utilization and conservation. TCM is about coordinating government and community efforts in natural resources management, and focuses on water catchments because they provide a convenient and readily identifiable part of the ecosystem on which to concentrate these efforts. Catchment Management Committees, which are joint community and agency based committees, are responsible for overseeing and coordinating TCM and related natural resource management activities at a regional or entire river basin level. A key program under TCM is Salt Action which is specifically directed at mitigating the impacts of soil and water salinization in irrigated and dryland areas.

A broad range of state-based strategies, policies and plans is in place for natural resources management. From a water perspective, these include strategies, policies and plans for: wetlands, sand and gravel extraction, state rivers and estuary management, coastal management, floodplain management, integrated drainage for irrigation areas, nutrient management, algal management and numerous policies for sharing water between consumptive users and the environment. Specific activities related to water resources management include:

-   Strategic Water Management Plans for the eight major regulated river systems of NSW. The objectives of these plans are to provide a clear indication of the status of the water resources and associated aquatic environment in each system, identify key water resources management issues and provide a regional framework for water management by government and community groups. They are compatible with other plans covering land management, forests and the environment generally. The initial life expectancy of these Plans is five years before review.

-   Development of Land and Water Management Plans for major irrigation areas, such as the Murrumbidgee Irrigation Area, Coleambally Irrigation Area and the four main Murray irrigation areas. These plans are developed jointly by Government and the community under the National Landcare Program and the Salinity and Drainage Strategy. They are intended to enable land use and water use to be managed to ensure long term viability of agriculture, prevention of land salinization and minimization of saline drainage outflows, and are consistent with the relevant Strategic Water Management Plan. The plans have led to a move away from construction of large scale drainage works to a greater emphasis on improved farm management and on-farm works to minimize saline drainage and groundwater accessions.

-   Development of floodplain management plans for urban and rural areas, including most country towns in the State, parts of Sydney and other major urban areas, and rural areas such as the Liverpool Plains in the north of the state. They cover urban

drainage systems as well as rivers and creeks. These plans comprise combinations of structural and non-structural measures to minimize socio-economic impacts of flooding. They provide an integrated approach, covering land use planning, ecological, water quality, social, economic and heritage issues as well as hydrologic and hydraulic factors in determining the best mix of works and measures for the whole floodplain area.

-   Preparation of Nutrient Management Plans for all major river catchments in the state. These are developed through collaboration between Government agencies and Catchment Management Committees. The aim of these plans is to reduce the delivery of nutrients to streams from both point and diffuse sources.

-   Development and implementation of Environmental Flow Policies or River Flow Objectives for regulated and unregulated streams in NSW. These are aimed at improving river health through restoring key components of the natural flow regime. They include a five part package comprising passing some low flows through major dams, contingency allocations in storages, quotas and limitations on access to unregulated flows, greater variability in release flows from storage and modifications to weir structures and management practices for fish passage and other environmental benefits. There are also replenishment rules for major wetland areas such as the Macquarie Marshes which include rules for prolonging inundation due to small to medium floods by releases from storage if needed to ensure completion of a bird breeding cycle.

-   Development of Water Quality Objectives, complementing the River Flow Objectives and relating river water quality to desired uses and environmental needs.

All significant water users in NSW are licensed, and the licenses have conditions attached to them which specify the circumstances under which water may be diverted. Licenses are also being issued for discharging to water bodies, and these have water quality performance criteria attached to them. Trading of water use and discharge licenses, or of some of the entitlement conferred under the licenses is permitted. For example, in a regulated river system an irrigator who does not require all the water allocated to that license in a given season may sell that unused allocation to another irrigator, and there is a well established market in operation for this. Temporary transfers in NSW have exceeded 300 million m^3/yr, but vary widely depending on climatic conditions and water availability. Transfer of discharge license rights is being trailed in practice.

As part of the COAG Water Reform Framework, action is in progress to better define property rights for water diversions and water and pollutant discharges. Water pricing structures are being reformed to better reflect the costs of storage and supply, and to reflect usage. Privatization or corporatisation of urban water supply authorities and irrigation areas is also in progress. Licensing, monitoring and performance audit procedures are being implemented to ensure that public and environmental interests are protected after privatization or corporatisation.

New developments in data collection and management, analytical tools and presentation tools are supporting the integrated approach to natural resources management and the community involvement. These include:

- Telemetry systems, electronic instrumentation for water quantity and quality measurement,

- Decision support systems to present information in a manner that is understandable by experts, managers and the community, and

- A new generic, hydrologic, river system simulation package for investigating water resources management policy options that operates at a daily time step, known as the Integrated Quantity/Quality Model (IQQM). IQQM is designed for investigating water management issues at the river basin, inter-state or international level, and between competing users including the environment. It is particularly well suited to investigating issues where short duration variability is important, such as for environmental flow rules.

E. Conclusion

Australia is pursuing an approach to water resources management that recognizes the inextricable links between land and water management. There is a wide range of strategies, policies and plans being implemented at all scales of application from the individual property to the river basin. There is a strong focus on community involvement and ownership, as this is seen as the key to success in natural resources management.

In addition, new developments in data collection and management, analytical tools and information presentational tools are supporting the integrated approach to natural resources management and the community involvement. These developments are essential to the provision of the reliable information needed to enable planners, managers and the community to properly identify problems and issues, and to adequately evaluate alternative solutions.

IV. SUSTAINABLE DEVELOPMENT OF WATER RESOURCES IN BANGLADESH

A.F.M. Nurul Alam, Chief Engineer
Bangladesh Water Development Board, Dhaka, Bangladesh

Abstract

Water constitutes a unique resource in the delta of Bangladesh. The three mighty rivers, the Ganges, the Brahmaputra and the Meghna with their numerous branches and tributaries have played a key role in shaping its destiny from time immemorial. The civilization, cultural patterns, agro-ecological system and production structure have been shaped through the millennium by the water of these rivers. They provide water for agriculture, domestic and municipal use, fisheries, industries, forestry, navigation and maintenance of the delicate ecological balance. The entire ecosystem of the country is tuned to these river systems and any interference with the supply of these life giving flows would invariably bring about changes in the coexistence of its population, flora and fauna with nature and the environment. The balance between man and nature in the river basins of Bangladesh rests essentially on water. Unfortunately the balance has been severely disrupted by substantial diversion and blockage of various rivers in the upstream outside the territory of the country. This has changed the level and nature of water supply in Bangladesh, which in turn affects the hydrological system and environmental balance of the country. The resultant consequences of hydrological changes include, siltation and rise of river beds leading to floods, destruction of river embankment and changed river courses, decreased soil moisture and increased salinity leading to possible desertification; decreased water level adversely affecting agriculture, industry, irrigation, navigation, fishery and domestic use, increased saline intrusion in the coastal areas and damage to the mangrove forest at Sundarban. Consequently, appropriate measures to restore Bangladesh's rightful share of the upstream flow in dry season become imperative for sustainable development of water resources in Bangladesh.

Introduction

Bangladesh has an area of 147,570 km^2 and a population of about 120 million. It lies in the floodplains of three mighty rivers, the Brahmaputra, the Ganges and the Meghna. Although it is one of the densely populated countries, its production of foodgrains comes close to self-sufficiency. Water resources development activities, initiated in the 1950s paid its dividends. Steady gains in agricultural output in the 1980s have come largely from the exploitation of ground water for dry-season cropping and from many FCDI (Flood Control, Drainage and Irrigation) projects all over the country.

Unfortunately, the gains in production have been matched by rapid growth in population. The farm size has dropped from 1.5 ha to 0.9 ha over the past 20 years and the proportion of landless has risen from 35 per cent to 45 per cent. Unemployment in rural areas at present is about 30-40 per cent, and in recent years there has been a secular decline in wage rates and landless household incomes. With water having so much influence on the socio-economic attributes of the country, there seems to be no alternative to increased emphasis on developing a strategy for sustainable development in the water sector.

A. Sustainable development of water resources

1. Environmental sustainability of water resources development

(a)   Overview of water resources availability

Bangladesh has a network of about 250 rivers crossing the entire land. More than 90 per cent of the flooding of Bangladesh originate from outside. There are 54 common rivers between India and Bangladesh.

There are three sources of water in Bangladesh: rainfall, surface water and groundwater.

The water availability of the country from these sources are as indicated below:

Annual average rainfall	2,320 mm
River discharge: Maximum outflow of surface water (in August)	111.25 km^3
Ponds and lakes	0.61 km^3
In stream storage	0.50 km^3
Groundwater	9.60 km^3

(b)   Overview of water resources use (present and future)

In Bangladesh, water resources are used for navigation, agriculture, fisheries, hydro-power, industrial and domestic use.

	1996	1997
Domestic and Municipal	2.00 km^3	6.00 km^3
Industry	0.42 km^3	0.90 km^3
Irrigation	8.80 km^3	14.29 km^3
Other purpose	10.98 km^3	9.91 km^3

(c)   Incidence of overexploitation and overuse of water resources and measures to prevent such incidence

As the surface water storage area in the country is limited, surface water is increasingly becoming insufficient and polluted. As a result, the agricultural and industrial sectors as well as the city water supply systems have to turn to ground water for alternative supplies. At present, overexploitation of ground water is becoming a serious issue.

Due to continuous withdrawal of river water in the dry period by the upper riparian country, recharge of ground water decreases and the water level in the wells went down from 0.35 m to 5.98 m resulting in acute shortage of water for drinking and irrigation.

To encourage growth of irrigation in private sectors, no restrictions have yet been imposed on installation of shallow and deep tube wells.

(d)   National Master Water Plans

1964 Master Plan: In pursuance of the recommendations of the Crug Mission, the then East Pakistan Water and Power Development Authority (EPWAPDA) was set up in 1959. A Master Plan for water development was drawn up in 1964 that conceived flood protection for 5.8 million hectares of land, mainly by the construction of flood embankments

with gravity drainage, tidal sluice drainage and pump drainage.

National Water Plan: By the 1980s, the need for a long-term water resources development plan became apparent. In 1983, the government initiated the National Water Plan Project for the purpose of preparing a comprehensive plan for development of water resources. Under Phase I of the National Water Plan (NWP) a comprehensive assessment of the land and water resources available and future demand by different users was carried out. The NWP period of development was taken as the 20-year period between 1985 and 2005. Short-term and medium term plans proposed for ground water and regional surface water development were expected to be completed by the year 2000. Long-term water resources development was expected to depend upon construction of major barrages on the Ganges and Bhahmaputra Rivers. Full development was not expected until about 2018 or thereafter.

The objective of the Phase I of NWP was to maximize agricultural growth and production and contribute to achieving foodgrain self-sufficiency by providing investment strategies and guidelines for water allocations to:

- meet domestic and industrial water needs on a priority basis;
- improve or maintain water quality in critical areas;
- maintain effective water transportation;
- develop water resources to increase agricultural development contributing to foodgrain self-sufficiency;
- expand and maintain inland and coastal fisheries production; and
- control flooding and improve drainage over a large portion of the country.

The Phase II of NWP was started in 1988 and completed in 1991. It is predominantly an agricultural development plan for the period 1990-2010 which is being administrated by Water Resources Planning Organization (WARPO), a national coordinating body under the Ministry of Water Resources.

(e)   Environmental impacts of water development projects

Bangladesh has given top priority to the integration of environmental concerns into economic planning at all levels. The impact of potential water sector projects on the environment is a key concern in developing a national water resource development strategy.

Flood protection, flood management and flood proofing projects are designed to improve the environment for people by reducing flood damage and enabling more productive use of land and water resources. However, such projects also have adverse impacts.

(f)   Institutional and legal frameworks for water resources development

Institutional arrangements for developing and managing water resources are the critical link between policy objectives and field-level performance. Institutional frameworks are established by legislation that provides basic operative norms, and its various elements (customs, laws, regulations, organizations) are closely interdependent. The three primary areas of government institutional involvement are legislation, regulation and operation. Organization involved in sustainable development of water resources in Bangladesh are given in table 2.

Water legislation in Bangladesh has two basic functions:

(i)   Conferring necessary powers over water and land on the government, while preserving or granting such rights to individual users are consistent with the goals of the country: and

(ii) Establishing a basic administrative framework and necessary institutions to execute the various functions assigned.

Meanwhile, the Ministry of Water Resources has issued a guideline for Peoples Participation in Water Development Projects in August 1995. To ensure sustainable water development planning, implementation and management, and to provide diverse socio-economic groups of people affected by project development with the opportunity to articulate their needs, identify problems and work out solutions.

(g)   Human resources development (training at all levels) in water resources development

In order to achieve sustainable water resources development in Bangladesh, human resources development is considered as a prerequisite. The roles of various organizations in human resources development in various fields of sustainable development of water resources are indicated in table 2.

(h)   Nature of assistance required by the country to improve national capabilities in water and sustainable development

Bangladesh would require assistance in the following areas in order to strengthen national capabilities in water and sustainable development:

-   Planning, pilot projects and supporting activities and studies to broaden the scope of water sector planning and identify essential and justifiable structural and non-structural interventions;

-   Flood forecasting, mitigation and disaster management projects;

-   River management and coastal protection projects to protect about seven million people from severe river flooding, tidal flooding and storm surges. These projects would protect rural communities and agricultural land;

-   Urban protection projects to protect about six million people and industrial areas in Dhaka, Chandpur, Bhairab Bazar, Munshiganj, and selected secondary towns;

-   Water and flood management projects to conduct feasibility studies for small number of projects in north-central, north-east and south-east Bangladesh, aimed at increasing agricultural and fisheries production in flooded areas.

Table 2. Organizations involved in sustainable water development

Name of organization	Overall planning and data management	Project preparation, design and implementation	Operation and maintenance	Monitoring and evaluation
1. WARPO (Water Resources Planning Organization)	x	-	-	x
2. BWDB (Bangladesh Water Development Board)		x	x	x
3. LGED (Local Government Engineering Department)		x		
4. BIWTA (Bangladesh Inland Water Transport Authority)		x		
5. BADC (Bangladesh Agriculture Development Committee, Ministry of Agriculture)	-	x		
6. DPHE (Department of Public Health Engineering)	-	x	-	
7. WASA (Water and Sewerage Authority)	-	x		-
8. DOE (Directorate of Environment)		x		
9. SOB (Survey of Bangladesh)		x	-	
10. NGOs (Non-governmental Organization)	-	x	x	x

2. Financial sustainability of water development projects

(a) Overview of social and economic conditions and their relationship with resources development

Utilization of surface and groundwater resources in an optional manner is essential for the future economic development of Bangladesh as the available water resources of the country do not meet the water requirement of the country. Water is the key input in agriculture but equally important to non-agricultural sector like fisheries, navigation, domestic and industrial water needs.

It has been estimated that with a private investment of Taka 64,740 million (US$1 = 31.4 Taka) and public investment of Taka 74,320 million under the National Water Plan, the benefits could be 5.44 million ha of irrigated land; 27.5 million Metric tons of food grain; 115 billion Taka of value added; 2,371 million mandays of employment.

Continued employment opportunity and ability to produce needed food grain have positive impact on the socio-economic condition of Bangladesh.

(b) Cost recovery from water development projects in the country (Capital and O & M)

Responsibilities for water resources development lies largely with two public sector agencies, Bangladesh Water Development Board (BWDB) of the Ministry of Water Resources, and the Bangladesh Agricultural Development Corporation (BADC) of the Ministry of Agriculture. BWDB is responsible for the construction and operation of facilities for Flood Control Drainage and Irrigation by gravity and pumps while BADC is responsible for provision of minor irrigation facilities through tube wells and lowlift pumps.

BADC have made efforts for recovery of capital cost towards the installation of tubewells and lowlift pumps, but due to non recovery of investment, installation of pumps and tube wells were handed over to the private party (Committee) on down payment.

In Bangladesh no cost recovery arrangement has been made for capital investment against the BWDB Projects. Efforts have been made since 1963 for partial cost recovery of operation and maintenance

(O & M) for irrigation projects without much success for a number of reasons. The funds collected from BWDB and BADC are treated as the general revenue of the government while their annual budget is allocated by the government. Experience has confirmed that partial cost recovery for O & M may be achieved only when water users are satisfied with the quality of services and when their active participation towards the collection of water charges becomes effective. While the shortage of annual budget for O & M is a constraint for provision of proper services of the users, the inability to achieve full cost recovery of O & M has become an issue for the sustainability of water resources development projects in the country.

The BWDB has already initiated assessing and collecting of water charges on irrigation projects under Irrigation ordinance 1963, "Bangladesh Irrigation Water Rate ordinance, 1983" and "Irrigation Tax Regulations 1992". The 1963 ordinance provided for 3% incremental benefit; the 1983 ordinance provided for a fixed rate per acre per crop season (flat rate was different for different projects); and Regulation 1992 provided tax collection based on outlet and irrigation equipment (pumps) capacities. The assessment and collection of taxes under the above ordinances for an irrigation area of 0.677 M ha. of land as of May 1996 are as follows:

(c) Relationship between water-related natural disasters and water development projects and measures to mitigate to those disasters

Ordinance/ Regulation	Assessment	Actual tax collection	Percentage
1963	45.36 M Taka	1.18 M Taka	2.60
1983	159.38 M Taka	9.02 M Taka	5.66
1992	210.12 M Taka	41.76 M Taka	19.87

Floods and storm surges are two water-related natural disasters frequently faced by Bangladesh. Flood control and drainage improvement projects, disaster management study projects and the Coastal Embankment Rehabilitation Project are being implemented to combat these disasters. The mitigation measures to water-related natural disasters include:

(i) Flood forecasting and warning. The Flood Information Center is located at the Head Office of the Bangladesh Water Development Board. The North-East

Flood Warning Project is designed to provide timely and readily understood warnings in flash-flood prone areas;

(ii) Flood proofing. A combination of structural and non-structural measures that include flood proofing of public buildings, assistance to households to raise plinth levels and providing shelter areas above flood levels.

(iii) River management and coastal protection. The Coastal Embankment Rehabilitation Project involves the repair and strengthening of sea-facing embankments to protect inland areas from storm surges and from saline tidal intrusion.

B. Sustainable use of water resources

1. Water conservation and wastage prevention through demand management

(a) Water allocation system and procedures

Water allocation attempts to distribute water among different sectors of the economy should follow a socio-economic, economic, geographical or other principle. The easiest economic principle would be to sell it as a commodity. To ensure a socially acceptable water distribution, a strong regulatory function has to be developed. At present there does not exist an allocation policy, and every sector takes whatever it needs. In the dry season this leads to problems with increasing demands in all sectors.

The important elements of an allocation policy are: (i) identification of allocation period; (ii) assessment of the total water volume available in the allocation period, both ground and surface water; (iii) prioritization of the sectors and sub sectors; (iv) zoning of the country; (v) enforcement of the policy.

To effectively implement an optional water allocation policy, huge data bases have to be prepared, changes in attitude of people have to be achieved, and a long term view on integrated water management has to be developed. Bangladesh is quite far away from this goal, but the first steps have been made with the initialization of a National Water Plan.

(b) Use of water saving devices

Water saving device should aim directly, at demand reduction for a specific activity. In Bangladesh water demand reduction through the use of water saving devices has not yet been considered as a pressing issue.

(c) Enhancement of irrigation efficiency

In Bangladesh, typical values of overall efficiency range from 30 to 50 per cent for a major surface water irrigation system and 40 to 60 per cent for a small scale irrigation project such as low lift pump, shallow tubewell and deep tubewell schemes.

Enhancement of irrigation efficiency has several objectives of which the most obvious one is reducing the demand of water. Others are reducing the wastage of other resources (fuel for pumped irrigation, run-off and leaching of fertilizer and nutrients, reducing the costs of irrigation and drainage systems and reducing water logging and related salination problems.

Higher irrigation efficiency of up to 85 per cent be attained by sprinkle and buried pipe irrigation systems. Both of these systems are being practiced in small scale. Because of high initial investment cost, large scale implementation has distant possibility.

(d) Use of water pricing policies and structures

Pricing policies can have different objectives: to recover the O&M of the water distribution system, with or without some charge for the sustenance of the source of water or cover the entire investment. In Bangladesh, usually only part of O&M cost for the supply of water is charged or reserved.

In Bangladesh, there is no administrative structure to determine water pricing policies and its collection. However, in urban and town areas there are certain public agencies which distribute water to users. The pricing policies set by these agencies are different.

(e) Recycling (reuse) of water

Recycling irrigation water, for either surface water or ground water systems, is a complex issue involving various assumptions on system water losses and the deposition of the lost water. Basically the concept is simple. Water diverted for irrigation use either goes upward to the atmosphere as evapotranspiration, or down ward as deep percolation to the aquifer, or runs off laterally to the stream flow system. However, allocation among these three distinctions is not simple.

With regard to irrigation potential from wastewater it was estimated that 40% of the total losses from irrigation could be re reused for irrigation during the same cropping period. This concept of recycling of water on a limited scale is being practiced in certain irrigation projects.

2. Water quality protection

(a) Recycling/reuse of water

Recycling and reuse of waste water are very important for all industries. These techniques not only reduce the production cost but also protect the surrounding environment from pollution. None of the industries of Bangladesh established before 1980 have any provision for recycling/reuse water. The Department of Environment, Government of Bangladesh has been continuing its effort to motivate all these industrial concerns for upgrading their plants with waste treatment and recycling facilities. As a result, three industries of Bangladesh namely, Zia Fertilizer Factory, Ashuganj; Urea Fertilizer Factory, Chittagong; and Bata Shoe Factory, Nayarhat have installed waste treatment plants while other two namely, Karnophuli Paper and Rayon Complex, Chittagong and Sylhet Pulp and Paper Mills, Sylhet have adopted partial regulatory measures for their effluent treatment and recycling. Moreover, Bangladesh Sugar and Food Industries Corporation is considering the waste effluent issues with top priority.

(b) Regulations concerning wastewater disposal, and their enforcement

In Bangladesh, there was no environmental legislation until the late sixties in relation to water pollution and its control. "The Factories Act" for controlling the discharge of toxic substances and "The Criminal Procedure Code" for punishing pollution activities were there but those were very seldom enforced in practice. At the time, the local Government bodies, like, Municipal Authorities and the Department of Public Health Engineering controlled, in limited degrees, wastewater related health problems through their own by-laws. The first regulation came into force after passing the "Water Pollution Control Act of

1973". Following this act a project called "Water Pollution Control Project" was formed under the Department of Public Health Engineering and this started some monitoring activities on surface water and groundwater qualities at about twenty locations on nine major rivers and also in some ponds, canals, wells, effluent outfalls/drains, etc. In 1977, the Government of Bangladesh promulgated the "Environment Pollution Control Ordinance" and this continues as the only effective law in respect of wastewater disposal and environment protection in the country to this date. In order to make the law more comprehensive and the penalties more stringent a revised ordinance, incorporating experiences of environmental laws in Bangladesh and abroad, named "Bangladesh Environment Preservation Ordinance" is underway.

(c) Application of clean technologies in industry and agriculture

Application of clean technologies in industry and agriculture has not yet started in Bangladesh. However, some steps have been initiated in order to have partial protection of surface water and ground water quality as follows:

(i) *Relocation of harmful waste producing industrial units to suitable places*. For example, tanneries in the Hazaribagh area, one unit of which is reported to discharge 2,500 gallons per day of wastewater containing mostly chromium into the Buriganga River, have been instructed to shift out of Dhaka city;

Parameter	Range of variation
pH	4-10
Total Alkalinity (as CaCO$_3$)	185-6,475 mg/l
Electrical conductivity	1,670-93,000 micro mhos/cm
Chloride	175-18,000 mg/l
Chromium	2.6-2,800 mg/l
COD	120-9,600 mg/l
Ammonia Nitrogen	12-1,970 mg/l

(ii) *Setting up of a system of environmental clearance (no objection) certificate for all new industrial establishments*. This clearance is issued upon thorough investigation and judgement about the wastewater produced and their treatment in the concerned industry. The Department of Environment usually issue no objection certificates in this respect;

(iii) *Imposing ban on the use of harmful pesticides in the agricultural sector.* For example, eight pesticide chemicals have already been banned and some others are under serious consideration. Control on pesticides use is being done through Plant Protection Unit of the Department of Agricultural Extension, Government of Bangladesh.

3. Monitoring and enforcement of the quality of wastewater for disposal into water bodies

(a) Wastewater quality monitoring (ground and surface water)

Most industrial units of Bangladesh, large an small, discharge their wastewater into nearby water bodies and this ultimately flows into four main rivers, namely, Buriganga, Sitalakhya, Kornaphuli and Bhairab through canals or oxidation lagoons. These rivers are also subject to pollution from untreated urban domestic waste and to a lesser extent run-off of agrochemicals. The Department of Environment, Government of Bangladesh conducts a monitoring programme on the quality of wastewater discharge form 905 identified polluting industries as well as the pollution level of the related river waters at different locations downstream of the discharge points, and has set up an informal data bank containing these information. The typical quality of wastewater from tannery industries in Hazaribagh, Dhaka is shown below:

The above information indicate that industrial waste discharge to rivers are relatively less offensive than sanitary wastes from urban areas. Bangladesh Water Development Board collects data on groundwater quality from a number of selected monitoring wells. The Department of Environment also collects ambient water quality data from 9 specific points of the major rivers of Bangladesh under the programme of Global Environmental Monitoring System (GEMS).

(b) Standards for the quality of wastewater for disposal to main water bodies

Type of wastewater	Parameter	Standing limit
Domestic sewage	Temperature	30°C
	Nitrate-Nitrogen	58 mg/l
	Phosphate	35 mg/l
	BOD	40 mg/l
	Total coliform	1,000/100 ml sample
Industrial effluent	Temperature	40-45°C
	pH	6.0-9.0
	Dissolved oxygen	4.5-8.0 mg/l
	Electrical conductivity	1,200 micro mhos/cm
	Ammonia	5 mg/l
	Nitrate-Nitrogen	58 mg/l
	Iron	2 mg/l
	Zinc	5 mg/l
	Manganese	5 mg/l
	Chromium (+6)	0.1 mg/l
	BOD	50 mg/l
	COD	200 mg/l
	Total coliform	10,000/100 ml sample
	Faecal coliform	100 mg/l

The Department of Environment, Government of Bangladesh has classified wastewaters, depending on the source, into five categories namely, domestic sewage, sanitary sewage, house sewage, storm sewage, and industrial waste. The Government of Bangladesh has set the Environmental Quality Standards (EQS), wherever possible, for these wastewaters for disposal into main water bodies. The following shows discharge standards for domestic sewage and industrial effluent into recipient water bodies.

(c) Wastewater quality management

In Bangladesh, wastewater arises mainly from two sources: domestic/community and industrial. The domestic wastewater usually has high BOD and bacteria content, while the industrial wastewater is mostly polluted with BOD, COD, and heavy metal elements like, lead, chromium, cadmium, mercury, copper, etc. There is no specific treatment method in use in the country for managing the quality of domestic/community wastewater. This type of water is normally self-treated by natural means like lagoon treatment upon disposal into the water bodies. A survey conducted by the Department of Environment in 1990 showed that out of a total of 6,313 industrial units in Bangladesh, 2,152 are water polluters at various degrees. Among these water polluting industries only a few large scale industries treat the wastewater and monitor the quality to maintain the discharge standards. All other remaining industries do not follow any technique for wastewater quality management.

Conclusion

Scarcity of freshwater poses a serious and growing threat to sustainable development and protection of the environment. Human health and welfare, food security, industrial development and the ecosystems on which they depend, are all at risk, unless water and land resources are managed more effectively in the present decade and beyond. Reduction of dry season flows in Bangladesh due to increasing upstream withdrawals has also aggravated saline intrusion. Appropriate measures to restore Bangladesh's rightful share of the upstream flows and assured share of dry season flows become imperative for sustainable water resources development of Bangladesh.

V. WATER AND SUSTAINABLE DEVELOPMENT IN CAMBODIA

Ouk Sisovann
Environmental Science Specialist and Assistant to the Minister
Ministry of Environment

A. Water resources and hydrology

The Mekong River, one of the earth's major rivers, originates in Tibet. It enters Cambodia from Laos and then flows south for about 500 km before entering Viet Nam. The Mekong system drains 86 per cent of Cambodia with an average annual discharge of more than 300 billion m^3 at the border with Viet Nam. The average flow in the lower basin is 12,350 m^3/s, and in the dry season amounts to about 1,600 m^3 /s. A major feature of the Mekong system is Tonle Sap (the Great Lake) which varies in size from about 2,600 km^2 at the end of the dry season, to some 10,500 km^2 at the end of the rainy season. Tonle Sap fills by means of flow reversal from the Mekong river during the wet season and then discharges back to the river during the dry season.

There are approximately 20 major tributaries in Cambodia that enter the Mekong system. Nine of the tributaries discharge into Tonle Sap. Over the ages, the silt load from these tributaries and the river has resulted in deposits of fertile soil in the lowland areas which are the main source of the country's rice and other crops. A number of the tributaries are developed for water storage, hydro-electricity, flood control, or irrigation.

Changes in the hydrological regime of the Mekong system, due to upper catchment deforestation, water storage and diversions for irrigation without natural flow consideration, in particular during the dry season, and proposed construction of dams in the system will have major impacts on the ecology of wetlands, floodplain, fisheries, and existing land use patterns in the country.

Although silt transported by the Mekong system is beneficial for depositing fertile soil for agriculture, sedimentation in Tonle Sap poses a major problem. Bed aggravation in the Tonle Sap could lead to environmental degradation and would be a major loss of aquatic biota.

B. Water quality

The water quality of the Mekong River is a regional issue, and Cambodia is highly dependent on the policies and management of upstream countries. The water quality in the Mekong River system is characterized by a great variety of hydrological conditions.

The deterioration of the water quality in most rural areas of Cambodia is expected to take place through agricultural run-off (containing pesticides and fertilizers) and household waste disposal. There are no proper sanitation facilities, and people defecate in fields or by water bodies, resulting in contamination of drinking water sources.

In Phnom Penh, most of factories and handicrafts are situated close to the river bank and thus pour out their waste directly into the rivers. Moreover, the navigation of all kinds of vessels, and the operation of a number of night clubs, floating houses and hotels along rivers and lakes, contribute to degeneration of water quality. Almost all factories, enterprises, handicrafts and services have not been equipped with a chemical reaction or filter tank to treat their waste before discharging into public sewers, or rivers and lakes. Industrial waste disposal will cause a major problem in the near future, because no pollution standards currently exist.

C. Water supply and sanitation

Cambodia has abundant water resources from the Mekong River. Despite the abundance of groundwater resources, access to potable water and environmental sanitation facilities are limited. During the rainy season there is heavy reliance on rainwater for clean water supplies - which is collected in large jars in both urban and rural areas, although this provides safe water for only some five months of the year. During the dry season, the rural population relies mostly on discriminate and often highly contaminated surface water from ponds, lakes, rivers, etc., while the urban population use water in both seasons that is obtained from wells, private vendors or dilapidated public systems. Bottled drinking water is widely available but, although reasonably priced, is often beyond the reach of the poorest and most vulnerable members of society.

While precise comprehensive data on access to water supply are not available, it is estimated that only some 3.2 million people (32 per cent of the population) have access to clean drinking water, about 65 per cent of the urban population (mostly in Phnom Penh) and 25 per cent of the rural population. These data hide the wide variations in both the quality and quantity of water available, as well as the frequent interruptions in urban supply, and they also hide the fact that there is no treatment of sewage even where sewage systems exist are often a water source as well.

The current situation with respect to water supply, sanitation and drainage has obvious implications for public health, particularly for children. The provision of potable water and sanitation facilities in both rural and urban areas is the high priority of the Royal Government planning.

Waste water management in Phnom Penh and other large municipalities is extremely poor. The combined sewage/storm drainage systems have not been maintained over the past two decades, and are in a state of disrepair, with 80 per cent of the piping damaged in Phnom Penh. Drainage water and drinking water mix, with obvious health implications. Diarrhoeal diseases are common throughout Cambodia and cholera outbreaks occur frequently. There are frequent floods in the city during the rainy season, as the sewers become rapidly clogged. The problems of urban waste water are particularly acute in the larger urban areas such as Phnom Penh and Battambang, where dramatic population growth is placing additional burdens on the overloaded system.

Cambodia does not have a national water management policy addressing the multi-sectoral interests of water use. The lack of sufficient water for both irrigation and domestic use is considered to be the most pressing problem in many areas. In addition, the water quality of the Mekong River in Cambodia is highly dependent on water management policies of the countries with territory in the upper catchment of the Mekong River.

The Ministry of Environment has worked together with institutions involved in preparing managerial principles consistent with environmental techniques, especially, the preparation of country wide water quality standards. A comprehensive water management policy is needed which will rationalize water use in the areas of agriculture, fisheries, domestic use, hydropower, transportation and tourism.

D. Wetland

In Cambodia, the most important wetlands are the Mekong River and its floodplain, the Great Lake and the Tonle Sap River floodplain, marshes and grasslands around Stung Sen, and the coastal wetland. Cambodian wetlands provide rich nutrients and spawning habitats for fish, water birds, reptiles, and amphibians.

All types of wetlands are used for gathering fuelwood and the production of charcoal. Fish, waterfowl, edible vegetation, and animals are directly used as a sources of food. Aquaculture and agriculture are both supported by water from the wetlands.

Threats to Cambodian wetlands are numerous and vary with wetland type and location. They are summarized below:

For the Mekong river and its floodplain:

- water pollution by agricultural run-off carrying pesticides, fertilizers and domestic waste;
- high pressure on the natural resources, forests clearing for firewood and charcoal;
- poor planning and management of development projects (irrigation and hydroelectric dams) and growing industry will form a threat in the near future.

For the Great Lake and the floodplain of Tonle Sap river:

- illegal, forest clearing for charcoal and firewood, affecting fish and other biodiversity habitats;
- construction of fish traps,
- transformation to agriculture land,

- over-exploitation and the use of destructive fishing gears,
- increase in siltation as a result of deforestation in the upper watersheds;
- water pollution due to domestic waste, mining and agricultural run-off.

General recommendations regarding wetland conservation are:

- institutional capacity building of involved governmental agencies;
- strengthening the cooperation among governmental agencies and local authorities and people;
- promoting living standards of local people by offering new proper employment;
- development of wetland policy, legislation and enforcement instruments, e.g. Environment Impact Assessment (EIA);
- initiation of research programmes on ecology and socio-economic aspects of wetlands;
- starting environmental education and training programmes at higher institutions;
- stimulating the Cambodian government towards international cooperation, e.g. Ramsar Convention;
- encouraging the proposal of nomination of the Great Lake to the World Natural Heritage List.

E. Fisheries

Fish is the second most important component of the Cambodian diet (consumption for 1991 was estimated to be 13-16 kg per capita), next to rice. Up to 75 per cent of the population's dietary animal protein intake is from fish.

The fisheries sector plays a significant role in the economy representing up to 5 per cent of the GDP. Total commercial fisheries output between 1990-1992 averaged 113,500 tons per year, of which 70,000 tons (61 per cent) were inland fish, 37,000 tons (32 per cent) marine fish and 7,000 tons (about 6 per cent) aquacultural products.

Currently, over-exploitation, poor management and environmental degradation are claimed to have irreparably damaged these fisheries. The Tonle Sap lake was once one of the richest inland fishing lakes in the world. It accounts for 60 per cent of the country's

inland fisheries. However, the fish stock in Cambodian waters is now believed to be under stress. Hence, the ecological threat, environmental degradation, over fishing, and unregulated coastal development, pose serious threats to Cambodia's fisheries.

Fish productivity is very closely linked to environmental quality. Environmental causes of declining fisheries production in Cambodia are cited as the following: loss of fish spawning grounds through deforestation (especially inundated forests) and conversion of land to agriculture; sedimentation of the Great Lake and siltation of the Mekong River system; efforts of a poorly-designed irrigation network of canals; barrage systems that have altered the spawning environment; and water pollution due to gem mining activities in the upland areas.

1. Constraints

Some of the constraints faced by the fisheries sector include: the Fishery Department (FD) does not have enough budget to fully execute its responsibilities; limited number of staff of the FD have the capacity for administration and management; uncontrolled fishing, over-fishing, and environmental degradation; fisheries research activities are very weak, the existing Freshwater Fishery Research Station is only producing fish fry of limited types, and the facilities and equipment are ill-designed; there were Freshwater, and Oceanic Fisheries Research Institutes before the war, but these were all destroyed during the Khmer Rouge period; there seems to exist fish marketing problems, for instance in the production areas, there is a difficulty of fish sales in the fishing season, while in remote provinces, the people need stable supply of fish; lack of coordination between FD and relevant agencies; lack of legal instruments and enforcement; and lack of knowledge in the field of fisheries and public participation, etc.

2. Recommendations

In order to restore sustained production of fisheries in Cambodia the following actions are recommended: rehabilitation of inundated forests to re-establish spawning habitats; preparation of EIAs on dam projects on the Mekong River, and the barrage project on the Tonle Sap; capacity building of the staff of FD and Ministry of Environment; implementation of marine reserves and national parks; data and information gathering; development of a sustainable fishery management policy; development of appropriate legislation and reforcing instruments; regulation; and initiation of integrated studies.

F. Irrigation

France and the USA had provided substantial assistance in the development of irrigation systems in Cambodia. During, the Khmer Rouge period, a gridwork of canals was built without a technical understanding of hydraulic works. The scale of work was such that it has caused massive damage to the landscape and hydraulic regime. Since 1974, no large irrigation projects have been implemented, and most medium-sized projects have failed. Some small scale projects have been successful.

At present, the Department of Hydrology defines three categories of irrigation works: (i) large scale projects, which include multi-purpose hydro-electric and irrigation schemes, such as reservoirs and dams; (ii) medium scale projects, which cover an area of more than 500 ha and serve as single-purpose irrigation systems such as colmatage canals. and (iii) small scale projects, which cover irrigation works in an area of 500 ha or less, such as construction of weirs, culverts, ponds, dikes, canals, and control structures. A comprehensive study of large and medium scale irrigation systems was recently undertaken by UNDP and Mekong Secretariat to prepare an inventory of existing systems, and to develop a procedure for irrigation rehabilitation works and prepare a rehabilitation strategy.

1. Constraints

- No large scale irrigation systems are currently under construction due to the on-going study by the Mekong Secretariat of about three to four systems for possible rehabilitation; uncertainty due to the large financial commitments which are required; continuing security problems; possible effects of upstream development projects on the Mekong River; and the fact that such projects are beyond the Government's capability to design, construct and maintain.

- Recent attempts at medium scale projects have run into difficulties, and some have failed entirely. The ten medium scale projects identified in the UNDP/Mekong Secretariat Irrigation Reha-bilitation Study are considered to be economically

justifiable in the pre-feasibility stage and, if implemented, should encompass sustainable operations and maintenance measures.

- Although small scale irrigation systems are less costly and are more easily implemented with the participation of the local people, they are still complex in nature and require significant materials and strong technical support. Several systems have been completed, but problems of operation and maintenance have occurred.

2. Recommendations

- Detailed studies are needed to understand the complex relationships between water and its purposes in Cambodian society;

- EIA studies need to be included in irrigation development projects;

- Capacity building of the Hydrology Department's and Ministry of Environment's staff;

- Strengthening the cooperation between governmental institutions involved and international and NGOs;

- Stimulate local people to take part in maintenance of the existing irrigation;

- Promotion of public participation.

G. Navigation and transport sector

Inland water ways constitute one of the most traditional and, most efficient mode of transportation in Cambodia. The inland water transport system in the country comprises the Mekong, the Tonle Sap and Bassac rivers, and their tributaries having a total navigable length of about 1,800 km, of which more than a third can be used throughout the year. During the last twenty years of warfare and hostilities, the navigable system has been dramatically destroyed. However, after the recent restoration of peace, it is envisaged that the demand for water transport will be increasing again due to the recovery of industrial and agricultural productivity in the country.

Environmental issues mainly relate to the risks of transporting hazardous goods. Oil spill poses the greatest risk of polluting the Mekong and Bassac

Rivers and Great Lake. Erosion of the soil of the river banks due to river transport is not yet a real problem.

1. Constraints

As in other development sectors, data/information on the existing inland navigation facilities and their respective conditions in Cambodia are limited. The existing navigation facilities are believed to be in bad shape, due to many years of internal disturbance and lack of proper maintenance. The capacity of the responsible agencies to carry out the operation and maintenance of the navigation facilities is insufficient both in terms of manpower and training.

2. Recommendations

- A clear strategy for development of inland navigation to optimally utilize the rich water resources in the country and for national economic development is required to ensure its appropriateness and its full complementarity to other modes of transportation.

- It should be of interest to enhance the role of inland navigation in Cambodia in promoting economic cooperation among countries in the region.

- Development of inland navigation should take advantage of an effective use of the scarce resources, such as development fund, experts, skilled labours, equipment and materials.

- Improving legal instrument and enforcement for navigation.

H. Hydropower development

1. Power demands, potential and development plans

The electricity supply in Cambodia is totally dependent on imported fuel and consists of a number of isolated systems serving Phnom Penh and the major provincial towns. Following the rehabilitation of the Kirirom Project (11 MW) over the next two years, another hydropower project is being considered for priority development; namely, the Kamchay project in southern Cambodia, with an installed capacity of around 100 MW. In addition, a number of small-scale hydropower projects are also being considered as priorities for local supply, such as the Battambang (36 MW) and Stung Chinith (8 MW). The Sambor project (3,300 MW) on the mainstream is viewed as an important long-term project. The total potential on the Mekong tributaries is estimated at 2,200 MW, with a further 1,000 MW on the rivers outside the Mekong basin. Most of the identified projects have only been studied at desk/reconnaissance level, and are not ready for implementation in the near future. Therefore the immediate demand has to be met by diesel/thermal plants and energy imports.

2. Inventory of hydropower potential

A study, based on the findings of earlier studies in 1970, 1973 and 1983, namely "Review and Assessment of Water Resources for hydropower Development and Identification of Priority Projects in Cambodia" was completed in June 1995. The result of the study is summarized table 3.

3. Short and medium term development projects

With the review of the present situation of power demand and supply in the country, the following projects indicated in table 4 were recommended for short and medium needs.

4. Long-term development projects

Based on these results, together with the recently completed Mekong mainstream run-of-river hydropower study, and other on-going sectoral studies, the newly established Mekong River Commission will prepare a Basin Development Plan, in which hydropower is a major component. The hydropower projects for long-term development in Cambodia are given in table 5.

The projects mentioned above are considered as the best possible projects for long-term or energy export-oriented development. However, the preparation of feasibility studies, mobilization of funds, and detailed design are expected to take 8-10 years or more.

Table 3. Hydropower potential in Cambodia

No.	Items	Unit	Site number/installed capacity
1	Number of potential hydropower projects	-	65
2	Number of potential irrigation projects	-	18
3	Total number for installed capacity	MW	5,300 or 8,135*
3.1	Mekong	MW	1,445 or 4,280*
3.2	Mekong tributaries and other rivers	MW	3,855
4	Total energy generation	MW	41,400
5	North eastern region		
	Highest hydropower potential	GWh/year	13,000
	Sre Pok	GWh/year	5,000
	Se Kong	GWh/year	4,000
	Se San	GWh/year	3,000
	Prek Chlong	GWh/year	1,000
6	South western region		
	Stung Ta Tay	GWh/year	460
	Russei Chrum	GWh/year	220

*Depending on the alternative development scheme of Sambor Project (installed capacity 465 MW or 3,300 MW).

Table 4. Short- and medium-term development projects

No.	Projects	Max installed capacity (MW)	Annual energy production (GWH/yr)
1	Western Kirirom	13	70
2	Stung Piphot Alternative 2	25	140
3	Kamchay	127.5	558
4	Stung Atay	110	558
5	Bokor Plateau	28	147
6	Stung Battambang Alternative 2	36	187

Table 5. Long-term development projects

No.	Projects	Max installed capacity (MW)	Annual energy production (GWH/yr)
1	Sambor CPEC	465	2,800
2	Sambor 1994	3,300	14,780
3	Sambor 1984	3,600	18,820
4	Lower Stung Russei Chrum	125	656
5	Upper Se San 4	350	1,812
6	Upper Se San 1	900	4,740
7	Stung Areng Alternative 2	260	1,358
8	Upper Se San 3	375	1,977
9	Lower Se San and Lower Sre Pok	480	2,537

5. Environmental and socio-economic impacts

As compared to other sources of energy supply, hydropower is considered to be a better option since it is renewable, relatively clean and does not cause air pollution and global warming. However, hydropower development may affect the river ecosystem in terms of loss of land and forests, have impact on fisheries and other resources. It may also affect the livelihood of population, particularly when it requires resettlement. Due consideration should be given to these impacts in identifying and selecting project options for sustainable development. The Mekong River Commission and Cambodian National Mekong Committee should pay considerable attention to these issues, even at the planning stage, by using information from several research programmes on the environment, management of regional fisheries resources, including fish migration, watershed and forestry protection and erosion control, etc. These programmes provide essential basic data and information for the studies on hydropower projects.

(a) Regional cooperation for sustainable development of the Mekong River Basin

The Governments of Cambodia, Lao People's Democratic Republic, Viet Nam have agreed to cooperate in sustainable development, utilization, conservation and management of the Mekong River Basin water and related resources under the following Protocol Agreement:

Areas of Cooperation. To cooperate in all fields of sustainable development, utilization, management and conservation of the water and related resources of the Mekong River Basin including irrigation, hydro-power, navigation, flood control, fisheries, timber floating, recreation and tourism.

Projects, Programmes and Planning. To promote, support, cooperate and coordinate in the development of projects and programmes through the formulation of a basin development plan, that would be used to identify, categorize the projects and programmes to seek assistance for and to implement at the basin level.

Protection of the Environment and Ecological Balance. To protect the environment, natural resources, aquatic life and conditions, and ecological balance of the Mekong River Basin from pollution or other harmful effects.

Sovereign Equality, and Territorial Integrity. To cooperate on the basis of sovereign equality and territorial integrity in the utilization and protection of the water resources of the Mekong River Basin.

Reasonable and Equitable Utilization. To utilize the water of the Mekong River system in a reasonable and equitable manner in their respective territories, pursuant to all relevant factors and circumstances.

Maintenance of Flow on the Mainstream. To cooperate in the maintenance of the flow on the mainstream from diversion, storage, release or other actions of a permanent nature; except in the cases of historically severe droughts and/or floods.

Prevention and Cessation of Harmful Effects. To make every effort avoid, minimize and mitigate harmful effects that might occur to the environment, especially the water quantity and quality, the aquatic (ecosystem) conditions, and ecological balance of the river system.

State Responsibility for Damages. Where harmful effects cause damage to one or more riparians from the use of and/or discharge to waters of the Mekong River by any riparian State, the party(ies) concerned shall determine all relative factors, the cause, extent of damage and responsibility for damages caused by that State in conformity with the principles of international law relating to State responsibility, and to address and resolve all issues, differences and dispute in an amicable and timely manner by peaceful means.

Freedom of Navigation. Freedom of Navigation shall be accorded throughout the mainstream of Mekong River without regard to the territorial boundaries, for transportation and communication to promote regional cooperation and to satisfactorily implement the projects.

Emergency Situations. Whenever a party becomes aware of any special water quantity or quality problems constituting an emergency that requires an immediate response, it shall notify and consult directly with a party(ies) concerned and the Joint Committee without delay in order to take appropriate remedial action.

VI. SUSTAINABLE DEVELOPMENT OF WATER RESOURCES IN CHINA[*]

Introduction

China is a country having a great number of rivers. There are more than 50,000 rivers with catchment area each over 100 km^2 and about 1,500 rivers each over 1,000 km^2. According to analysis and calculation of the synchronous precipitation and runoff data for 24 years from 1956 to 1979 the mean annual runoff in the whole country is 2.72×10^{12} m^3, and the mean annual depth of runoff is 288 mm. There are about 2,300 lakes each with area larger than 1 km^2, and the total storage of about 709 $\times 10^9$ m^3, of which the freshwater portion constitutes 33 per cent. The total glacial area of the country is about 58,500 km^2, the glacier storage is around 5.1×10^{12} m^3, and the mean annual amount of glacier melt water is about 56×10^9 m^3. It is one of the recharge source for western rivers in the country.

The total average annual groundwater resources potential for whole country is 828×10^9 m^3. The amount of groundwater resources in plain areas of the north part of China is 146.8×10^9 m^3, which accounts for 78 per cent of groundwater resources in whole plain areas. For the whole country, the long term mean annual potential of surface water resources is 2,712 m^3 and that of groundwater resources is 828 km^3. As the duplicative amount is 728 km^3, the long term gross mean annual potential of water resources is estimated at 2,812 km^3.

A. Environmental sustainability of water resources development

1. Present situation of water resources development

The Chinese government has given high priority to the development of water resources as a basis for the development of its national economy. Water projects have been developed rapidly since the founding of the People's Republic of China. By the end of 1995, the country had constructed over 80,000 reservoirs with a total storage of 472 billion m^3, one million water diversion projects , about four million pumping projects, about half a million irrigation and drainage stations with a total installed capacity of about 21 million kw, about four million wells with a total installed capacity of 60 million kw.

In addition, the interbasin water transfer projects have been developed including water transfer projects from Luanhe River to Tianjin, from Luanhe River to Tangshan, from Qinglonghe River to Qinghuangdao, from Yellow River to Qingdao and from Daqinghe River to Shaanxi, etc. Water supply through the transfer projects has already accounted for 23 per cent of the total water supply in the Haihe River Basin. These projects have played an important role in the control and mitigation of floods and guaranteeing adequate quantities of water supply for domestic and industrial uses.

2. Situation concerning water use and water availability

The shortage of water resources and water pollution is increasingly serious and restrict social and economic sustainable development. For improvement of macro-management of water resources, sustainable development and better use of water resources, effectively preventing and controlling flood and drought to meet water demand, relevant efforts have been made which include the "The medium-long term planning for the water supply and demand in China"; the "Planning for the sources of water supply for the main water shortage cities in China"; the "Planning for the irrigation development in China"; the "Planning for water resources development in Ninth Five-Year Plan and to the year 2010 in China" and the "Planning for water supply to the villages and small towns in China to the year 2000".

In 1995, the total capacity of annual water supply was about 538 billion m^3 or about 19 per cent of the gross annual mean water resources. Of this total,

[*] Consolidated from papers presented by Messrs Li Qi and Liu Ping, Ministry of Water Resources, and Messrs Xu Xinyi and Wang Yan, China Institute of Water Resources and Hydropower Research at the ESCAP Seminar on the Establishment of Guidelines on Water and Sustainable Development, Bangkok, 9-13 December 1996 and a paper presented by Ms Wanjun, Ministry of Water Resources at the ESCAP Ad Hoc Expert Group Meeting on Sustainable Development of Water Resources, Bangkok, 10-12 July 1996.

actual surface water constituted about 441 billion m³, or 82 per cent of the total; groundwater 93 billion m³, or 17 per cent of the total and treated wastewater 3 billion m³. Of the surface water supply, the contribution from storage projects constituted about 34 per cent, from diversion projects about 37 per cent, from pumping projects about 21 per cent and other projects 8 per cent. Compared with 1980, the total amount water supply increased by 94 billion m³, of which surface water was 60 billion m³ and groundwater 4 billion m³.

In 1995, the actual water consumption was about 527 billion m³, comprising municipal and domestic consumption 30 billion m³ (5.7 per cent); industrial consumption 95 billion m³ (18 per cent), rural consumption 24 billion m³ (4.5 per cent); agriculture consumption 378 billion m³ (72 per cent). In 1995, the net increase in total water consumption in China was about 82 billion m³ compared with the consumption in 1980. This comprised the increase from the rural areas of about 10 billion m³ (consumption for irrigation was nearly the same as 1980); increase from urban and industrial water use of about 72 billion m³. In Northern China, water-saving efforts for municipal water use have been carried out to solve the problem of water shortage and the limitation of available water resources. Over the past ten years, the industrial water consumption has been found to increase at a much slower rate than the municipal/domestic water consumption. In Southern China, especially in the mid-downstream areas of Yangze River and the coastal zones in Zhujiang River area, both industrial and the municipal/domestic water consumption has increased rapidly along with the rapid development of industry, urbanization and improved living standard. In river basins in the south-east coastal areas, the urban water consumption in 1995 has increased by about 3.5 times compared with 1980. The largest increase in industrial water use had occurred in the Zhujiang River basin and other basins in South China where the increase during the period 1980-1995 was 4 times. The annual mean rate of increase of industrial water consumption in the Haihe River basin in the same period was only 2.6 per cent.

Although the water supply capacity in 1995 was relatively larger compared with that of 1980, the rate of increase was far behind the rate of economic development in China. For example, the annual growth of GNP was about 11.34 per cent between 1980 and 1995, while the water supply capacity grew by only 1.31 per cent. Water shortage has increasingly become serious with the rapid social and economic development in China. Economic growth and living standards therefore depend on the efficient use of existing water supply capacity, practising water-saving measures and reducing the agricultural water consumption. An additional water supply capacity of 40-50 billion m³ is planned for the year 2000 together with water-saving measures to provide sufficient drinking water in rural areas and meet water demand for social and economic development.

3. Water resources use in future

In order to predict the water use and water availability in 2000, a national water management model has been developed. Computations using the model demonstrated that for an average year with the probability of exceedence of 75 per cent, some 667.8 billion m³ of water will be available for the whole country in the year 2000, a net increase of 194.3 billion m³ compared with that of 1980, constituting a total increase of 28.9 per cent over the during the 20 year period.

Of the total amount of 667.8 billion m³ available for the nation's consumption in the year 2000, 586.0 billion m³ (or roughly 88 per cent) will be surface water extracted from rivers, and 81.8 billion m³ (or roughly 12 per cent) will be groundwater. With the total consumption of 667.8 billion m³, the annual per capita water consumption will increase from 483 m³ in 1980 to 557 m³ in 2000. Out of 586 billion m³ of surface water to be tapped from rivers in 2000, the percentage to be supplied by reservoir storage will increase slightly from 30 to 35 per cent while the remaining will be shared by diversion and lifting.

4. Overexploitation and overuse of water resources and measures to prevent such situations

At present, the per capita freshwater reserve in China is 2,500 m³, which is about one-fourth of the world's average. With the increase in population and economic development, more and more cities will be facing serious water shortages. Although the bulk of China's water supply projects were completed during the 1950s and the 1960s, their supply capacity has gradually declined owing to lack of maintenance. A long term plan for development and protection of water resources is required to solve the problem of water shortage which has become a constraint to socio-economic development. Thus, the task of solving the continuing water shortage in Northern China, East Jiaozhou Peninsular, mid-South Liaoning, Northwest China and many coastal cities has been given high priority by the central government.

In general, Southern China is rich in water resources while Northern China is short of water resources, and it is more difficult to construct water development and utilization projects in the Northern part of the country. The level of water utilization, on the contrary, increases from South to North. In 44 years after the establishment of the People's Republic of China, a large number of water development and utilization projects have been built with capacities reaching 500 billion m^3 per annum. However, it still could not meet the nation's water demand. The annual water shortage for agriculture totals 30 billion m^3. The actual area of irrigated land amounts to 48.7 million hectares and 80 million people in rural areas still have shortage of safe drinking water. Three hundred cities in China are reported to be water-deficient as a result of (or a combination of) limitation of water resources availability, low water use efficiency, degradation of water quality, and insufficient capacity of water treatment plants and water distribution systems.

At present, the freshwater supply in most of China's cities is threatened by the deterioration of water quality and the destruction of water ecosystem. Almost 80 per cent of the country's wastewater is discharged directly into rivers. This caused high pollution levels in more than one-third of the country's rivers and in 90 per cent of the water bodies of all cities. Thus, water sources in more than 50 per cent of China's major towns are no longer suitable for drinking. Besides, water ecosystems have been severely impaired, and aquatic life, especially fishery resources, is threatened by large-scale reclamation of marshes, inappropriate application of pesticides and chemical fertilizers, and soil erosion. As a result, the length of rivers void of fish and shrimp totals 2,400 kilometres, and the number of lakes has decreased by 543 over a thirty year period, and some of the remaining lakes have become eutrophic. The loss in freshwater fish yield caused by the destruction of water ecosystem has reached eight thousand tons annually. This situation calls for the protection of water quality and the water ecological environment without delay.

In 1990, China's urban population was about 26 per cent of the country's total. It is estimated that by 2000 the urban population will reach 460 million,

which is about 35 per cent of the country's total. The fast growth of urban population and industrialization are putting increasing pressure on water resources and the environment in many cities. Over three hundred cities are having a daily shortage of 16 million m^3 of water. In southern cities, pollution causes 60 to 70 per cent of the total shortage. Water shortages are especially felt in northern and coastal cities. According to the current rate of economic growth, the annual water shortage in cities is expected to exceed twenty billion m^3 by the year 2000. Besides, population growth, increase in industrial wastewater discharge and over-exploitation of water resources, could threaten the country's coastal environment and supply of fresh water.

Groundwater is an important source of China's urban, industrial and agricultural water supply. About two-third of China's cities and one-fourth of its agricultural fields depend on groundwater. Agricultural use accounts for 81 per cent of the total groundwater being extracted. At present, there are many problems associated with groundwater development and protection, such as steadily lowering of groundwater table, and increased pollution of aquifers in urban areas. These problems directly affect the sustainable utilization and protection of the groundwater resources. To rectify such adverse effects, a long-term groundwater utilization strategy is urgently needed.

According to the statistics of twelve hundred rivers presently monitored, 850 are found to be severely polluted and some major lakes are already in various phases of eutrophication. Besides, coastal areas are hit by sea water intrusion. General speaking, water quality in China is steadily deteriorating which is aggravated by the widening gap between the water supply capacity and water demand. Severe water pollution and water shortage have become the two main obstacles in China's efforts to provide adequate water supply for sustainable development. While water cannot be substituted, it can be subjected to natural self-cleansing processes or man-made treatment processes. Treatment of urban wastewater into reusable water will therefore reduce pressures on existing scarce water supply, and reduce water pollution. In fact, the treatment of wastewater is an important water quality protection measure for enabling long-term water utilization.

Studies indicated that the water resources shortage or deficiency problem would arise in the long run. The yearly demand of water based on an expected fourfold GNP growth in China by 2000 is expected to reach 600 billion m^3, if conservation and rational use of water could take effect and a medium-drought weather would prevail. If the water demand in the first decade of the 21st century were to increase by 2-3 per cent annually, the total water demand in 2010 would reach 720 billion m^3, which means that the increment of water demand in ten years will comprise over 100 billion m^3.

By the turn of century, North China, Shandong, Northwest China, mid-South Liaoning and dozens of coastal cities will be seriously hit by freshwater deficiency. As a result, the economic and social development of various regions in the country will be adversely affected due to shortage of water for irrigation in North China, industrial use of water for energy base in Shanxi and water supply in mid-South Liaoning and Shandong Peninsular.

Measures undertaken to alleviate the problem of water shortage include:

Groundwater pollution control

- Comprehensive evaluation and assessment of the negative impacts of over-extraction of groundwater with the purpose of establishing a unified management plan for the rational utilization and development of groundwater resources in different areas and regions of the country;

- Enactment of legislation for groundwater resources utilization and protection;

- Identification and establishment of groundwater resources protection zones to improve groundwater recharge;

- Survey and exploration for new utilizable groundwater sources, introduction of measures for preventing overexploitation, enhancement of groundwater artificial recharge and adoption of rational water pricing policy to prevent wastage of both surface water and groundwater resources;

- Conjunctive use and management of both surface water and groundwater resources;

- Enactment and promulgation of laws, regulations and technical standards for water pollution control, for both surface water and groundwater;

- Strict control of discharge of industrial wastewater, disposal of solid wastes, poisonous and hazardous matters to prevent groundwater pollution.

Protection of aquatic ecosystems

- Improvement of the water resources management system by using river basins as management units and adopting an integrated approach to water resources utilization and protection of aquatic ecosystem;

- Setting-up and improvement of the biological, sanitary, physical and chemical standards for water quality monitoring for all kinds of water bodies;

- Preparation of environment management plans for protection of freshwater bodies and shoreline ecosystems, with particular attention paid to fishery, aquaculture, agricultural production and biodiversity conservation;

- Improvement of the water quality monitoring network for better water supply source protection;

- Strict control of discharge of industrial and urban waste water and use of agricultural fertilizers and pesticides in rural areas and reducing unit water consumption levels in all economic sectors;

- Dredging drainage canals and improving irrigation and drainage facilities in areas prone to waterlogging and schistosomiasis infection particularly in the south of the country to upgrade the quality of environment.

5. National master water plan

China has set up the following main targets in its national master water plans scheduled for the year 2000 and 2010 respectively. The essential features of these plans are as follows:

- Acceleration of the water management and flood control programme for nation's major rivers and lakes, with main emphasis placed on the safety of people in flood prone areas. Before the end of the century the flood control capacity of the main stem of all seven major rivers in the country is expected to become adequate to protect against the largest flood recorded since the founding of the People's Republic of China. It is also expected that the rehabilitation and strengthening of unsafe reservoirs nationwide as well as the construction of the first stage of flood control facilities near the key major cities would be completed and provide protection to the nation's industrial and agricultural areas, transportation facilities and main cities in the country. Before 2010 the country's flood control capacity of the major rivers would be further enhanced. Thus, on the Yangtze river a complete flood control system would be built up on its middle and lower reaches, and on the Yellow river further efforts would be made to upgrade the existing capacity on its lower reaches to control the one thousand year flood. In addition, the level of flood protection in all key cities would be raised up to the standards specified by the Ministry of Water Resources.

- Improving water development and management to increase the country's annual grain production to 50 million ton by the year 2010. To achieve this target some 6.66 million ha of farmland would be placed under irrigation by the year 2000 (with half as new irrigation establishment and the rest as water-saving irrigation), and another 6.66 million ha would be placed under irrigation by the year 2010. In the meantime efforts would be made to upgrade middle and low yield farmland through the dissemination of water-saving irrigation techniques as well as amelioration of waterlogged and salinized farmland.

- Enhancement of the rational exploitation, utilization and protection of water resources to provide adequate water supply of acceptable quality to the nation's industry, agriculture and cities. In order to achieve this target, a large number of key water control projects and the trans-basin water transfer project from south (from the Yangtze river) to north of the country would be carried out. With the commissioning of those projects, an additional water supply capacity of 60 to 80 million m^3 per annum would become available by 2000 improving the water supply capacities in the north of the country and in coastal regions. By 2010 the water supply capacity to some water-short regions and cities would be further improved.

- Acceleration of medium and small-scale hydropower construction and township water supply programmes. By the year 2000 an additional 10 GW installed capacity of hydropower would be commissioned and some 8,000 new township and village water supply facilities would be completed to provide water to 65 million villagers in remote areas. By the year 2010 another 20 GW installed capacity of hydropower would be commissioned and some 30,000 new township and village water supply facilities would be completed.

- Implementation of national programmes for water and soil conservation, water resources protection and ecological environment improvement. Main emphasis would be placed on accelerating the implementation of water and soil conservation in the Yellow river, Yangtze river and Pearl river basins. It is expected that the national water and soil conservation programme covering an area of 250,000 km^2 would be completed by the year 2000. At the same time, efforts would be made to assist the National Environment Protection Agency and its subordinate bureaus in controlling the river pollution, improving the quality of ecological environment and protecting the nation's water resources. By 2010 it is expected that the national soil conservation programme would cover another 400,000 km^2 of the nation's territory.

The overall goal of the development and protection of water resources is to combine the development and utilization of water resources with a full-scale saving of water to alleviate water supply crisis in the country and to maximize the economic, social, and environmental benefits resulting from the utilization of water resources. Another goal is to satisfy the demand for a greater quantity and better quality of water generated by higher living standards. Specific objectives are as follows:

(a) To meet China's water demand and assure continued economic development especially in regions with water scarcity through supply and demand management that would take into account the needs of national economic and social development as well as the management of state lands and drainage areas. These plans would then be included in the state and local development programmes at national and local levels. They are expected to function as a basis for action by the state and local governments;

(b) To develop preliminary solutions to the problems of pollution of drinking water sources and water systems in scenic spots by the year 2000, and improve the status of rivers, lakes and reservoirs to conform to state standards. Thus, groundwater used as urban drinking water sources should meet the state's quality standard. In rural areas, the centralized supply of potable water will be gradually expanded to reduce the incidence of water borne diseases, and prevent further degradation of the water quality;

(c) To achieve sustainable usage and protection of water resources, effective management and replenishment of groundwater will be carried out and groundwater pollution in over exploited areas will be controlled by the year 2000. Furthermore, legislation will be introduced and enforced to put groundwater resources under legal protection;

(d) To make the tap water available to 95 per cent of the population in 108 cities with insufficient water supplies by the year 2000. After the year 2000, following the completion of large scale water transfer projects and water source projects, sufficient domestic and industrial water supply in all cities will be ensured;

(e) Surface water and groundwater sources of water supply networks will be declared as protection areas by 2000. As a result, over 80 per cent of the surface water sources is expected to attain quality level B[1], at least 75 per cent of groundwater sources is expected to reach the national standards, and the environmental quality of major water bodies is expected to improve to some extent. Before 2000, pollution discharges will be controlled to maintain the water quality of major rivers and lakes (the Yangtze River, the Huaihe river, the Yellow River, the Pearl river, the Songhua River, the Taihu Lake, the Boyang Lake and the Dongting Lake) at quality level B, while the water quality of other heavily polluted rivers and lakes will be maintained at level C[2]. By the year 2000, 20 to 30 per cent of sewage effluent and 84 per cent of industrial waste water will be treated, and 10 per cent of the treated urban wastewater will be reused. By 2010, the treated volume of wastewater is expected to reach 40 to 50 per cent, and the reuse rate in water-scarce regions and cities will reach 30 to 40 per cent;

(f) To increase the overall irrigated land area from the present 48.7 million hectares to 53.3 million hectares by 2000, the increase in water demand will be met by the construction of farmland irrigation projects, medium and small reservoirs, water transfer and water lift projects which will provide additional water supply of 30 to 50 billion m^3 per annum. In the meantime, dissemination of water-saving techniques in irrigation such as low-pressure pipelines, sprinkling, trickling and microsprinkling techniques will be carried out. Besides, leveling of land and reduction of water losses in canal systems will lead to a saving of irrigation water of eight to ten billion m^3, thus guaranteeing the irrigation of 53.3 million hectares of land;

(g) To formulate appropriate strategies for the forecast and control of the influence of climate changes on water resources, and adopt effective measures to reduce the negative effects. At the same time, study of the potential influence of climate changes shall be carried out in regions with high drought and flood concentration to determine the best ways of controlling them;

(h) To reform the existing water management system and pass new legislation to promote the integrated planning and management. For effective

---

[1] Good for drinking without treatment but after disinfection.
[2] Good for drinking after treatment and disinfection.

development and protection of water resources, efforts will be made to improve the competence of management and technical personnel, and promote public participation in the integrated management of water resources.

The following measures are planned to be undertaken to achieve the above objectives:

(a) Advanced technology and methods will be adopted to enhance the effectiveness and efficiency in the protection of freshwater resources, land use control, development of forest resources, allocation water resources, and effective distribution of water resources. Public awareness of the importance of protection of water resources will be promoted through media and education. Community participating in water conservation, planning and managing, water resources assessment and other water related activities will also be encouraged;

(b) The entire catchment area will be treated and managed as a complete system. Water quality standards for all uses will also be set up. Pollution by fertilizer and pesticides in the rural area will be reduced. The efficiency in utilization of water resources will be improved to reduce water consumption. In flood prone areas of the South and lowland areas, rivers will be dredged to improve drainage and prevent the occurrence of water-borne diseases;

(c) The present over exploitation of groundwater resources will be examined and better planning and management of groundwater resources will be carried out. Legislation to control regional and trans-regional development and protection of groundwater resources will be introduced. Artificial recharge of groundwater and conjunctive use of surface and groundwater will be promoted. Control of groundwater pollution caused by industrial wastewater, solid waste and toxic pollutants will be strictly implemented;

(d) For trans-regional control of water pollution, urban water sources protection areas will be set up and the cost of upstream pollution control works will be matched with the benefit of downstream utilization. Water usage quotas will be set up for all industries as part of the implementation of the country wide water quota programme. Clean and water-saving manufacturing processes, recycling and reuse of water will be encouraged;

(e) Prevention and control of water pollution will be implemented by setting cross-boundary water quality standard in administrative districts, defining liability of each administration and by issuing waste discharge licenses. Public education in the protection of drinking water sources will be carried out and deadlines will be served to polluting facilities to either improve or move out of the catchment areas. Water quality monitoring and water pollution control will be carried out. Plans for the treatment and utilization of wastewater and standards of waste water quality for use in different industries will also be formulated. Efforts will be made for the establishment of enterprises specialized in the treatment, recycling and reuse of waste water;

(f) Existing policies, laws, and regulations related to development and protection of water resources will be revised to enhance the integrated management of water resources. Groundwater exploitation licenses will be issued based on a distribution quota system at the local levels to balance the supply and demand and improve the quality of water resources.

6. Institutional and legal frameworks for water resources management and development

At present water resources development, utilization and management are the main mandate and responsibility of the Ministry of Water Resources which will be supported by the major river basin commissions and local governmental agencies at the provincial, prefectural and county levels. The institutional organization of all relevant governmental agencies and institutions as well as their functions are summarized in figure 2.

The "Water Law of the People's Republic of China" was promulgated in 1988. Shortly after promulgation of this law, the Ministry of Water Resources started working on setting-up the water-related legislation framework. These water-related laws and regulations can be classified into seven categories, namely, water resources development, utilization and protection; water and soil conservation; flood and drought control; management and protection of water projects; operational management; supervision and administration of law enforcement; and others.

Two other national laws that have been promulgated include the "Law on Water Pollution

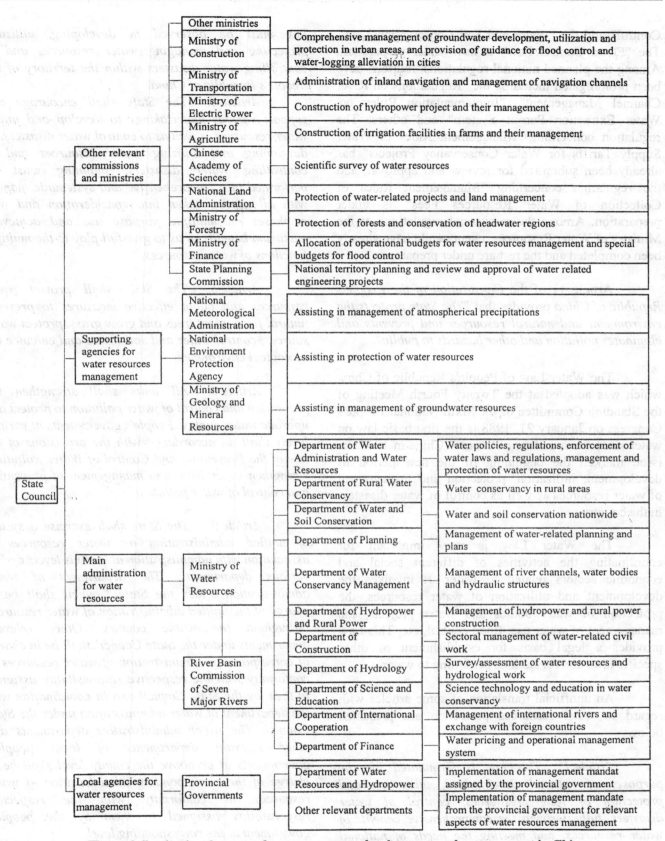

Figure 2. Institutional set-up of water resources development and management in China

Control" and the "Water and Soil Conservation Law". The "Flood Control Law" is now under preparation. Among the planned national regulations, fourteen have been promulgated including the "Regulations on River Channel Management", "Implementation Rules on Water Extraction Permit System" and others. The regulation concerning "Management Rules of Water Supply Tariffs for Water Conservancy Projects" has already been submitted for review and approval, and the regulation concerning "Management Rules of Collection of Water Resources Fees" is under preparation. Among the ministerial regulations of the Ministry of Water Resources, twenty eight have already been completed and the rest are under preparation.

Article 11 of the *Constitution of the People's Republic of China* provides that *"The State protects the environment and natural resources and prevents and eliminates pollution and other hazards to public".*

The Water Law of People's Republic of China which was adopted at the Twenty Fourth Meeting of the Standing Committee of the Sixth National People's Congress on January 21, 1988 is the first basic law on water since the founding of the new China in 1949. Its issue marked the beginning of the new period of development, utilization, protection and management of water resources as well as control of water disasters in the country.

The Water Law is very important for coordinating the activities of different social and economic sectors related to water. It involves the development and utilization of water resources, the protection of water bodies and water projects, the management of water use, flood control, etc. This Law provides a legal basis for establishment of other specific laws and regulations pertaining to water.

An unofficial translation of some articles with regard to water resources protection are presented below:

Article 1. This law is formulated for the purposes of rational development, utilization and protection of water resources, control of water disasters, fully deriving the comprehensive benefits of water resources, and meeting the needs of national economic development and the livelihood of the people.

Article 2. For the purpose of this law, "water resources" means surface water and groundwater. This

law must be observed in developing, utilizing, protecting and managing water resources and in controlling water disasters within the territory of the People's Republic of China.

Article 4. The State shall encourage and support various undertakings to develop and utilize water resources as well as to control water disasters. In developing and utilizing water resources and in controlling water disasters, planning must be performed in a comprehensive and systematic manner with all aspects taken into consideration and with emphases on multiple purpose use and achieving maximum benefits so as to give full play to the multiple functions of water resources.

Article 5. The State shall protect water resources and adopt effective measures to preserve natural flora, plant trees and grow grass, protect water sources, control water and soil losses and enhance the ecological environment.

Article 6. All units shall strengthen the prevention and control of water pollution to protect and upgrade water quality. People's governments at various levels shall, in accordance with the provisions of the law of the Prevention and Control of Water Pollution, strengthen supervision and management of prevention and control of water pollution.

Article 9. The State shall exercise a system of unified administration on water resources in association with administration at various levels and by various departments. The department of water administration under the State Council shall be in charge of the unified administration of water resources throughout the whole country. Other relevant departments under the State Council shall be in charge of corresponding administration of water resources in conformity with the respective responsibility assigned to them by the State Council and in coordination with the department of water administration under the State Council. The water administrative departments and other relevant departments of local people's governments at or above the county level shall be in charge of the corresponding administration of water resources in conformity with the respective responsibility assigned to them by the people's government at the corresponding level.

According to the Water Law and the administrative division of departments, the Ministry of Water Resources (MWR) is the department of water administration under the State Council and responsible for the unified administration of the development, utilization, protection and management of water resources throughout the country, establishing the administrating laws and regulations of water management, working out the long term and annual plans of water resources development jointly with other departments concerned, the comprehensive harnessing and development of rivers and so on. As MWR's agencies which have been authorized to exercise partial management functions of the MWR, there exist seven Water Resources Committees (WRC) administrating the Yangtze River, Yellow River, Pearl River, Songthuajiang and Liaohe Rivers, Haihe River, Huaihe River and Taihu Lake respectively. Each WRC has set up a water resources protection organization (bureau or office) under the dual leadership of NEPA and MWR.

7. Human resources development

(a) System for human resources development

To enhance human resources development, the Ministry of Water Resources has set up a guideline for the management system to incorporate provision of guidance, coordination, evaluation and offering of technical services as a component of its operational responsibilities. In 1994, the Ministry of Water Resources prepared and published a number of working documents, including the "Regulations on Professional Education for Employees in the Water Conservancy Sector", "Some Opinions and Considerations on Reform and Development of Professional Education in Water Conservancy Sector", "Planning Outline of Professional Education of Water Conservancy Sector in the Period of 1994-2000" and "Trans-century Human Resources Development Planning of Water Conservancy Sector". Those documents are expected to serve as the foundation for nationwide standardization of professional education for employees in the water conservancy sector.

(b) On-the-job training and continuing education

To explore the effective means of on-the-job training and continuing education and to introduce the registration system for the employees' desirous of receiving continuing education in the water conservancy sector, the Department of Personnel and Labour Management and the Department of Science and Education, Ministry of Water Resources, jointly prepared and issued a circular in 1995 to entrust the

Yellow River Water Conservancy Commission and the Jinan Yellow River Engineering Bureau in Shandong province to carry out a pilot project for the on-the-job training and the Water Resources Protection Bureau under the Yangtze River Water Conservancy Commission to continue with a pilot project on the registration system of continuing education.

(c) Skill training for operational management

To meet the demand of trained nationals in the water sector in the country, the Minister of Water Resources indicated at its "National Working Meeting on Water Conservancy Economy" in 1993 that it planned to train 10,000 managers with skills and expertise of operational management within two years. In this connection, the Ministry of Water Resources issued a circular in June 1993 entitled "On the Notice about Enhanced Training on Modern Operational Management" in which an action plan and a working schedule was prepared on the operational management training to be conducted in 1994 and 1995.

The planned operational management training had been carried out at different levels according to the Ministry's schedule. The Department of Personnel and Labour Management and the Department of Science and Education took the lead in this work by providing training programme, curricula and teaching staff. The two departments also organized supervision, assistance and coordination for conducting training courses. By the end of 1994 altogether 92 training courses were organized under the Ministry of Water Resources and some 4,800 leading cadres at different levels participated.

8. International support and assistance to enhance China's capabilities in water and sustainable development

China is facing tremendous challenge to improve its national capabilities in the sustainable development of water resources. On one hand, the country needs some financial support and technical assistance from the international organizations and foreign financial institutions. On the other hand, exchange of knowledge and experience with other countries and institutions are considered necessary and beneficial. The main purposes of seeking support and mutual assistance include:

- Adoption of advanced techniques and experience of developed countries in the domain of water resources assessment;

- International cooperation for water source protection and setting up of strategies and action plans for the global, trans-boundary, country-wide and basin-wide protection and management of water resources in general and of drinking water supply sources in particular.

- Conducting of joint studies on pollution control of water supply sources, restoration of aquifers, prevention of salt water intrusion, treatment and natural purification of wastewater and joint development of international rivers.

- Introduction of proven planning and management models for water resources development and recycling of wastewater as well as construction of pilot projects of different types for wastewater recycling.

- Active participation in international technical exchange and cooperation programmes concerning staff training and human resources development in the field of water resources management, water pollution control and environment protection.

- Active participation in international programmes for the study of climate changes and determination of their impacts on water resources as well as training of technical staff in this field.

9. International and regional cooperation

(a) China will cooperate with neighboring countries in the water resources assessment using advanced techniques;

(b) China will carry out international cooperation in the protection of water resources, and through consultation, devise strategies and action plans for global, trans-national, nationwide and trans-regional protection of drinking water sources;

(c) China will participate in the research on techniques for pollution control of drinking water sources, groundwater recharge, prevention of saline water intrusion, wastewater treatment and utilization of international rivers;

(d) China will use successful foreign technology, experience and equipment in wastewater recycling and reuse, and set up various types of demonstration projects for wastewater recycling and reuse;

(e) China will participate in international cooperation and exchange programmes for the training of its technical personnel in the fields of water resources management, water pollution control and remediation;

(f) China will participate in international cooperation to study climate changes and their influence over water resources, and train professionals in this field.

B. Financial sustainability of water development projects

1. Social and economic conditions for water resources development in the country

China's per capita water resources potential is far below the world's average. In addition, temporal and spatial water resources distribution in the country is very uneven. Thus, many regions in the country demonstrate unbalanced demand and supply of water.

At present, North China and the southern part of the Northeast are facing a significant shortage of water gradually widening the gap between demand and supply. The northwest of the country is short of water resources which is considered a serious constraint for further economic development in the region. The vast areas to the south of Yangtze river are comparatively abundant in water resources, yet insufficient water storage and regulation capacity has resulted in water shortage in some areas. It is believed that China's fast economic development will lead to the rapid increase in water demand which will eventually produce water resources management problems in some regions of the country.

In view of the steadily increasing water resources problems, the Central Government has formulated an overall strategy and target for China's water resources management that will ensure the country's sustainable development. This strategy and target can be summed up as "*to eliminate all water-caused disasters and to enhance all water-related benefits so as to meet all demands from country's social and economic development*". In other words, under the formulated overall strategy and target, the economic benefits, social benefits and environmental benefits should be maximized from all kinds of use of water resources, and water supply should meet the demand of country's social and economic development as well as the improved living standards of the people. In addition, the natural hydrological and ecological cycle should be maintained and all water-related diseases should be prevented and eliminated.

2. Cost recovery from water development projects

Before 1985, projects for flood control, irrigation and drainage were considered as public projects for the common benefit of the society. Therefore, the capital investments for these projects were allocated by the governments at different levels. As regards costs for operation and maintenance, the majority of water management agencies charged only nominal water fees for water supply and other services which were not enough for the recovery of operation and maintenance costs.

As the investment and financial reform gained some progress in the water conservancy sector, the Ministry of Water Resources promulgated the " Methods of Calculation, Collection and Management of Water Fees for Water Resources Projects" in 1985. In this document the Ministry clearly stated that all water-related projects in China should introduce the concept of cost recovery and to charge water fees for completed water projects. It was also stated that the water fees should be determined based on water supply costs including operation, management, maintenance and depreciation costs. For agricultural water supply, the direct investments and indirect investment (in form of labour input) made by farmers should not be incorporated.

According to the document, the annual operation, maintenance and management budget for flood control projects to be incorporated into comprehensive water utilization projects should be allocated by the Central Government and the local government at different levels depending on the project's scale and importance. For other projects such as regulating sluices, embankment, seawalls, water-draining installations and other water-related facilities, which have clearly identified beneficiaries, the expenditures incurred by the operation, maintenance

and management of projects should be covered by the beneficiary institutions. For water supply projects, irrespective of whether it is for industrial, agricultural or residential users the management agencies should collect the relevant water fees to recover their operation, maintenance, management, maintenance and rehabilitation expenditures. Based on this principle, the management agencies of all irrigation districts in China is practising the full financial autonomy in all aspects of water management.

3. Relationship between water-related natural disasters reduction and water development projects

The main water-related natural disasters in China include floods, drought, mud flows and others, out of which the most frequently occurring and the most devastating are floods and droughts.

Floods. During the period B.C. 206 to A.D. 1949, there were altogether 1,092 severe floods in China. After the establishment of the People's Republic of China the damages and economic losses from floods were reduced significantly due to the large scale construction of flood control projects in the country. However, as the economic development continued to take place in the flood prone areas, floods are still causing significant damages to the country. In the period from 1950 to 1994 China suffered regularly from floods and the total annual flooding area reached 8.93 million ha, causing damage to 5.06 million ha of cropped land per annum. In this period the total-affected area with significant economic losses exceeded 6.66 million ha.

Droughts. In the 45-year period from 1959 to 1994 the annual average drought-affected farmland area constituted 21.47 million ha, which accounted for 60 per cent of the total land area of the country.

The Government has been giving priority attention to alleviating both flood and drought disasters. After the founding of the People's Republic of China, a relatively complete floods and drought control system has been set up in the country.

The flood control system of the main river basins is composed of two categories of measures, the engineering measures and non-engineering measures. Engineering measures include: construction and strengthening of river embankments of about 245,000 km and tide-protection embankments of about 2,900 km; dredging and enlarging of some important flood-prone river courses and lakes, namely, Liaohe river, Haihe river, Huaihe river, Taihu lake, etc. to provide free passage of floods; construction of more than 80,000 water-storage and flow regulating reservoirs with a total storage capacity of 461.7 billion m^3. Of these, 358 were large and medium-sized reservoirs with a total storage capacity of 335.7 billion m^3. Other engineering measures being implemented include construction and establishment of more than 100 flood-diversion passages and flood retention areas on the main rivers in the country with a total storage capacity of 120 billion m^3; implementation of the national water and soil conservation programme on more than 500,000 km^2 of erosion-prone land areas; construction of the microwave digital communication between Zhengzhou and Sanmenxia on the Yellow river, Xinyang and Bangbu, and between Bangbu and Xiuzhou on the Huaihe river, as well as 800 MB communication systems from Lanfang to Tianjing and from Beijing to Zhouzhou in the Haihe river basin; construction and establishment of more than 8,500 flood information reporting stations and 1,000 hydrological forecasting stations; development and improvement of software for flood forecasting on the main rivers in the country; construction and establishment of more than 20 automated hydrological measuring, recording and reporting systems on the Yellow river, Yangtze river, Huaihe river, Yongding river, Liaohe river and Taihu lake, comprising about 500 remote measuring stations; construction and establishment of 85 central flood-warning transmission stations and 10,428 flood-warning receiving stations in the Yellow river, Yangtze river, Huaihe river and Haihe river basins; installation of devices for receiving Japanese GMS satellite clod images. Map of major rivers in China is shown in figure 3.

Among the non-engineering measures being implemented include establishment of the flood-control command centres at all the five levels of government organization (Central Government level, the provincial level, the prefectual level, the municipal level and the county level) and introduction of the system of accountability; establishment of ad hoc flood control teams in some important areas; enforcement of the relevant national laws and regulations such as the "Water Law of the People's Republic of China", the "Flood Control Regulation", the "River Course Management Regulations" and others; development of

the flood protection programmes and design of emergency action scenarios to protect against extraordinary floods on the major rivers in the country; and preparation and implementation of the flood insurance pilot projects in selected flood-prone areas of the country.

C. Sustainable use of water resources

1. Water conservation and wastage prevention through demand management

(a) Use of water saving devices and enhancement of irrigation efficiency

At present the water consumption of the agricultural sector constitutes about 80 per cent of the nation's total. Therefore water conservation in the agricultural sector is considered very important. Studies on water-saving irrigation technologies dated back to 1950s and 1960s. In the early 1970s some water-conserving technologies were used on large areas of farmland. From the middle of 1970s to early 1980s, the advanced irrigation methods such as sprinkling and drip irrigation were introduced in hilly areas, soil with high permeability, and areas with extreme water shortage. These methods were also used during drought spells in the north and for growing cash crops in the south of the country. Shortly afterwards, the low pressure pipeconduit irrigation technique was used extensively in the 1980s.

In the early 1990s, China's water conservation technology entered a new stage. In addition to engineering measures, agronomical measures and water management measures for saving irrigation water were introduced. Dissemination of high efficiency water utilization techniques for farmland irrigation, such as the optimized wheat irrigation technique, shallow watering technique for rice cultivation, on-membrane watering technique for corn, and on-water sowing or planting of dry land crops was carried out.

According to the results of a nationwide survey completed recently by the Ministry of Water Resources by the end of 1992, the total area of farmland equipped with water-saving engineering facilities reached more than 12 million ha and the total area of farmland irrigated with the high efficiency on-field water utilization techniques reached 45.3 million ha. Among the total farmland area equipped with water-saving

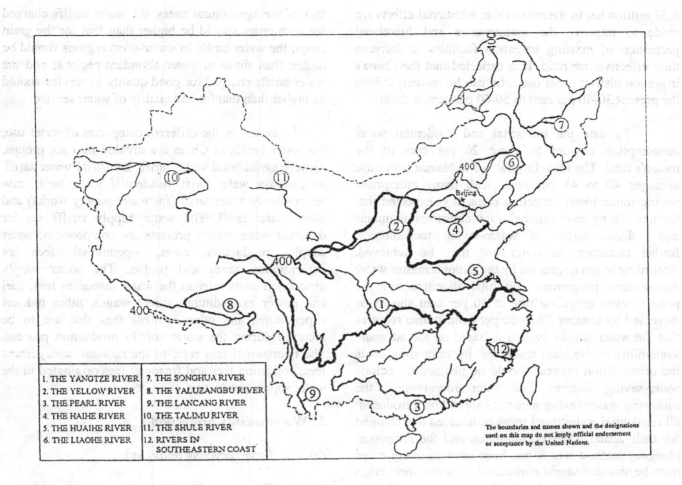

Figure 3. Map of major rivers in China

1. THE YANGTZE RIVER	7. THE SONGHUA RIVER
2. THE YELLOW RIVER	8. THE YALUZANGBU RIVER
3. THE PEARL RIVER	9. THE LANCANG RIVER
4. THE HAIHE RIVER	10. THE TALIMU RIVER
5. THE HUAIHE RIVER	11. THE SHULE RIVER
6. THE LIAOHE RIVER	12. RIVERS IN SOUTHEASTERN COAST

The boundaries and names shown and the designations used on this map do not imply official endorsement or acceptance by the United Nations.

irrigation facilities the coverage by the lined canals reached 9.33 million ha, low-pressure pipe irrigation 2.06 million ha, sprinkling irrigation 0.8 million ha and the drip irrigation 40 thousand ha.

The experience of farming with the water-saving irrigation in China indicated that it was always associated with dual results of less water use and increased harvest. Some statistical studies were conducted under three water-saving irrigation demonstration projects implemented in Henan, Shanxi and Hebei provinces. The results from those studies showed that dissemination of water-saving irrigation led to a unit production increase of crops by 39.7, 71.5 and 104.0 per cent and a water saving by 30.4, 45.4 and 55.0 per cent for three demonstration projects respectively.

At present China manufactures the majority of water-saving equipment for irrigation and is able to meet basically its domestic demand. The Ministry of Water Resources has organized and carried out technical training for water-saving irrigation at many levels among irrigation technicians and local farmers for effective dissemination of technical knowledge. The Ministry has also established a large number of district irrigation stations and a nationwide technical dissemination network for water-saving irrigation.

It has planned to further increase the cultivation areas under sprinkling, drip and pipe irrigation. The planned targets for 2000 are to add another 0.66 million ha of sprinkling and drip irrigation and another 3.33 million ha of pipe irrigation so that the total pipe irrigation area in China is increased to

5.33 million ha. In the mean time, additional efforts are made to improve the maintenance and functional perfection of existing irrigation facilities to increase their effective use ratio. It is expected that the China's irrigation district canal use ratio can be increased from the present 30-40 per cent to 50-60 per cent in 2000.

To date the industrial and residential water consumption amount to about 20 per cent of the nation's total. The recycling rate of industrial water use averages 40 to 45 per cent, with many enterprises having much lower recycling rates. It is expected that through setting up of rational water consumption quotas and dissemination of water-saving technologies, further reduction in water use may be achieved. According to the targets set by the nation's master water conservation programme, by 2000 all cities with the present water recycling rate of 50 per cent should be increased by another 20 to 30 per cent. It also requires that the water supply system is based on the adequate availability of the local resources. In water short areas the urbanization process should be planned to include water-saving features. For water conservation, the following water-saving measures should be introduced: all residential water users must be metered and charged for their actual water consumption and the lump-sum charging method which has been used in many cities must be abandoned and eliminated; in water-short cities the new apartment blocks, hotels, restaurants and other public facilities should be equipped with dual water supply systems wherever possible; and all new residential buildings and public installations must use advanced water-saving equipment.

(b) Water pricing policies and structures

The main concepts involved in water pricing are the following:

- Low operational profitability, differentiated prices for different categories of water users and cost-break-even zero-profit water supply to the agricultural sector;

- Enhancing conservation and protection of water resources;

- Higher prices for good quality supplies in terms of both guaranteed service assured quality.

According to these concepts, the water tariffs of industrial and residential users should be higher than that of the agricultural users, the water tariffs charged for cash crops should be higher than that for the grain crops, the water tariffs in water-short regions should be higher than those in water abundant regions, and the water tariffs charged for good quality of service should be higher than that for bad quality of water service.

Based on the different categories of water use, the water tariffs in China are divided into six groups, namely agricultural water tariff, industrial water tariff, hydropower water tariff, residential water tariff, raw water supply water tariff (for water supply works) and other water tariff. The water supply tariffs set for different water supply projects are composed of water supply production costs, operational fees or expenditures, taxes and profits. The water supply production costs refer to the water resources fees, fuel and power expenditures, direct wages, other indirect expenditures and other indirect fees that are to be incurred during the water supply production process. The operational fees refer to the rational management fees, collection fees and financial fees originated in the water supply production.

2. Water quality protection

(a) Water recycling and reuse

Water recycling and reuse rate in China is rather low at present. It is planned that by 2000 the residential sewage treatment rate in cities will reach 20 to 30 per cent, and the industrial wastewater treatment rate will reach 84 per cent. At that time, the urban residential sewage reuse rate will reach 10 per cent of the treated sewage. By 2010, the urban residential sewage treatment will reach 40 to 50 per cent and the urban residential sewage reuse rate in water-short cities and regions as well as medium and small-sized cities will reach 30 to 40 per cent.

(b) Wastewater disposal regulations and their enforcement

Laws and regulations issued by the Government to deal with wastewater disposal include the "Water Pollution Prevention Law", "Regulations on water Quality Management for Enforcement of Water Extraction Permit System", "Regulations on the Environment Protection Design of Construction Projects", "Temporary Rules on Collection of Fees for Wastewater Disposal" and others. There are relevant enforcement stipulations in those laws and regulations.

(c)   Watershed management to reduce erosion and sedimentation problems

The two important documents entitled "Water and Soil Conservation Law of the People's Republic of China" and "Regulations on River Channel Management of the People's Republic of China" have articulated the following policies and stipulations for watershed management to reduce erosion and sedimentation problems:

- Water and soil conservation work should be based on integrated planning and comprehensive use of mitigating measures relevant to local conditions;

- Water and soil conservation planning should be based on survey and assessment of water and soil resources;

- Land reclamation and cultivation on steep slopes of more than 25 degrees is not allowed;

- Construction of railroads, highways and water-related projects should minimize their impacts and damages on the existing vegetation coverage;

- All kinds of abandoned sand, soil and rock should be transported and stored at the specified places and should not be dumped into rivers, lakes and reservoirs;

- Barren land should be planted with trees and grass to prevent water and soil erosion;

- In areas of hydraulic erosion, small watersheds formed and bordered by natural streams or gullies should be protected with soil and water retention systems;

- Adoption of effective soil and water retention measures on flood plains to prevent water and soil erosion;

- River channel management organizations should include in their work programmes afforestation of flood control embankments and river banks.

In these two documents some punitive articles and stipulations are included, specifying relevant

warning, fines and confiscating of illegal revenues for violations of above policies and stipulations.

(d)   Measures for protection of water quality

Since the launching of systematic water quality protection all over the country in the 1970s, a number of water quality protection works have been planned to be implemented. First, plans for elimination of polluting sources in local areas were drawn up. Afterwards, plans for comprehensive prevention and control for water pollution in some rivers, such as the Yanghe River, Songhuajiang River, Yiluohe River, Baiyangdian Lake and Wuhan Reach of the Yangtze River, etc. were being formulated.

The water resources protection plans for the seven major river basins cover 135 tributaries and 271 cities and nearly 46 per cent of the whole country.

3.   Monitoring and enforcement of the quality of wastewater for disposal into water bodies

(a)   Wastewater quality monitoring and assessment

From 1950 to 1970, water quality monitoring was focused on the characteristics of natural water chemistry. The monitoring network had 718 monitoring stations spread all over the country. In 1974 there were 22 water analysis laboratories. All data concerning natural water chemistry were collected and published in the *Hydrological Year Book*. By the end of 1960s, when some parts of rivers, lakes and reservoirs in China became polluted the investigation of water pollution was made by hydrologists in cooperation with specialists of public health. With the development of water quality monitoring network in 1984, there were 2,689 water quality monitoring stations, 244 water analysis laboratories and more than 1,000 staff.

The investigation of pollutant sources distribution showed that the main pollutant sources were composed of the industrial wastewater and municipal sewage from cities and towns. The total wastewater discharge per day amounted to 86.33 million tons (not including the cooling water of thermal power stations and the mine drainage), 83 per cent of which is from industrial wastewater, and 17 per cent from municipal sewage. Most of the wastewater was directly discharged into rivers, lakes and reservoirs without treatment.

During the investigation, 18,903 samples from 2,774 monitoring sections were collected to assess the water quality of 874 rivers, 4 lakes and 111 reservoirs. The total river length assessed was 92,000 km, 20.9 per cent of which has been polluted by organic matters, 21.8 per cent by toxicant substances. The result of the investigation showed that 141 rivers (about 20,000 km) have been polluted. The main pollutants are COD, ammonia nitrogen, phenol and mercury. According to the assessment, 33.6 per cent of the total river length meet the national standard for drinking water, 89.1 per cent for irrigation and 5.7 per cent has been polluted seriously.

Since 1986, the *Water Quality Bulletin* has been issued monthly and the *Annual Report of Surface Water Quality Assessment* has been published by MWR. According to the *Report of Surface Water Quality Assessment (1995)*, the average daily discharge of wastewater in 1991 was 92.11 million tons. The report showed that in three river basins, namely, the Yellow River, Huaihe River and Haihe River, water pollution was more serious in tributaries and small streams than in main rivers, and in the northern part than in the southern part.

Another report, the *Prediction of Rivers Pollution in China by Year 2000*, published by MWR in 1986, stated that if further effective measures are not adopted to control water pollution, most of water bodies in China will be polluted seriously, especially in four river basins, the Yellow River, Huaihe River, Haihe River and Kiaohe River.

At present the quality of wastewater for disposal into surface water bodies and aquifers is monitored mainly by the water conservancy and environment protection agencies in the country. For this purpose, two separate water quality monitoring networks have been established, one under the Ministry of Water Resources and another under the National Environment Protection Agency.

(b)   Wastewater quality standards for disposal

To set up the specified standards for the quality of wastewater the state prepared and published the "Comprehensive Wastewater Disposal Standards" coded as GB 8978-88 which differentiates three levels of standards in accordance with the functional requirements of the receiving water bodies.

Within all water bodies and land areas under special protection, including the Class I protection areas of urban or township with concentrated drinking water supply sources, water bodies in the national parks and scenic areas, and water bodies used as habitats of valuable fish species new outfalls of wastewater or residential sewage is not allowed while the existing outfalls must be kept under strict control by relevant environment protection agencies to limit the pollutant load so that the water quality of receiving water bodies can be protected.

To enhance wastewater management and prevent water pollution the Ministry of Construction jointly with the National Environment Protection Agency prepared and published the "Environment Protection Design Criteria of Construction Projects". Articles 33, 34, 37 and 38 in this document clearly stipulate that:

- The concept of separated system should be considered and adopted in wastewater conveyance design depending on the wastewater quality, amount and selected treatment technologies;

- The selection of optimal treatment methods and process for industrial wastewater and residential sewage (including sewage disposed by hospitals) should consider the targeted water quality requirements after treatment and the area's special features;

- The quality of industrial wastewater and residential sewage should meet the water quality standards specified for municipal sewage systems before they are discharged into the municipal drainage;

- For canals, ditches, underground pipelines and monitoring wells for conveying and transporting wastewater containing poisonous, hazardous or corrosive matter the necessary anti-seepage and anti-corrosion measures should be adopted; and

- Non-poisonous and non-polluting chemicals should be selected and used for water treatment.

VII. WATER AND SUSTAINABLE DEVELOPMENT: INDIAN SCENARIO

R. Vidyasagar Rao, Commissioner (Water Management and Minor Irrigation)
Ministry of Water Resources, Government of India

Introduction

All development projects have environmental, economic and social consequences, some beneficial and others adverse. Water resources projects are no exception to this. With the increase in economic activities and the consequent potential for stress on ecosystems and natural resource stocks, the study and recognition of linkages between freshwater issues and other sectoral and cross sectoral issues are becoming increasingly important.

The main challenge facing the management of water resources is how to maximize all the positive impacts and minimize the adverse impacts; how to ensure reliable water supply and efficient use in the agricultural sector, mitigate flood damages, control water pollution and at the same time reduce environmental and social impacts, such as rehabilitation and resettlement of displaced people, mitigate the problems of waterlogging and salinity and reduce the spread of waterborne diseases and the problems associated with pollution. The idea of environmentally-sound water management or sustainable development and management of water resources is to convey the concept that development is to be accomplished with minimum damage to the environment. However, experience shows that translating the concept into a reality remains rather a difficult task.

A. Environmental sustainability of water resources development

1. Water resources of India

India, with a geographical area of 329 million hectares experiences extremes of climate. Normal annual rainfall varies from 100 mm in Western Rajasthan to over 11,000 mm at Cherapunji, in the north-eastern part of the country. The annual average rainfall is of the order of 1,170 mm, which together with snow melt yields nearly 4,000 km³ of water. After deducting for infiltration and evaporation, the average surface flow in the river systems of the country is estimated at 1,869 km³. The constraint in exploiting the available water is that the major part of the flows occurs as floods during short periods and there are obvious limitations in storing all the quantity. The utilizable surface flow is estimated at 690 km³. The utilizable groundwater potential is estimated at 432 km³. Thus, the total utilizable water resources of the country is about 1,122 km³. A summary of water resources in India is given below.

(a)	Rainfall	1,170 cm or 4,000 km³
(b)	Geographical Area	329 M ha
(c)	Utilizable water:	Surface flow 690 km³
		Groundwater 432 km³
		Total: 1,122 km³

2. Water resources assessment

(a)   Surface water

The Central Water Commission, Government of India has a network of 877 key stations throughout the country in collect and compile hydrological data, as well as to take measurements of river flows on a regular basis. In addition, silt observations and water quality observations are made at a few selected sites. Most of the hydrological data collection activity is manual, though automation has been introduced at some of the stations. Snow melt and glacial ice melt provide a major part of the run off in the mountainous areas of the Himalayas. The snow melt forecasts provide an important input to the river management. Remote sensing techniques have been found useful in predicting the snow melt run off.

To improve India's institutional and technical capability to measure, collate, analyze, disseminate and use data concerned with quantities and qualities of surface and ground water, including the use of data for hydrological design a project entitled "Hydrology Project" is being implemented in peninsular river basins of India under the World Bank Assistance.

(b) *Groundwater*

With the increased emphasis on groundwater in the last few years, a scientific assessment of the groundwater potential of the country was undertaken and extensive exploration work was carried out in the country. In the reassessment based on guidelines laid down by a Ground Water Estimation Committee of 1984 and the additional available data, the annual replenishable ground- water is estimated as 432 km^3. The present annual utilization is 115 km^3 through 15.3 million groundwater structures. A hydrographic network of about 15,000 stations monitors the levels and the quality of groundwater. Monitoring shows that some areas are exhibiting signs of over-exploitation. There is a proposal to extend the network to 17,000 stations.

(c) *Storage created*

Out of the average annual flow of 1,869 km^3 a live storage of only 171 km^3 of water has been developed through about 3,000 large dams. An additional live storage of 3 km^3 is estimated to have been created through medium projects, each having a capacity less than 10 million m^3. Thus, the total live storage is about 174 km^3 at completed projects. Dams to create additional live storage of 72 km^3 are now under construction and for 132 km^3 are being planned. With the live storage of 25 km^3 of minor tanks, the ultimate live storage would be 403 km^3 would be around 22 per cent of the average annual flow of the rivers.

3. Water use

Owing to spatial and temporal variation of flows, the amount of water that can be actually put to beneficial use is much less. The constraint in creating sufficient storages results in non-utilization of all the available water resources. The recent estimates made by CWC (Central Water Commission) indicate that the water resources that can be actually utilized by constructing surface structures is about 36 per cent of the total available resources, that is, 690 km^3. Greater environmental and social consciousness could reduce this quantum further. On the other hand, the utilizable quantum can be increased by about 250 km^3 by undertaking inter-basin transfer of water.

(a) *Present water use*

Principle consumptive use of water is in irrigation. The irrigation potential has increased from

22.5 M ha in 1950-1951 to 76.5 M ha in 1989-1990, comprising 41 M ha irrigated by 300 km^3 of surface water and 35.5 M ha from 160 km^3 of groundwater. The present use on account of irrigation is estimated to be around 460 km^3. Water use by industries has not been assessed precisely. Based on the water requirements of the industrial products, it has been approximately assessed as 15 km^3. The present water uses by thermal and nuclear power plants is estimated as 4 km^3. For hydropower generation, the consumptive use of water is only by way of evaporation from reservoirs, which is estimated to be of the order of 15 km^3. Approximately 33 km^3 of water is being used for other miscellaneous activities. Out of the present total use of 552 km^3, 362 km^3 has been estimated to be from surface water and 190 km^3 from groundwater.

(b) *Future requirements*

The population of the country is expected to increase to about 1,020 million by the year 2000 and to 1,394 million by the year 2025. It is expected to stabilize at 1,700 million by the year 2050. In order to meet the foodgrain requirements of the future population, irrigated agriculture has to expand considerably. It is estimated that by the year 2000, the water use for irrigation would increased to 630 km^3 and by 2025 it may reach a level of 770 km^3. Table 6 shows the demand for water for various uses in the years 1990, 2000 and 2025.

(c) *Water resources development*

By the dawn of the twenty-first century, the country will be fast approaching a situation when nearly all the utilizable water resources will be put to beneficial use and by the year 2025 no additional surface water source would be available for meeting the increased demand. This situation calls for an urgent need to formulate suitable strategies for planning, development, conservation and management of available water resources in the country.

4. Over-exploitation of groundwater

When there is overexploitation of ground water, the water table goes down progressively until a stage is reached, when the rainfall will not be able to replenish it within a reasonable time. In coastal areas, this induces intrusion of saline water of the sea into the freshwater aquifers. The country is already witnessing such a situation in many areas, particularly in

Saurashtra and in the Pennar basins. In years of drought, overexploitation of ground water becomes inevitable, leading to irrecoverable damage to the groundwater table. Some states like Gujarat have imposed legal measures for regulating groundwater exploitation. However, legal measures alone may not be enough to solve the problem. Wherever economically feasible, artificial recharging measures should be undertaken. Artificial recharging by spreading excess surface water over sider areas or injecting water into the aquifers through tubewells is advocated in coastal areas.

Table 6. Present and future water requirements for various uses (km^3)

Purpose	Demand in 1990	Demand in 2000	Demand in 2025
Domestic use	25	35	52
Irrigation	460	630	770
Energy	19	27	71
Industrial use	15	30	120
Others	33	30	37
Total	552	750	1,050
Surface water	362	500	700
Groundwater	190	250	350

5. National water policy

The National Water Policy adopted in 1987 considers that water is a prime natural resource, a basic human need and a precious national asset. It recognizes that water resources planning has to be done for hydrology units, such as a drainage basins or sub-basins as a whole. As far as possible, the projects should be a planned and developed as multipurpose projects. Provisions for drinking water should be given the highest priority. There should be an integrated and multi-disciplinary approach to the planning, formulation, clearance and implementation of projects including catchment treatment and management, environmental and ecological aspects, and the rehabilitation of affected people in command area development. The integrated and coordinated development for surface and ground waters and their consumptive use should be envisaged right from the planning stage and should form an essential part of the project. The policy further suggests that recycling and

reuse of the water should e an integral part of water resources development. It lays emphasis on preservation of the quality of environment and ecological balance in planning, development and operation of the projects and suggests that adverse impacts, if any, on the environment should be offset by adequate remedial measures.

With regard to setting up of multi-disciplinary units for preparing comprehensive master plans, some state governments such as Karnataka, Kerala and Rajashan have already taken up the lead and others have reorganized their irrigation departments in this direction.

6. Master plans

Though comprehensive master plans are not yet fully ready in the specified format for many river basins, master plans for part of the areas and for specific purposes like irrigation and flood control have been drawn up for a very large part of India.

A comprehensive River Basin Plan for Water Resources Development of the Zone Sub-basin of the Ganga basin (catchment area 70,055 km^2 and water availability 19,095 km^3) was prepared in the year 1988 by the Sone River Commission. The Ganga Flood Control Commission set up in April, 1972 for preparation of an integrated plan to tackle the flood, erosion and drainage problems (861,000 km^2) has prepared 23 sub-basinwise comprehensive master plans. The Brahmaputra Board, established by an Act of Parliament in 1980 for the planning and implementation of measures for the control of floods and bank erosion in the Brahmaputra valley is currently drawing up the master plans keeping in view the optimum utilization and development of the water resources of the sub-basins of the valley. So far, Master Plans for nine tributaries of Brahmaputra have been completed.

7. Environmental aspects

India is a land of rivers having predominantly agriculture based economy. Development of river valley projects has become a lifeline of progress and prosperity of the country. Water Resources Development (WRD) Projects are indispensable as they are inextricably linked to the country's economy besides their need for the welfare of the people. However, in the last two decades, a very strong opposition has been voiced to the construction of large dams arguing that irreparable damage to the environment may result due to such projects. On the one hand a fear syndrome has been created in recent years against WRD projects by exaggerating the likely or assumed adverse environmental impacts and by ignoring or suppressing their tremendous benefits. On the other hand, controversial debates are generated on the grounds that the possible environmental impacts are not properly evaluated in many projects. As a result, many potential economic development activities, which could generate wealth and employment to people have been blocked in several large cities, towns and villages due to acute shortage of water especially during the dry season. At the same time, progress floods routinely continue to affect the economic causing large scale loss of lives and properties.

(a)   Guidelines   for   environmental   impacts assessment

There was no proper mechanism for assessing the environmental impacts of the River Valley Projects (RVP) in India until 1978. In 1978 the Department of Environment and Forests (DOEF) has prepared the guidelines for environmental impact assessment of river valley projects. It was aimed at subjecting each river valley project to rigorous assessment of its environmental impacts so that necessary mitigation measures could be incorporated in the project right from its inception stage. These guidelines concerning site selection as well as incorporation of mitigation measures were prepared and circulated among the project authorities through the planning commission. It was made imperative to analyze whether the adoption of environmental measures is going to result in any short or long term social and economic benefits or not. Special emphasis was laid on the health effects, plant genetic resources, aquatic life, water logging, salinity of irrigated lands, deforestation and soil conservation for considering the techno-economic viability of the project. It was made mandatory in the DOEF guidelines that the ecological considerations should be incorporated at every stage of planning and construction phases.

The Union Ministry of Irrigation, had set-up a working group in 1979 to prepare the comprehensive guidelines for the preparation of project reports for major River Valley Projects (RVP). The working group considered the importance of soil conservation measures in the catchment of RVPs and was of the view that they should be implemented as a complement to river valley projects. Aspects recommended for consideration in site selection included immediate and long-term impacts on human settlements, flora and fauna in the vicinity, impacts on monuments and mineral resources, groundwater levels etc. The items mentioned in the guidelines include effects on the environment such as (i) involuntary settlement of project affected persons, (ii) sedimentation, (iii) water-logging, (iv) salinity, (v) monuments/shrines, (vi) submergence of flora and fauna, (vii) aquatic life, (viii) health, (ix) climate, and (x) water quality.

Under the Forest Conservation Act passed by the Indian Parliament in 1980 all the states concerned have to get the proposed river valley projects cleared before commencement of construction that would result in the submergence or deforestation of land.

In 1985, Ministry of Environment and Forests (MOEF) prepared a list of data and basic information necessary for environmental impact studies along with the Guidelines for Environmental Impact Assessment of River Valley Projects, which were sent to the project authorities.

In 1992, the Central Water Commission has published "The Guidelines for Sustainable Water Resources Development and Management" to meet the requirement for data collection and analysis, impacts assessment and management plans. Together with Environmental Impact Assessment (EIA) for water resources projects, Environmental Management Plan (EMP) is also essential to ensure sustainable development and to limit the stress on the system to be within its carrying capacity. Special attention has to be given to rehabilitation and resettlement, compensatory afforestation and catchment area treatment.

The overall efforts while preparing such guidelines and studies of various river valley projects is in ensuring rapid economic development on a sustained basis with due consideration for safe-guarding the environment.

(b)   Environmental clearance and monitoring

At present, all new development projects and/or proposals for expansion of existing projects in the public sector are referred to the Ministry of Environment and Forests (MOEF) for environmental appraisal. The Environmental Impact Assessment

(EIA) of the projects is carried out by the Impact Assessment Division (IAD) of the Department. The IAD, which has a multidisciplinary base, carries out EIA of project with the hope of inter-ministerial appraisal committee, comprising experts from related disciplines. The feasibility reports along with questionnaires and Environmental Management Plans (EMP) furnished by the project authorities are first scrutinised by the IAD and the project proponents are advised to plug the information gaps, if any. The project is then considered by the Expert Environmental Appraisal Committee (EAC). Site visits are undertaken by the sub-committees constituted as and when necessary to supplement the information submitted by the project authorities. The MOEF has developed guidelines, checklists and questionnaire to hope the project authorities collect the relevant information for EIA.

MOEF through its field offices spread over the country regularly monitor the implementation of environmental safeguards stipulated by the ministry while according environment clearance to the development of projects including river valley projects. Besides, a high level Environmental Management Committee (EMC), headed by Member (WP & P), Central Water Commission (CWC) and comprising several inter-ministerial/inter-agencies, constantly monitors the environmental status of the major and medium water resources projects. It regularly reviews the mechanism established by various project authorities to monitor the ecology of the project area and provides guidance on additional compensatory measures. To date, 84 projects have been selected out of which 17 important projects are being closely monitored by the national level EMC. State and project level EMCs have also been set up for review, coordination and ensuring the implementation of environmental safeguards in WRD projects.

(c)   Compensable measures

Two main problems associated with the construction of water resources projects are the displacement of people and submergence of forests.

(i)   Resettlement and rehabilitation of people from project sites

The problem relating to resettlement and rehabilitation (R&R) are far more complex than are generally perceived by the public

policy makers or the project implementing authorities. The objective of any R&R package should be to provide the same quality of life, if not better to the affected persons than what they have been enjoying before displacement. Generally suitable compensatory measures such as providing alternative land to the affected persons should be made. A number of state governments such as Andhra Pradesh, Madhya Pradesh, Karnataka, Orissa and Maharashtra have their own rehabilitation policies.

Recently a draft national policy for resettlement and rehabilitation of displaced people has been evolved by the Government of India which is under consideration for adoption.

(ii) Compensatory afforestation

It has been internationally acknowledged that about one-third of the total geographical area must be under good forest cover for balanced environment and ecosystem. The forest cover in India has decreased from about 75 ha in 1947, to 40 ha due to the demands for fuel wood, timber and indiscriminate felling of trees. The country is at present reported to be losing forest cover at an alarming rate of 1.5 ha per year. Deforestation on account of water resources projects is estimated at 4 per cent of the total forest during the last 3 decades, and compensatory forestry has become an essential and integral part of all the new water resources projects.

As per the Indian regulations afforestation is to be undertaken in an equal area of non-forest land and where non-forest land is not available it should be undertaken in degraded forests on twice the extent of the area.

8. Institutional and legal framework

The Union Government as per entry 56 of List I of Constitution of India has been charged with the responsibility for "Regulation and development of inter-state rivers and river valleys to which such regulation and development under the control of the Union is declared by the Parliament by a law to be expedient in the political interest". As per Entry 17 in

List II, the State Governments have been provided with the responsibilities for water resources development for irrigation and flood control development etc. subject to the provision of Entry 56 of List I.

Article 262 of the Indian Constitution authorizes the Parliament to enact a law to adjudicate the disputes in distribution and control of inter-state waters. The River Boards Act 1956 authorizes the Indian Government to set up Advisory River Boards on the inter-state river, in consultation with the inter-state states.

Under the planning mechanism, established in 1951 for the preparation of National Five Year Plans; all the new major and medium water resources development (WRD) projects are cleared by the National Planning Commission for inclusion in the Five Year Plans. All WRD Projects are cleared from techno-economic aspects by the Technical Advisory Committee (TAC) chaired by Union Secretary (Water Resources). The Environmental Appraisal Committee (EAC) under the Ministry of Environment & Forests (MOEF) accords the environmental and forest clearance for major and medium irrigation and hydro-electric projects.

The Central Government acts as a coordinator and promoter of development in the water sector. The Central Ministry of Water Resources with the assistance of Central Water Commission (CWC) and Central Ground Water Board (CGWB) plays in important role in formulating the National Policy and in coordinating the activities of the States. It also deals with Inter-state and International problems in the use of water. The Central Water Commission attached to the Ministry of Water Resources functions as a repository of technical information with regard to water resources development in the country and carries out all technical work concerning water resources development. It provides at the national level, facilities for investigation design and execution of various projects and assists as well as conducts various types of research work in the field of water resources. It also carries out a technical examination of major and medium projects submitted by the States before they are approved by the National Planning Commission for implementation under the national Five Year Economic Development Plans. The Central Ground Water Board attached to the Ministry of Water Resources is responsible for exploration, assessment, development and regulation of groundwater exploitation.

Control Boards have been set up for large projects particularly the inter-state projects undertaken in different parts of the country. These Boards comprise representatives of the State Governments concerned and those of Central Ministries of Water Resources, Finance and Central Water Commission. The Boards periodically review the progress of projects and give direction for the speedy implementation by taking steps to remove bottlenecks.

9. Human resources development

Recently 11 States (Andhra Pradesh, Karnataka, Kerala, Madhya Pradesh, Maharashtra, Bihar, Gujarat, Orissa, Rajasthan, Tamil Nadu and Uttar Pradesh) have set up Water and Land Management Institutes (WALMI) in their States to promote innovative concepts in improved water management practices. These institutes provide training to the staff and farmers in irrigation management. They also carry out action research programmes in operational irrigation projects for optimization of irrigated agricultural production. Such training programmes undertaken by WALMIs have contributed towards improved water management practices and increase of overall irrigation efficiency. The Central Training Unit of CWC imparts short and long term training to water resources engineers in the field of integrated basin planning. A detailed study carried out in 1985 indicated that 500 senior engineers 6,200 middle level engineers and 20,000 junior engineers need to be trained in the planning, designs, operation, maintenance and management of water resources projects. In order to meet the growing demand of training of the above personnel, WALMIs and State Engineering Training Institutes would be strengthened, besides setting up of new institutes in the States where they have not so far been set up. The strengthening would also take into account the requirement for training of field level functionaries in water management. Efforts are being made to set up the National Irrigation Management Institute (NIMI) to coordinate the activities of all WALMIs, Command Area Development Agencies as well as to establish linkage with international institutions.

10. Required assistance to improve national capability in water resources and sustainable development

The Ministry of Environment and Forests has set out guidelines for preparing Environmental Impact

Assessment of river valley projects Central Water Commission has brought out detailed guidelines for sustainable water resources development and management. These guidelines, no doubt, would provide useful information to the field agencies vested with responsibility of preparing environmental impact assessment and environment management plans, which are mandatory for taking up water resources development projects, the same may not be adequate for preparing these detailed reports. Creation of infrastructural facilities for providing hands on training in preparation of environmental impact assessment and environment management plans in water resources sector will be of immense benefit and of urgent need.

Water pollution is a serious problem affecting many parts of the country. It is necessary to monitor the quality of the surface and ground water, before any suitable measure for controlling or abatement of pollution is contemplated. The Central Board for Prevention and Control of Water Pollution, Central Ground Water Board and Central Water Commission are regularly monitoring the water quality parameters through a wide network of stations. Sophisticated instruments and latest technology may help in accurate determination of the quality as well provide facility in monitoring surface as well ground water quality in expeditious way.

Basin level management for sustainable development is a new concept catching the attention of the water resources planners of the country. Exposure to the systems adopted in other countries such as France through training programmes and field visits will go a long way in improving the capability in water resources management in sustainable manner.

B. Financial sustainability of water development projects

1. Overview of social and economic condi-tions and their relationship with water resources development

The National Water Policy of 1987 sets out the following uses in order of their importance: (1) drinking; (2) irrigation; (3) hydropower; (4) navigation and (5) industrial and other uses.

The sequence of priorities is designed to ensure ecological security, economic efficiency and social equity towards achieving sustainable development. The

water development projects have contributed to the increase in foodgrains production from 51 tons in 1950-1951 to 191 tons in 1994-1995. However, due to the increase in population, the per capita availability of foodgrains has increased only marginally from 395 gm per day in 1951 to 502 gm in 1995 which is below the required normal standards.

2. Cost recovery from water development projects

There are no uniform set principles in fixing the water rates and a multiplicity of principles are followed such as recovery of cost of water supply service capacity of formers to pay based on gross earning or net benefit of irrigation, water requirement of crops, sources of water supply and its assurance, classification of land, linked with land revenue system and a combination of various elements.

Irrigation is one of the key inputs for crop production and pricing of this input as one method of raising the efficiency of water use. A revision in the level and structure of water rates is necessary in the interest of both efficiency and equity. The revision should be such as to achieve full cost recovery, promote water saving, and create disincentives for wastes. Revision of water rates should go hand in hand with measures to improve the quality of services. Rates should be based on O&M norms and capital charges (interest and depreciation). Some sort of averaging of rates by region and/or category of projects is desirable. There should be two part tariff: (a) a flat annual rate on per hectare basis and (b) variable rate linked to actual expenditure of service (volume of area). Rates as per volumetric basis could be assessed for only a small group of farmers. Rationalization of fixing of water rates etc. are suggested in three stages. The objective of the first stage should be to rationalize and simplify the existing system of assessment (based on cropwise irrigated area on an individual basis) to a system of season specific area rates. The variable part of the tariff in the case of major and medium projects should be fixed on this basis. In the second phase the aim would be to shift to a fully volumetric system. As system efficiency and productivity improve, the targets of cost recovery can be progressively increased. Volumetric system of charging is best decided in consultation with the Water Users Association. Phase III which will be spread over a much longer period should seek to extend and consolidate the system of Farmers Group Management and implement with the involvement and participation of such groups.

3. Relationship between water related natural disasters and water development projects

There are about 3,600 dams in India of which more than 2,342 are 15 m and above in height. Out of these dams, 45 have been classified as dams of national importance which have heights of 100 m and above and/or having storage capacities of 1 cubic km or more. These dams provide the much needed water for irrigation and hydropower generation. They also pose potential hazards in the unlikely event of a failure. In view of this the Dam Safety Organization was created in Central Water Commission in the year 1979 to assist the state governments to locate the causes and potential distress areas affecting the safety of dams and allied structures.

Reservoir induced seismicity is generally considered as a source of the man made disaster associated with the creation of a reservoir. Koyna dam in Maharashtra is often cited and example. Though it has not been conclusively proved that the creation of reservoir induces seismicity, yet as a precautionary measure a number of seismological stations are set up at the dam sites for conducting seismological observations and analyzing the results for planning necessary preventive measures. Dams are also designed to withstand the seismic forces considering the maximum design flood. Dam break analysis is also carried out as an integral part of the design activity of large storage structures so as to plan and take necessary mitigative measures in the event of occurrence of unlikely disaster.

C. Water conservation and wastage prevention through demand management

1. Water allocation systems and procedures

The priorities for allocation of water in the planning and operation of system as laid down by the National Water Policy are in the following descending order: drinking water; irrigation; hydropower; navigation; and industrial and other uses.

The policy thus gives an overriding priority for irrigation over industrial use. Apparently any type of industry gets the least priority for allocation of water. In some regions of the country, this may cause hardship, particularly in the case of agro-based industries like the dairy products, sugar and textile industry. The water requirement for most of the agro industries is hardly a fraction as compared to the irrigation requirements of

some crops. In the rural society, the agro based industry has a distinct socio-economic role to play. It is, therefore, felt necessary that the water allocation priority for the agro industries and the related irrigated agriculture should almost receive the same priority as for irrigation.

2. Use of water saving devices

Water conservation measures comprise not only creation of reservoirs for storing the water that would otherwise be running waste into the oceans but also prevention of losses, promotion of efficient use, recycling and reuse of wastewater. Future saving may also come from irrigation through the application of modern technologies. In water short basins, industrial and domestic sectors need to go in for recycling and reuse on a large scale. Some of the means of saving water are as follows:

(a) Creation of storage reservoirs

A major part of river flows that occur as flood flows during three to four months may be stored up for use by creating a reservoir.

(b) Control of water loss through evaporation

Large quantities of water are lost by evaporation from the surface of the reservoirs, from the open channel irrigation system and from the irrigated farms. In vast arid and semi-arid regions of the country the annual loss through evaporation is as high as 3 metres of water. Irrigation in summer months may have to be essentially from ground water. Application of chemical retardants over water surface has been experimented which proved to be very costly.

3. Improving water use efficiency

In irrigation, the efficiency of water use can be increased by improved methods of irrigation such as drip and sprinkler irrigation and by careful planning of conjunctive use of ground water with surface water. Lining of canal distributaries are also tools for controlling water losses. In the industrial sector there is a vast scope of water saving by recycling and reuse of the wastewater.

4. Pricing of water

The National Water Policy recommends that water rates should be such as to convey the scarcity value of the resources to the users and to foster the motivation for economy in water use.

5. Recycling and reuse

The water intake by the industries is affected by the extent to which water is reused. Reuse is common in large scale industries using substantial quantities of water. Pollution of water by the effluents discharged by the industries is a serious hazard increasingly being faced by the country. Although fresh water is a renewable resources, generation of new and complex wastes by industries is adding to the complexity of water pollution. Both surface water and ground water are affected by such pollution.

Recycling and reuse of wastewater is, therefore, being increasingly resorted to wherever fresh water supplies are inadequate. Wastewater discharged by an urban centre or an industry at a particular point in a river gets diluted by the river and another city or industry on the downstream draws the river water and uses it after the necessary treatment. This is generally referred to as indirect reuse. Apart from this, even within an industry a certain amount of water is normally recycled after necessary treatment for specific purposes. A high percentage of demand for industrial water is for cooling purposes. Recycling of industrial processed water should be introduced for cooling purposes wherever economically feasible, since cooling can tolerate low quality of water. Reuse of processed water reduces fresh water consumption as well as the quantity of waste products.

Treating municipal wastewater and reusing it for industrial purposes has been successfully accomplished by certain industries in the city of Bombay. Other cities are now being encouraged to adopt the same as far as feasible.

To encourage water conservation measures tariff for water conservation equipment and effluent treatment plans should be very low. Since the emphasis should be more on management of water usage rather than management of pollutants, technology and equipment that support low water usage should be encouraged with lower due level.

D. Water quality protection

1. Water quality criteria

Any stretch of river or coastal water may be subjected to more than one organized use. The list contains irrigation, drinking, industry, power generation, fisheries and wild life propagation, navigation, recreation and aesthetics, and even receptacle for treated wastes. In any stretch there would be one use which would be demanding the highest quality of water and that stretch is designated by that best water quality use (designated best use). The recognized designated best uses along with nomenclature (class of water) and primary water quality criteria are listed in table 7. Based on critical analysis of water quality carried out by them the Central Pollution Control Board (CPCB) has classified four rivers as in table 8.

(a) Ganga Action Plan Phase-I

The Ganga Action Plan Phase I was initiated in February, 1985 to combat the problem of pollution of the Ganga. The Action Plan envisaged diversion and treatment of domestic wastes in 27 important towns situated along the river. In all, 261 schemes were undertaken for sewage interception and diversion, sewage treatment, low cost sanitation measures, electric crematoria and river front development. The various schemes have been aimed to reduce the pollution in the Ganga by at least 75 per cent. Of the 261 schemes, 211 have been completed by now and the remaining are expected to e completed in the next two years.

(b) Ganga Action Plan Phase-II

The second phase of Ganga Action Plan (GAP) for pollution abatement of Yamuna and Gomti rivers at an estimated cost of Rs 4,210 million[1] has been approved. The second phase of GAP has also envisaged formulation of Action Plan for Pollution Abatement of River Damodar. The works that were required but were not included in the first phase of GAP are proposed to be covered under this phase.

---

[1] US$ = Rs 31.4

Table 7. Water quality criteria for different uses

Designated best use	Nomenclature (class of water)	Primary water quality criteria
Drinking water source without conventional treatment but after disinfection	A	(1) 6.5 to 8.5 (2) 6 (3) 2 (4) 50 (5) 10 (6) unobjectionable (7) Tasteless (8) 500 (9) 300 (10) 100 (11) 250 (12) 400 (13) 20
Outdoor bathing	B	(1) 6.5 to 8.5 (4) 500 (2) 5 (5) 300 (3) 3 (14)
Drinking water source with conventional treatment followed by disinfection	C	(1) 6.5 to 8.5 (8) 1500 (2) 4 (11) 600 (3) 6 (12) 400 (4) 5000 (13) 50 (5) 300 (14) 1.5
Fish culture and wild life propagation	D	(1) 6.5 to 8.5 (15) 1.2 (2) 4 (16) 6
Irrigation, industrial cooling or controlled waste disposal	E	(1) 6 to 8.5 (12) 1000 (8) 2100 (17) 26 (11) 600 (18) 16

Legend:

1. pH value
2. Dissolved oxygen (mg/l, min)
3. Biochemical oxygen demand (5 days at $20^{o}C$)
4. Total coliform organisms (MPN/100 ml, Max)
5. Colour, Hazen units (Max)
6. Odour
7. Taste
8. Total dissolved solids (mg/l, Max)
9. Total hardness (as $CaCo_3$) (mg/l, Max)
10. Magnesium (as $CaCo_3$) (mg/l, Max)
11. Chlorides (as Cl) (mg/l, Max)
12. Sulphates (as SO_4) (mg/l, Max)
13. Nitrates (as NO_3) (mg/l, Max)
14. Fluorides (as F) (mg/l, Max)
15. Free ammonia (as N) (mg/l, Max)
16. Free carbondioxide (as CO_2) (mg/l, Max)
17. Sodium absorption ration (Max)
18. Percent sodium (Max).

Table 8. Classification of critical rivers in India

River	Total length (km)	% of length in various categories				
		A	B	C	D	E
Ganga	2, 525	-	11	56	33	-
Yamuna	1, 376	-	36	64	-	-
Brahmni	799	-	23	77	-	-
Subarnarekha	395	-	-	90	-	10

(c) National River Action Plan

An approach paper on the National River Action Plan (NRAP) has been approved by government at an estimated cost of Rs 10,000 million spread over a period of 100 years. NRAP will include grossly polluted stretches of all those rivers of the country not covered in the GAP Phase I and II.

2. Regulations concerning water quality

The Constitution of India (Article 48-A) requires the State to endeavour to protect and improve the environment and to safeguard the forests and the wild life. As per Article 51-A, it is the fundamental duty of the citizens to protect and improve the natural environment including forests, lakes, rivers and wild life and to have compassion for living creatures.

The Water (Prevention and Control of Pollution) Act, 1974 is the first enactment by the Parliament for prevention and control of water pollution and maintaining or restoring the wholesomeness of water. Another related legislation enacted was the water (prevention and control of pollution) Cess Act, 1977 in order to conserve this vital natural resource and to augment the finance of the regulatory agencies.

The Water (Prevention and Control of Pollution) Act, 1974 and the Environment (Protection) Act, 1986 deal with the prevention and control of water pollution. The Environment (Protection) Act, 1986 is considered to be an Umbrella Act covering all aspects of environment such as water, air and land and the inter-relationship which exists among and between water, air and land, and human beings, other living creatures, plants, micro-organisms and property. Under this Act, the Central Government has the powers to take all such measures as it deems necessary or expedient for the purpose of protecting and improving the quality of environment and preventing, controlling and abating environmental pollution.

The Ministry of Environment and Forests has circulated a policy statement for Abatement of Pollution, during 1992, which lays emphasis on pollution prevention in place of the conventional end-of-the pipe treatment and also identifies adoption of best available and practicable technologies as the key element for pollution prevention. The focus of various programmes, as such has shifted from merely identifying changes in disposal techniques to issues such as promotion of clean and low-waste technologies, improvement of water quality, formation of standards, institutional and human resource development.

3. Watershed management to reduce erosion and sedimentation

Sediment flow in rivers is a natural process and water resources development projects do not contribute to increase in the sediment inflow in the rivers. All reservoirs in India have deal storage for trapping of sediments and soil conservation and watershed works are being undertaken in a number of catchment areas to reduce the sediment flow in rivers as well arrest erosion in the catchments.

During the third Five Year Plan (1961-1966), the soil conservation programme was initiated in 13 multipurposes river valley projects which during the successive plan periods has been extended to more catchments. After the floods of 1978 and 1979, a centrally sponsored scheme of integrated watershed management was undertaken in the Ganga basin. The scheme covered 240 watersheds in 8 catchments in the Indo Gangetic plain spread over 7 states and Union Territory of Delhi. It was reported that the soil conservation programmes undertaken in Kankedigedda, Pathalagedda and Onderuvagu watersheds in the catchment of Machkund project have shown declining trends in soil erosion. Many soil conservation measures such as trenching, contour bounding, planting vetiver grass are proving (extremely beneficial and cost effective. In 1978, the Government formed a Reservoir Sedimentation Committee to carry out an indepth study of sedimentation process, sedimentation transport and deposition mechanics, sedimentation sources and yields and to review the actual reservoir sedimentation situation and formulate recommendations for future

sedimentation policies. The recommendations and observations of the Committee are as follows:

(i) There is a need for scientific and technical evaluation of soil conservation programmes which should be carried out by project authorities in consultation with agricultural universities and other academic institutes such as the Indian Institute of Technology.

Comprehensive watershed management programmes provide multiple benefits at micro level resulting from small centres of intensive activity, generate larger income for the local people, greater employment opportunities and a more stable ecology. Therefore, it is recommended that soil conservation programmes should be interwoven with comprehensive watershed management.

4. Application of clean technology

Economic development of any nation depends upon several factors such as energy production and conservation, raw materials like water, minerals, forest produce and capability and skill to manage the resources optimally. Adoption of cleaner modes of production helps in resource conservation and minimization of gaseous, liquid or solid wastes.

Clean technology therefore requires waste prevention and reduction by reduced consumption of raw materials, modification and upgradation of the technological processes so that optimal utilization of natural resources is made possible, and adoption of preventive rather than corrective approaches to pollution control.

The Government is currently considering a proposal to set up the Indian Centre for Promotion of Clean Technology (ICPC) with World Bank Assistance for collection, collation and dissemination of information on clean technologies.

E. Water quality monitoring

1. Surface water quality

The Central Water Commission (CWC) is carrying out water quality monitoring at 319 sites spread over all the major and medium river basins in the country. Initially, the water quality investigations were aimed at ascertaining the status of water for irrigation use. Hence, 24 parameters associated with irrigation were monitored through tests on water samples at CWC's 18 water quality testing laboratories spread throughout the country. Since 1978, additional 22 parameters are being monitored at 42 sites in the Ganga basin under a special programme.

The Central Pollution Control Board (CPCB) is the modal agency for organizing the water quality monitoring network throughout the country. The State Pollution Control Boards are also carrying out functions similar to those of the CPCB within their respective states. Since 1977, the CPCB in collaboration with the State Pollution Control Boards has been monitoring the water quality parameters at selected locations under different programmes. Thus under the Global Environmental Monitoring Systems (GEMS) there are 51 monitoring stations and under the Monitoring the Indian National Aquatics Resources 402 monitoring stations.

In addition to the above, CPCB is collecting water quality data at 27 stations on River Ganga under a separate programme called Ganga Action Plan. The monitoring network of CPCB is expanded from a size of 17 stations on river Yamuna to the present size of 480 stations throughout the country. Though it is desirable for a single agency to collect and analyze the water quality data, considering the varying interests and responsibilities of the different agencies, work at different locations along the rivers has been continued to be undertaken by different agencies. Efforts are now being made to ensure uniformity in practices so that the data from all the agencies can be compiled and published together to give a total picture of the river systems.

2. Groundwater quality

A national status report on water quality was brought out in 1979 by the Central Ground Water Board (CGWB). In the hydrological map of India, revised in 1989, the groundwater quality parameters have been indicated. The statewide maps were prepared for the groundwater quality in the year 1987.

Unlike surface water, groundwater pollution may remain localized for a long time and escape detection at the monitoring well. Hence, micro surveys are needed to know the correct status of the quality of ground water, particularly near the cities, industrial areas or sewage irrigation farms. This aspect is being considered by the CGWB while locating the monitoring stations.

3. Standards for quality of wastewater for disposal

For the purpose of protecting and improving the quality of environment and preventing and abatement of environmental pollution, standards for emission or discharge of the industries, have been specified in the Environment (Protection) Act, 1986. As per the guidelines for sustainable water resources development and management, CWC tolerance limits prescribed for industrial effluents are given in table 9

4. Management of wastewater

The approach to management of wastewater pollution by the industries begins at reducing the generation of industrial wastes. The emphasis should shift from the management of pollutants to the reduction of generation of wastes. In general, the generation of wastes can be reduced by taking any of the following steps:

(i) changing the raw materials;

(ii) modifying the production process equipment, operational parameters or the technology itself;

(iii) improving the production efficiency and procedures;

(iv) recovering, recycling and reusing the wastewater within the plant;

(v) modifying or reformulating the products;

(vi) reusing of the wastes as raw material by other industries.

Many of the industries in India discharge their effluents after partial treatment to agricultural fields. Such discharging for irrigation purposes should not be done as a matter of course because of the inherent detrimental effects on the soils and crops and possible contamination of nearby groundwater aquifers. Studies should be undertaken to evaluate the contamination due to discharging of effluents to agricultural fields to explore the steps to be taken to remedy the situation.

In the case of highly polluting industries, regular monitoring of the quantity and quality of the effluents by an independent agency should be made mandatory.

Table 9. Tolerance limits preseribed for industrial effluents

Characteristics*	A**	B***	C****
Particle size	should pass 850 µ IS sieve		
Pesticides	Absent		
Total suspended solids	100	600	200
Total dissolved solids	2,100	2,100	2,100
pH	5.5-9.0	5.5-9.0	5.5-9.0
Oil and grease	10	100	30
Total residual chlorine	1	-	-
Ammonia nitrogen	50	50	-
Total Kjeldahl nitrogen	100	-	-
Free ammonia	5	-	-
Biochemical oxygen demand	30	350	100
Chimcal oxygen demand	250	-	-
Arsenic	0.2	0.2	-
Mercury	0.01	0.01	-
Lead	0.1	2.0	-
Cadmium	2.0	1.0	-
Hexavalent chromium	0.1	2.0	-
Total chromium	2.0	2.0	-
Copper	3.0	3.0	-
Selenium	0.05	0.05	-
Boron	2.0	2.0	-
Nickel	3.0	3.0	-
Zinc	3.0	15.0	-
Percent sodium (%)	-	-	60
Residual carbonates	-	-	5.0
Cyanides	0.2	2.0	0.2
Chlorides	1,000	1,000	600
Fluorides	2.0	15.0	-
Dissolved phosphates	5.0	-	-
Sulphides	2.0	-	-
Sulphates	1,000	1,100	-
Phenolic compounds	1.0	5.0	-

*   All parameters are in mg/l except particle size, pH, per cent sodium
**   Effluents discharged in surface water
*** Effluents discharged in sewers
**** Effluents discharged on land

While pollution from specific sources including towns and industries have been addressed, non-point pollution from run-off of agricultural inputs such as pesticides, insecticides, fertilizers, etc. has not been death with. This is gaining increasing proportions, which is polluting not only water bodies but even sub-soil water resources and would affect the health of human beings. A long-term policy for pesticides use, including the introduction of environmentally acceptable pesticides, particularly biopesticides and non-persistent biodegradable ones, and integrated pest management together with the phasing out of the proven harmful toxic and persistent ones, would be formulated in collaboration with the concerned Ministries and infrastructure involved for its effective implementation. A similar policy for fertilizer use will also need to be formulated.

VIII. WATER AND SUSTAINABLE DEVELOPMENT: CURRENT STATUS AND FUTURE TRENDS IN INDONESIA

Sutardi, Assistant for Director of Planning and Programming
Directorate General of Water Resources and Development
Ministry of Public Works, Jakarta

Introduction

Indonesia, an archipelago country with over 17,000 islands as a unified nation or known as "Wawasan Nusantara", covers a land area of 1.92 million km^2 with a coastline exceeding over 84,000 km. The country is blessed with abundant rainfall, which is approximately 6 per cent of the world's freshwater resources.

Currently over 5.5 million ha of agricultural land have been served with modern irrigation systems while another 1.6 million ha are irrigated through village irrigation systems. This has involved either construction or rehabilitation of about 12,500 diversion structures and 40 reservoirs. Indonesia has been able to progressively extend water resources utilization to support its 2,200 MW of hydropower generation which now forms about 20 per cent of the nation's generating capacity. Rural and urban water supply systems deliver close to 100,000 litres per second of piped drinking water. Over 3.3 million out of the 33.4 million ha of swamp land have been developed and major flood control and drainage projects have been implemented. In addition, nearly 18,000 ha of fishponds have been developed mostly in Aceh, North Sumatra and Sulawesi. In all about 1.96 million ha of lowland and urban area is provided with flood protection infrastructure along with 15 km of coastal protection. Industrial production, which requires large quantities of good quality water, has increased substantially over the past decade.

As in many other countries, the condition of water resources in Indonesia has come to a stage where integrated action is needed to reverse the present trends of over consumption and wastage.

A. Water resources availability and demand

1. Water resources potential

Indonesia is a tropical country affected by tropical monsoon rainfall (dry season and wet season). Total land area is 1.9 million km^2 across 13,667 islands. Total population according to the 1990 census was 179.4 million with the increase of population at about 1.98 per cent per annum. The country is divided into 27 provinces, 241 districts, 55 urban municipalities, 3,625 sub-districts and 67,033 villages.

Indonesia has abundant water resources with the annual average renewable potential of about 2,986 km^3. Owing to the uneven rainfall distribution and variability of stream flow between low and high flow conditions, only part of the renewable water resources can be used, unless large storage reservoirs are constructed. Since much of the water discharges to the sea during periods of high flows, the actual volume of useable flow is only about 30 per cent to 50 per cent of the total renewable resources.

Groundwater potential in Indonesia is limited and can support only part of the urban and rural needs for water supply while providing irrigation water for very limited areas. The demand on water resources has rapidly increased as the country implements its development programme to meet the sharply increasing needs of irrigation, drinking water, industrial water, energy, etc. The irrigation, domestic and industrial water demand formed the bulk of the demand in 1990.

In some river basins the available water resources are inadequate to meet the current needs. Java has already a shortage during the low flow season. The on-going industrialization and urbanization have put a further strain on the water resources due to water quality degradation. Hence, Indonesia is putting a greater emphasis on holistic planning approach to meet the challenges of the 21st century.

Indonesia has over 5,590 rives. Except for rivers in Kalimantan and a few rivers in Java, most rivers are short with limited flood carrying capacity. In general the rivers originate from volcanic mountains and have a distinct upper reach were the bed slopes are steep, a short middle reach with moderate bed slopes and a meandering lower reach where bed slopes are flat. Because of high rainfall intensities and upper watershed erosion, most rivers carry large quantities of sediment. Because of the flat slopes and inadequate carrying capacity in lower reaches, many rivers experience flooding in the lower reaches.

To facilitate planning, development, management and administration, the river basins are grouped into river territories called Satuan Wilayah Sungai (SWS). Thus, the country has been divided into 90 SWS or river territories. Of these, 73 SWS which are fully located in a province are termed as provincial SWS. The remaining 17 SWS which are located in two or more provinces or are of strategic importance are termed as central SWS.

It is estimated that water would become a limiting factor in national socio-economic development when water withdrawal exceeds 20 per cent of the total renewable water resources. While it is difficult to generalize, a higher level of water use relative to water supplies implies that role of water in socio-economic development is becoming more important. Water availability may therefore become a limiting factor in national development.

A water balance carried as part of the FAO/UNDP background studies for the National Water Resources Policy Project estimated that in 1990, at least eight out of the 15 river basins in Java have reached a critical situation in that there are already serious water deficits during the dry season, low-flow periods.

2. Water resources development

River basins of Indonesia could be categorized into the following three development types, namely, **Development Basin** which has great development potential, **Conservation Basin** which can be developed if the basin environment and conservation assessment allows its development, and **Management Basin** which should be developed under the strict control of overall water resources management.

A study on Formulation of Irrigation Development Programme by Japan International Cooperation Agency (JICA) in 1993 indicated that Java is covered by Management Type basin while Sulawesi, Nusa Tenggara, and north-eastern part of Sumatra is covered by Conversion Type. Development Type is extended to the whole of Kalimantan and Irian Jaya.

3. Water resources demand

For the second 25-year (1994-2019) development plan (PJP-II), water resources development will continue to support other sectors such as agriculture, industry, energy, tourism. urban and rural water supply, transportation and transmigration. However, the needs for raw water in these sectors have changed substantially, both in quality and quantity due to the progress achieved in national development. The rapid development of industries, requires increased supply of raw water at a certain quality.

Despite Indonesia's remarkable achievement in reducing the population growth rate, population still continues to grow. An average rate of 1.2 per cent, will push the population level to about 250 million in 2020. This growing population will create an increasing demand for food and ever greater pressures on land and water. Also, the labour force will grow at an appropriate rate of 2.2 per cent, requiring a rapid growth in employment opportunities.

Along with increasing urbanization which follows the current rapid growth in industry and service sectors, particularly in Java, the demand of water for domestic, municipal and industrial uses will substantially increase. This will trigger the competition among different water use sectors. Furthermore, pollution resulting from industrial and domestic waste will pose severe threats to water quality.

Based on the population growth rates and the corresponding requirements for domestic, municipal and industrial (DMI) uses, it is possible to project the total DMI demand in the year 2020, just after at the end of PJP-II. Similarly, predictions can be made for irrigation demands, based on population projections and food (rice) requirements to maintain self-sufficiency. River maintenance water demand is estimated by multiplying projected urban population by per capita flushing water requirement. Total annual water demand on each island in the year 2020 is shown in table 10.

Out of 1,847 billion m^3 of available water (natural basin discharge per year), about 127 billion m^3 will be used for DMI, irrigation, river maintenance,

Table 10. Annual water demand and estimated natural basin discharge in 2020 (million m^3)

Region	DMI	River maintenance	Irrigation	Fishpond	Livestock	Total demand	Estimated natural basin discharge
Sumatra	2 630	2 733	15 992	1 257	155	22 766	482 173
Jawa & Bali	9 805	9 799	54 918	809	258	75 569	122 699
Kalimantan	768	820	3 643	753	29	6 014	556 700
Sulawesi	686	769	14 243	354	110	16 612	143 343
Maluku & Nusa Tengara	406	444	5 526	40	69	6 485	45 909
Irian Jaya	107	124	48	0	2	281	496 422
Indonesia	14 401	14 670	94 370	3 213	623	127 277	1 847 246

etc. The remaining 1,720 billion m^3 is Available for additional development of DMI, mining and agriculture. However, regulating reservoirs may be required to use the surplus water.

As there may be water shortages in some catchments during the dry season, "real-time management" of all water resources in each river basin is necessary with due regard to water allocation and the operation of each scheme under normal and emergency conditions. Consideration will also have to be given to the releases required from reservoirs for hydropower generation, for aquaculture, maintaining minimum flows in rivers and for flushing. This can only be achieved by adopting the integrated approach to river basin planning, with the necessary regulations and procedures in place, to provide the means of "managing" the water resources in the fullest sense of the word.

The Sixth 5-year Development Plan (REPELITA VI) 1994/1995 to 1998/1999 explicitly mentioned the following targets: providing water at a rate of 210 m^3/sec to meet the needs of 72 per cent of the population; supplying 3,700 m^3/sec to irrigate 6.2 million ha of rice land; supplying 380 m^3/sec of fresh water for 370,000 ha of fish ponds; supplying 20 m^3/sec to irrigate 50,000 ha of grazing land; and supplying 110 m^3/sec to fulfill the needs of industry and tourism. In addition to meeting these physical targets, the ability to master and apply water resources technology will be improved.

Policies for achieving these targets include: improving efficiency and productivity in water utilization; increasing the supply of water to human settlements, agriculture, industry, tourism, and electricity generation; extending irrigation networks; improving water utilization through development of fair and efficient allocation systems; controlling damage to the environment; strengthening water resources institutions; and supporting regional water resources development.

B. Current status of water resources development and management

1. Policy and strategy

The Government of Indonesia (GOI), as part of its continuing effort to improve and integrate water resources management, is in the process of introducing several strategies in the management of the nation's water resources. Of these, three are of particular importance to sustainable water resources development and management (WRDM). These are:

(a) Preparation of spatial plans at the regional, provincial and local levels to guide development on a sustainable basis taking into account the optimum utilization of all resources, natural and manmade for the achievement of development objectives;

(b) Preparation of basin integrated water resources plans at the river basin level linking ground and surface water, water quality and land use plans in harmony with spatial plans, and specifically laying the basic scheme-ne for infrastructure to deliver the water according to the demand;

(c) The Government will delegate greater responsibility to the local governments for decisions and activities.

These strategies will form an important basis in the management of the nation's water resources during the PJP-II (1994 to 2019) in terms of new investment and improved water resources management.

Adequate legal basis is available from Water Law No. 11/1974 and Government Regulation No.

22/1982 to undertake integrated water resources management (WRM) from which additional policies and strategies can be set up as required during PJP-II. Apart from these, a number of laws and regulations exist that provide the legal basis for water quality management, groundwater management, river basin management, decentralization of administration and coordination as explained below.

2. Institutional and administration aspect

Water is considered as a gift of Almighty God and must be used for the welfare of the people. This statement is clearly written in The Constitution of the Republic of Indonesia 1945. Therefore the water should be controlled and administered by the State, since the State is the only Body that has the power.

In the Water Law No. 11/1974 the state has empowered the Government to administer all water resources, including the natural riches contained therein. The Government authorizes the Central, Regional or Corporate Bodies, to exercise its power in the administration of all water resources.

This authorization has been distributed to several agencies. The Ministry of Mining and Energy, for Groundwater Administration and also for the development and management of hydroelectric power. The Ministry in charge of surface water resources is presently the Ministry of Public Works. The quality of all natural resources and the environment is managed and administered by the State Ministry of the Environment. The Ministry of Forestry is in charge of Watershed Protection, and Ministry of Home Affairs is in charge of administering Irrigation Service Fee (ISF) collection and formal establishment of Water User Association.

According to the Ministry of Public Works Regulation No. 48/89 and Government Regulation No. 22/82, the management of water resources of 73 river basin units is given to the Regional Government for co-management. The co-management means that the Lower Regional Government executes the management functioned as planned by the Government or upper regional Government.

However, two river basin units are still managed by Government owned corporations and fifteen river basin units by the Central Government because they cover more than one province or because they play a strategic role in the national economy.

Planning and programming of water resources development projects are carried out by the Ministry of Public Works in consultation with the BAPPEDAS (Regional Planning Board) and BAPPENAS (National Planning Board). The projects are then implemented by the Project Implementation Unit in accordance with the de-concentration or co-management principles. These principles are also applicable to the operation and management of completed projects.

Financial arrangements are carried out by the Central Government for major water resources projects especially those for irrigation, flood control, large dam, hydro-power generation, water supply, and watershed protection. The contribution of the regional government, especially for O&M of irrigation has been gradually increased since 1987, and some contribution from the Districts through Water Supply Regional companies (PDAMS) have been obtained to cover the investment cost of water headworks. The investment in WRD by the private sector has not yet been materialised because of constraints such as water concession, and lack of investment planning to inform the private sector of investment priorities and opportunities.

Society's involvement in water resources development and management (WRDM) has, at the early stage, also been principally regulated through Law 11/74 and Government Regulation 22/82. The philosophy of society's involvement was to generate the sense of belonging and responsibility of the society, who would receive the benefit of the water resources. The participation was considered necessary to ensure adequate recovery of O&M cost in order to sustain the function of the infrastructure. The original philosophy has now been developed to encourage participation in the investment required for water resources development.

Through the Government Regulation No. 22/1982, the administration of surface water has been broken down into the following major issues, namely, concept of water resources administration, coordination of water resources administration, priority of water resources utilization, licensing of water resources utilization, O&M of water resources structures, water resources financing system, and supervision for water resources management.

By the Presidential Decree No. 244/1994, the Government has given the Ministry of Public Works, the duty to implement Government Administration concerning Public Utilities and their development, which include the water resources. By the Ministerial Decree No. 211/1994, the Ministry of Public Works delegates the water resources administration and development to the Directorate General of Water Resources Development (DGWRD). In this Ministerial Decree, the new organization structure of DGWRD was established. It consists of 6 directorates, namely, Directorate of Water Resources Management and Conservation, Directorate of Planning and Programming, Directorate of Technical Guidance, Directorate of Implementation Guidance Western, Central, and Eastern Region. This reorganization is to reflect the regional approach and to strengthen WRDM to cope with the future challenges and problems anticipated in the Second Long Term Development Plan (PJP-II). In fact, it is also an improvement of the old structure that consists of Directorate of Planning and Programming, Directorate of Irrigation I and II, Directorate of River, Directorate of Swamp, and Directorate of Equipment which was in operation for almost 20 years (during PJP-I). Similarly, GOI has also initiated steps on institutional adjustments essential for integrated WRDM. A separate Bureau of Water Resources and Irrigation in BAPPENAS under the Deputy Chairman for Infrastructure has been created.

3. Achievement of water resources development during the first 25-year development plan (1968-1993)

(a) Irrigation

In the year 1967, the starting period of the new government, the economy was nearly collapse. The agricultural sector, the primary source of employment and income had grown only 1.4 per cent, while population growth was about double that rate. The existing irrigation system in Indonesia was in poor condition mainly because of insufficient maintenance. Moreover, the number of irrigation systems available was inadequate so that many cultivated areas were depending on rain. Consequently, the total production per ha was relatively low. As a result nearly two-thirds of the population who were in fact farmers, lived in poverty with income too low to meet their basic needs.

It had also made Indonesia the biggest rice importing country in the world. Since rice was identified as a major factor in maintaining stable

conditions in Indonesia. The agricultural sector was given the highest priority in the National Development Plan, and irrigation development was given the highest priority in the water resources development sector.

Development of agriculture for poverty alleviation cannot be separated from irrigation development as water is the main input for agriculture. Therefore, during the First and second Five-Year Development Plans (1969-1974 and 1975-1980), the emphasis was put on the rehabilitation of the existing irrigation schemes, to extend such schemes where water is available, and also to build new schemes especially the simple irrigation schemes (area < 500 ha) due to its "quick yielding" process (it only takes one to three years for the system to be fully effective). The result of such a strategy is encouraging. Indonesia has reached selfsufficiency in rice production in 1984.

In the Third and Fourth Five-Year Development Plans, the focus was to support transmigration and regional development through the construction of new systems (small, medium, and large scale) in less developed regions. In 1987 the Government of Indonesia (GOI) had issued a policy statement setting out priorities for: (a) sustained O&M of the existing infrastructure together with appropriate cost recovery from beneficiaries (introduction of Irrigation Service Fee); (b) turnover of less than 500 ha systems to WUAs; (c) completion of agricultural and land development on nearly-completed schemes off-Java so as to realize agricultural benefit quickly; and (d) development of new irrigation in the outer islands for poverty alleviation and mitigating regional imbalances as well as to cope with the increase of food demand during 1994-2019. The GOI has maintained a strong commitment to provide adequate levels of O&M funding to help secure efficiency and sustainability.

During 1968-1993, a total of 3.36 million ha located mostly in Java and several major schemes in Aceh was rehabilitated. North Sumatra, and South Sulawesi and a further 1.44 million ha were completed or expanded into new areas which are located off-Java. Also in this period, a total of 40 reservoirs, 164 ponds, and 36,354 weirs were completed resulting in the increase of irrigated laid by about 5.7 million ha annually. Besides, during the first three years of REPELITA VI (1994/1995 to 1996/1997), a total of 1.088 million ha of village irrigation scheme and 0.431 million ha of existing irrigation schemes were rehabilitated.

However, the objective is not limited to providing sufficient irrigation water but also to efficiently and effectively develop and manage water to be used on a sustainable basis with due regard to the complex hydrological interrelationship between rainfall, rural land uses and vegetative aspects, flooding, erosion and all the other relevant aspects of the natural ecosystem.

(b)   Swamp reclamation

Indonesia has a total of 33 million ha of swampy areas. These areas were mostly unproductive. To support the government's programme on transmigration, swamp reclamation has been carried out for the cultivation of paddy, coconut, palm oil, etc. as part of nucleus estates for small holders or private sector development of cash crops combined with transmigration. More than a million hectares has been opened during 1968-1993. Recently a mega-project on swamp reclamation covering an area of 630,000 ha has been started in Central Kalimantan in order to cope with the long term demand for agricultural area as well as to support the transmigration programme.

(c)   Flood and volcanic debris control

Rivers while providing water as one of the basic human needs, can at the same time cause devastating floods and damage to life and property. Floods have caused serious damage in and around the capital city of Jakarta and the northern coast of Java. Major flood control works have been carried out in Java, Sumatra and Sulawesi islands. In addition, the larger multipurpose dams constructed have helped to reduce flood peaks. During 1968-1993, a total of 44 1,000 ha of productive area has been protected from recurrent floods.

Indonesia has quite a number of volcanoes and some of them are still very active. The volcanic activity results in the destruction of human settlements and damage to structures as well as irrigation and transportation systems. The active volcanoes which are kept under monitor include Mt. Merapi in Central Java and Mt. Semeru and Mt. Kelud in East Java, Mt. Galunggung in West Java and Gunung Agung in Bali. These volcanoes are included in the programmes for volcanic debris control.

(d)   Coastal area protection and management

The large number of islands in Indonesia is synonymous with sandy beaches, natural lagoons and vast expanse of coastal eco-systems. These are all subject to deterioration by tidal wind effects as well as by human activities. Coastal protection has emerged as one of the latest activities managed by the DGWRD. The work has so far been carried out on a limited basis. Some coastal protection works have been carried out in Bali, West Sumatra, Bengkulu, and North Sulawesi. A natural lagoon conservation project has been started in Segara Anakan.

(e)   Provision of raw water supply

Only a few projects have been completed under this programme during 1968-1993, among them are Jakarta Pipeline Water Supply, Nusa Dua Estuary Dam and some on-going projects such as Wonorejo and Bili-Bili dams. Rural and urban water supply systems deliver close to 100,000 litres per second of piped drinking water.

(f)   Hydropower generation

Indonesia has been generating 2,200 MW of hydropower which now forms about 20 per cent of the nation's generating capacity.

4. Problems in water resources development

Confronted with the need to respond to water demand by rapid economic development in Indonesia, the following institutional deficiencies in WRDM would be addressed:

(a) The water allocation priority in the descending order is domestic use, agriculture, industry, and electricity generation. However, this prioritisation neither clarify the allocation amongst specific users, nor does it provide specific measures to be undertaken under long term and emergency shortages.

(b) Safe drinking water is available to only part of the population (piped water supply only cover 30 per cent to 40 per cent of the city population). Though there are plans for expanding the service funding constraints prevent their implementation. The quality of surface water supply is deteriorating due to indiscriminate discharge of urban and industrial waste into waterways. Measures to promote effective waste management, such as levying pollution charges and enforcement of effluent standards have not yet been introduced.

(c) Flood events are occurring with increasing frequency because of changes in the runoff pattern of deforested watersheds as well as changes in the land use of catchment areas. The primary reason for increased flood damage, however, is that habilitation and economic activities are expanding into flood prone areas. Land use zoning and construction of flood ways are effective, but these require joint land and water resource management plans, backed by project formulation guidelines and facility operation.

(d) The electricity company owns and usually operates large reservoir facilities as single purpose projects. Without basin wide multipurpose operation rules, maximum energy benefits cannot be realized. Neither can water supply and flood protection be optimized.

(e) Most local water agencies do not apply sound water management practices. Deficiencies in mid- and long-term planning, budgeting, accounting and financial control preclude them from becoming effective and self-sufficient entities.

(f) O&M of irrigation service are not commensurate with the programmes for expanding irrigated areas. Rehabilitation and maintenance overwhelm national budgets, and water-user groups contribute only minimally to financing of operation and maintenance.

(g) Financial responsibilities are a major issue of water management institutions and appropriate answers should be sought for the following questions. For what aspects of resource development and management should the society pay? To what extent should activities be subsidized? If the beneficiaries should pay, what facilities and responsibilities should the government relinquish to them? Can privatization for profit, as applied in some developed countries, be adopted by Indonesia ?

5. Sector policies for water resources development and management

The success of efforts to improve water resources management hinges on the adopted policies, the strategy for their application and timely implementation. It is urged that the initial set of policies focus on the most critical issues confronting the country and select the most effective line of action to deal with them.

The findings of the 1992 World Bank studies on the performance of policy and strategy in Indonesia and other Asian countries are given below.

(a)   Policy: Aggressively strengthen the water resources institutions

Action: Assess present institutions, identify deficiencies and undertake, on an urgent basis, a scheduled programme for improvement. This should include; establishing a water resources unit without line responsibilities to direct all water resources planning and related cross-sector work; separating the regulatory and line operations responsibilities; establishing specialized functional units with responsibility across the respective sub-sectors; devolving responsibilities, as possible, to the lowest governmental level and the private sector (including not-for-profit entities); and altering personnel policies to encourage staff specialization.

Status: The government recognizes the importance of strengthening water resources institutions. The government has created a separate Bureau of Water Resources and Irrigation in BAPPENAS under the Deputy Chairman of Infrastructure. DGWRD also has been reorganized to reflect the regional approach and to strengthen WRDM. Recommended decentralization and deconcentration, cost recovery measures and turnover of irrigation schemes have been initiated (Irrigation Policy 1987). Beginning with REPELITA VI (1994) the country is implementing an irrigation decentralization programme under which the O&M and management of all irrigation systems will be transferred to the District. To support this policy, the government has implemented a cost recovery programme termed Irrigation Service Fee (ISF) which gradually being implemented in all provinces. The O&M budget has increased by 243 per cent in the past five years and is currently at Rp. 27,000/ha[1] of irrigated land. Further, the government has instituted a turnover programme under which irrigation systems having less than 500 ha are being handed over to Water Users Associations for operation, maintenance and management. About 200,000 ha have thus been turned over in the past five years.

---

[1] US$1 = Rp 2,200

(b)   Policy: Institute a comprehensive water rights system

Action: Institute a system of water rights/licensing governing the use of surface and groundwater resources applicable to both government and private developers and water users. Appropriate legislation and the related regulations and procedures should be prepared and enacted.

Status: No effective surface water rights system exists and the administration of the groundwater licensing system is inadequate.

(c)   Policy: Turnover O&M responsibilities of water facilities to appropriate entities

Action: Provide the necessary ownership, water rights, organizational preconditions and beneficiary support and undertake orderly turnover of water facilities O&M to local government or not-for-profit beneficiary owned entities. O&M of flood control and larger features of other systems will require joint responsibility with the assigned government agencies.

Status: The government has set policy and launched a programme to turnover small irrigation schemes to farmer entities. Urban water supply is a local responsibility in several instances. But constraints remain.

(d)   Policy: Assign basin water operations to appropriate basin/system entities

Action: Institute real-time basin water quantity and quality management under all hydrologic conditions through small, capable entities that would provide real-time analysis and operating instruction to existing O&M systems unit as appropriate. This should comply with the principles of decentralization, maximum use of involved entities and minimal interference.

Status: This concept is being instituted in selected basins under the present and future projects. The preparation of the integrated basin WRDM is currently under way under a World Bank assisted programme which will outline the technical and institutional system, and by undertaking planning in three river basins located in Java. In later years the government will gradually decentralize the preparation of the long term basin WRDM to the provincial agencies.

(e)   Policy: Install comprehensive data service

Action: Establish and equip basic data collection, analysis, storage and dissemination unit(s) to fully support planning, regulatory and, in part, real-time operations by public and private entities.

Status: Very little data collection, processing and dissemination responsibilities are focused within government. It is typically provided under individual projects and to a limited extent under regulatory programmes. But even there the service is inadequate and unreliable, and timely data are not available.

(f)   Policy: Prepare emergency drought operations plans

Action: Assign responsibility and set timely work schedule for the preparation of emergency drought plans, including the mechanism for biannual updating, for every rural and urban community with large population or substantial industrial activities. Water, land and civil government units and public advisory groups will have to cooperate in this endeavour to detail the institutional, physical and operational features of the plan.

Status: Existing plans are of limited use.

(g)   Policy: Effect project performance standards

Action: Establish operating and maintenance performance monitoring programmes on all water storage, supply, drainage and flood control projects with clear unit and agency responsibilities. Subsequent performance should be reflected in formulating the agency's future programme and budget. Planned and actual performance of local service units should be published/posted within the beneficiary area with external oversight concerning their adequacy and completeness. This should be independent of the traditional monitoring and evaluation programmes, which should be conducted as well.

Status: No formal project performance monitoring exists.

(h)   Policy: Prepare financial overview of the water sector

Action: Analyse the projected financial needs of the anticipated programmes, projects and associated activities in the entire water sector. Identify sources of funding (government and customer) and the implication for the operational and regulatory functions and prepare a broad financing plan of priority actions for attaining the nation's goats. This should contribute to establishing the investment priorities and strategies in the water sector.

Status: No comprehensive financial projections linked to needed projects and programmes have been made that cover the mild and longer term.

C. Future trends on sustainable water resources development and management

1. Objective and strategy for the second 25-year development plan (1994-2019)

Water resources development policy during the first 25-year development plan emphasized the support for achieving national self-sufficiency in food. The result of Indonesia's agricultural, industrial and economic development, supported among others by WRDM, is reflected in a four fold increase in GDP per capita over the past twenty five years and in the reduction of poverty from 44 per cent (54 million people) to 13 per cent (26 million people) of the population. In the second 25-year development plan (PJP-II) for the period 1994-2019, Indonesia has set its course to continue this development but with a greater emphasis on sustainability, thus preserving the environment and permitting the consolidation of development.

The primary objective of water resources development in PJP-II is to achieve a well distributed water supply that provides sustainability of development in Indonesia and its people. The second objective is to establish an effective and efficient water allocation system that is inter sectoral and inter regional in nature to increase the productivity of the water resources. The third objective is to conserve water resources and enhance the quality of the environment.

The strategy for water resources development in the PJP-II is to improve efficiency and productivity in the use of water for human consumption, agriculture development, industry, tourism, and power generation while performing its role in reducing income gaps and

alleviating poverty, conserving natural resources and improving environmental quality.

The State Policy Guidelines of 1993 stipulates that in PJP-II the utilization of water resources will be well planned, rational, optimized, accountable and in accordance with its carrying capacity, with emphasis on promoting prosperity of the people as well as functional sustainability and environmental balance for continuing development. The spatial plan based on a national concept is the guide in the development planning so that the management of the environment and the utilization of natural resources, including water resources, can be done safely, orderly, effectively, and efficiently. Water management, land use, and watershed management will be implemented in an integrated manner.

The increase of population coupled with the growth of various strategic sectors will increase the demand for water of significant quantity and quality at different locations. On the other hand, indiscriminate exploitation of forests, destabilization of river channels due to unplanned excavations and excessive sedimentation, increased pollution from industries and households will seriously affect the availability of natural water resources and reduce water-use efficiency. In the PJP-II, which began with REPELITA VI in April 1994, the work on water resources development will continue as a follow up of PJP-I. The development will support in the fulfilment of the need of water for human needs, strengthen economic conserve water resources and environment, and mitigate flood damage.

2. General policies

General policies on the water resources development are to enhance the efficiency and productivity of water use and to improve the water supply for residential, agricultural, industrial, tourism, and energy development. Another major goal is to fight against poverty, to minimize social disparity, and to conserve the natural resources and improve the environment.

With a view to supporting the economic growth, particularly in the agriculture, industrial, tourism, and energy sectors, the policy towards development of water resources shall be to improve the efficiency of water allocation (inter-sectoral and inter-regional) and to develop new water resources and expand the irrigation system. This can be realized by improving the water resources management system, through acquisition of new knowledge and technology, and strengthening the institutions. The water allocation shall be based on the economic value of water through the application of market mechanism. However, water prices will be controlled to ensure the fulfilment of water needs of the community.

In order to support the regional development, the development of water resources and investment in the sector shall be in harmony with the regional socio-economic conditions and land use. Farmers participation in water resources development shall be further promoted.

To minimize inter-regional disparity, development will be devoted to the under developed areas situated mostly in the eastern and western part of Indonesia. Efforts will be made to facilitate farmers in cultivating their land to raise their standard of living.

Conservation work shall be carried out in the upstream areas, in order to prevent damage to the environment and degradation of water resources quality, which shall include rehabilitation of land, the improvement of catchment areas, harmonization of master water plan, land use pattern and other natural resources.

3. Specific policies

(a) Strengthening of water resources infrastructures

To strengthen the water resources infrastructures, the policy is to improve the efficiency of operation and maintenance through motivation of community participation in the process of maintenance; prevention of productive land from other uses; and the application of new technology.

(b) Optimization of water use

In order to continuously optimize the water use, it is necessary to carry out water allocation efficiently and equitably.

(c) Environmental protection

The protection of the environment is carried out by developing a well laid out water use pattern, developing land and water conservation, motivating community involvement in maintaining the environment and community's health condition.

(d) Strengthening of water resources institutions

Measures shall be taken to establish water users associations, involve the Cooperative (Village Cooperative Unit) in water resources management, to improve human resources capability, to acquire new knowledge and technology, to improve the enforcement of law related to water resources, and to promote water use efficiency.

4. Policy for water resources management

The water resources management (WRM) policies in line with the basic principles and national policies are:

(a) To carry out water resources management within the framework of responsibilities and authorities of central and regional governments, taking into account the national, regional, and local interests and the characteristics of river and groundwater basins, so that the utilization of water resources and management of environment can be carried out harmoniously, safely, effectively, and efficiently;

(b) The management of surface and groundwater resources is conducted in an integrated way through coordination and consideration of national, regional, and local interests so that the communities can avail and use water equitably and evenly to meet their needs;

(c) The development of water resources is performed by the government with the active participation of the community so that the management and utilization of water resources development and costs arising from its operation and maintenance are duly shared;

(d) To conduct integrated management of water resources, so that the quantity and quality of water resources utilization are within the environmental capacity to support future development needs;

(e) Cost recovery for providing water supply services is based on cost allocation procedures, with government retaining the option to grant subsidies to uses having impact on poverty alleviation and self-sufficiency in food; and to apply the principle of water allocation based on social, economic, and environmental values in accordance with the Constitution and the Law of Indonesia;

(f) To improve the institutional system at the central and regional levels, particularly in its operational capability toward achieving an efficient integrated water resources management;

(g) Enhance human resources development as an inseparable part of water resources management.

5. Strategy for water resources management

Integrated water resources management in line with the above mentioned policies will be pursued through the following strategies:

(a) To apply institutional and organizational systems for coordination between the central and the regional levels, in the framework of supporting the process of integrated water resources management;

(b) To delegate a larger role to Regional Governments in the responsibilities and authority for water resources management commensurate with their interests and capabilities;

(c) The Minister responsible for water resources shall formulate national level policies based on national strategic interest, in coordination with other Ministries and Institutions involved. At the provincial levels, the formulation of policies will be done by the Governors in coordination with other interests, while at the interprovincial levels, this will be done by the involved Governors through interprovincial coordination and in close consultation with the Minister responsible for water resources;

(d) To transfer water resources management to the Provincial Level-I Regions. The Provincial government Level-I Regions will be assisted by

Provincial Water Management Committees and Basin Water Management Committees to be organized in these regions. For interprovincial basins, the Provincial Level-I Regions will be assisted by an inter provincial Basin Water Management Committee. However, water resources management of river basins of strategic value to the nation will be the responsibility of the Minister for Water Resources;

(e) Water resources and environmental management will be governed by the legally established National, Provincial, and District Spatial Plans;

(f) River basin approach, defined as Satuan Wilayah Sungai (SWS) approach, will be used in water management for areas where water resources and corresponding hydraulic structures are located, even if this covers in one or more river catchment developments, based on a master plan prepared for the integrated, efficient and effective management and protection of water resources;

(g) To allocate water in accordance with the principles of Integrated River Basin Development and Management;

(h) Conjunctive use and management of ground and surface water based on the integrated water plan for development and utilization, taking into consideration the sustainability of the resources and environmental balance for future development;

(i) To manage water quality in rivers and water bodies through waste discharge control and flow management;

(j) To maintain the function and benefit of water resources development through adequate operation and maintenance, with the application of suitable technology for achieving effective and efficient water use;

(k) To create a favourable atmosphere and to provide facilities conducive to a broader community participation in water resources management;

(l) To improve the skills for increasing efficiency in the allocation and utilization of water (inter-sectoral and inter-regional).

6. Industrial water use

The need for water for industrial development is not limited to use of water in the production process. Water is only one of inputs to industrial production. As such, there is no fixed water demand for each industry but rather a range of values due to the substitution effects of different technologies. Even with alternative technologies, some industries such as petro-chemical, pulp and paper, and steam electric power generation, demand large quantities of water in their production processes. The demand and use of water in industry is a complex process which requires clarification. There are four parameters, namely, water intake, consumptive use, effluent quantity, and effluent quality, and two processes, namely, production process and waste treatment process that characterize the technical aspects of industrial demand.

The intake water is the amount of water that is withdrawn from the water body that is needed for the production process. A certain portion of intake water is consumed during the production process and this called consumptive use. Consumptive use may be the direct use in the output of the industrial product (for example, beverage industry) or in a cooling process (for example, petro-chemical industry).

The remaining intake water of the consumptive use plus liquidified by-products from other inputs to the production process are combined into process waste. Process waste is often passed through a waste treatment process before being discharged to the receiving water body. The effluent then is the output of the waste treatment process and can vary in quantity and quality (content of pollution) depending upon the technology treatment.

Water bodies have a natural ability to assimilate waste material from industrial processes through a self-purification process. However, each water body has a limit to the amount of waste that it can accept before the self-purification mechanism becomes overloaded. In this event, the quality of the water body begins to degrade. In some cases, the amount of industrial use of the water for disposal can be increased, if the industrial effluents are first treated by a waste treatment process thus reducing the concentration of pollutant. If the water quality due to waste disposal degrades and loses the ability to perform certain functions, it can have an adverse effect upon industrial development.

Water use for hydropower can be viewed as a direct industrial use as part of the electric power industry, or as in indirect use as part of an essential infrastructure for industrial development. In either case, water for hydropower use is non-consumptive use.

7. Agricultural water use

In many strategies for industrial development, agro-industry is stressed in areas where irrigated agriculture is needed. Water is an important input to provide sufficient agricultural production. The increased income generated by increased agricultural production will also provide a greater market for industrial products.

8. Municipal water use

Municipal water supply is part of the infrastructure necessary to foster economic and social development. The direct benefit of a good municipal supply system is that for small industries, the municipal supply system is the source of water intake for industrial production. As industries get larger, they tend to develop their own water supplies due to lower costs. Thus, a good municipal water system with low water rates can attract industrial development. Secondly, industrial development requires a viable labour force. A good municipal supply which is related to better public health will attract good workers and increase their efficiency through better health leading to increased industrial production.

9. Water quality

Water is sometimes used as a measure of increasing the self-purification potential of water bodies. By increasing the minimum flow in rivers, it allows for water quality to be improved. A high water quality level is important for uses such as municipal supply, fishery, and recreation, which are indirect benefits to industrial development.

10. Flood control

The damage caused to life and property as a result of floods is enormous. In selecting locations for industrial development in river valleys close to the source of water and main transport routes, it is important to protect these large investments from floods. At the same time, industry located in a high risk flood zone may find it hard to attract labourers.

11. Navigation

The use of water for navigation is an indirect benefit for industrial development. Navigation is part of the transportation infrastructure which is important for development. It can be substituted by rail or road transportation but it allows for cheap transport of bulk commodities. This is important to keep the costs down on industrial products.

D. Issues and constraints

The holistic, integrative and sustainable principles introduced into current water resources development and management (WRDM) policies are a real challenge because of the technical, institutional, as well as financial and budgetary complexities. The shift from the sectoral approach in PJP-I period to a multisectoral integrative approach in PJP-II period has to overcome number of problems. These are cultural issues such as preference for development over water management; continued functioning of WRDM institutions based on narrow sectoral irrigation development policies and resistance to change to the more integrative approach in WRDM; lack of proper WRDM basin plans which are based on sustainable inter-sectoral and integrative principles; in spite of the new planned approach, development activities in WRDM continues to be sector or project oriented and directed by the centre rather than by a programme driven approach; inter-sectoral programmes may suffer from a lack of adequate management and institutional support; water resources provide support to a number of development sectors, however, it lacks an effective coordination mechanism at the various levels which makes inter-sectoral coordination difficult; the national level coordination is solely the responsibility of the Ministry of Public Works and lacks a coordination mechanism (similar condition exists at the provincial level); lack of a well defined water rights system, fully developed licensing system and water allocation system makes water resources management at basin level difficult; on the financial side, the revenue is insufficient and poorly defined to undertake effective water resources management; the local government revenue raising capacity is limited; the highly centralized financing and budgetary procedures impede decentralization and autonomy; the institutional reorganization and decentralization process has been slow and institutional strengthening measures in WRDM suffer from deficiencies and difficulties in human resources development; the recruitment and personnel policies including benefits inherited from the past colonial regime are not conducive to effective and efficient management; lack of public awareness at the community level with regard to water quality maintenance and efficient use of water for irrigation and domestic needs and the limited involvement of the society in water management activities; the use of appropriate pricing for water is increasingly acknowledged as a way to achieve economic efficiency and better cost recovery but it is viewed with some concern in the light of present socio-political situation and consumers' ability to pay; steps are now being taken to recover costs from urban, and industrial users and partially from irrigation through Irrigation Service Fee; in a few cases, water charges are linked to the production value, however, pricing based on the concept of water as an "Economic Good" remains elusive and will have to be applied with caution in Indonesia's current state of development; and the Public-Private Partnership (PPP) and Private Sector Participation (PSP) projects in water resources development (water supply system) have experienced delays in their implementation due to many constraints such as non familiarity of the Local Government officials in making joint ventures with private companies, insufficient detailed guidelines provided by the Central Government to Local Government and Private Sector for sharing the risks and revenues between government and private investors during construction and operation of the facilities.

The Government, through a continuous process of policy and programme review and resource mobilization, plans to address the above issues and constraints with priorities as dictated by national development.

E. Conclusions

Indonesia has embarked on a major step in water resources development and management based on a "holistic and integrative" approach towards sustainable development for the nation's second twenty five years development period (1994-2019). The focus in water resources development and management policy will shift from narrow sectoral approach to the inter-sectoral character and promote the stated goals of autonomy and decentralization. Economic policies will be directed towards reducing subsidy, improving cost recovery through pricing and service charges and promoting community, public and private participation.

To support the water resources development and management policies, the Ministry of Public Works through the Directorate General of Water Resources and Development has launched a new planning and programming approach in the area of water resources development and management, beginning with REPELITA VI in 1994, as part of its efforts to achieve sustainability in development. The Ministry has plans to carry out its programme to support four major missions, namely, supporting self-sufficiency in food productions, raw water supply and management, flood control, and water resources conservation. For the development of the capital city and its surroundings, the Government will not only provide safe and reliable drinking water, but will also improve the sanitation and drainage system. The new programming structure has shifted from the project programming system to a more holistic mission programming system. While initial difficulties are being experienced in its implementation, this approach will enable the nation to use its water and resources in more efficient and sustainable way in the long run.

It is important that Indonesia continues to develop and promote the involvement of the community and private sector, if water resources are to be conserved and preserved for future generations.

IX. WATER RESOURCES DEVELOPMENT IN LAO PEOPLE'S DEMOCRATIC REPUBLIC

Phouang Phanh Souvannabouth
Water Resources Development Engineer
Ministry of Communication Transport Post and Construction
Department of Communication, Inland Waterways Division

A. Introduction

1. Physical feature of the Lao People's Democratic Republic

Lao People's Democratic Republic is a small land-locked country situated in Southeast Asia with five neighbouring countries: Viet Nam to the east, China to the north, Myanmar and Thailand in the west, and Cambodia in the south.

The country has an area of 236,800 km^2, abundant rivers including the 1,886 km segment of the Mekong river, which defines the border with Myanmar and the major part of Thailand. Most of the Mekong river is navigable throughout the year, but most effective during the rainy season, when it provides large alluvial deposits for the fertile plains.

About two thirds of the country is mountainous, ranging from 200 m to 2,820 m above mean sea level. The mountains pose transport and communication difficulties but the rivers provide a large potential for hydropower, some of which has been tapped and provides the major source of electricity for export earning. The forest cover is 47 per cent of the total country and comprises a variety of commercial trees, species suitable for production of plywood, raw timber, parquet and furniture.

Sizeable deposits of gemstones such as sapphire, zircon and amethyst are present. Other minerals are gold, iron ore, tin, potash, limestone, silver, zinc, copper, bauxite, coal and lignites.

2. Water resources

Lao People's Democratic Republic has a tropical monsoon climate with wet and dry seasons. The wet season starts from the end of April to the end of October, with the peak rainfall period in August and early September. Dry season extends from November to March with the coolest month being January and hottest in April. The annual rainfall ranges from 1,100 mm/year in the Northern valley to over 3,700 mm/year in the south. More than 1,000 mm of surface run-off can be expected over the country. The flow of the Mekong river and its tributaries follows closely to the rainfall pattern. Peak flow of the Mekong river was recorded at 26,000 m^3/sec in September 1966, 21,000 m^3/s in 1971 and 20,600 m^3/s in 1995. The average flow of the Mekong river at Vientiane station is 1,400 m^3/s and the minimum in April was 701 m^3/s on 28 April 1956. The flow in the Mekong river and its tributaries provides a large amount of surface water resources for socio-economic development.

These water resources can be utilized for irrigation in major lowland area, for hydropower generation in numerous valleys in the mountainous regions as well as for urban and rural domestic use and other industrial uses in residential and industrial areas. On the tributaries alone this is estimated at 13,000 MW, about one third of the Mekong potential. The rivers provide one of the most important means of communication in the country, as many boats of different types and sizes sail up and down carrying thousands of tons of cargo and hundreds of thousands of passengers each year. Furthermore, these rivers also provide a large stock of natural fish of numerous species.

Groundwater resources are also abundant, but their potential is not clearly known and has not yet been studied. At the moment only shallow wells are used to draw water for rural domestic use. Deep wells used for large-scale water supply and irrigation are negligible at present.

3. Economy of the country

In 1986 the Government of Lao People's Democratic Republic adopted the New Economic

Mechanism (NEM), an economic reform package transforming economic activity from a Central command system to a market-based approach, decentralizing economic decision-making and allowing the private sector to take an active role. An economic system based on market principles has been facilitated by many structural and policy changes which have had an overall impact on the economy.

In 1994 the economic growth rate was 8.1 per cent compared to 7 per cent in 1992. Growth rate has averaged 7.6 per cent annually since 1988 with a capital income was of US$ 325 in 1994. Economic growth is mainly due to increases in industry and the service sector. The agriculture sector has contributed less to overall growth in recent years. Trends in GDP show an emergence of the private sectors in the industrial and service sectors, which are changing the orientation of economic activities in the country.

The agriculture sector grew 2.7 per cent from 1992 to 1994 and contributed 5.5 per cent of GDP. The industry sector grew 10.3 per cent from 1992 to 1994 and contributed 17.3 per cent of GDP. The service sector grew 7.7 per cent and contributed 24.3 per cent of GDP. The agriculture production losses are partially attributable to weather conditions.

4. New policy on economic reform

The government recognizes the need for further changes for economic growth to take place and further market-based activities to develop. The major macro economic component of the government's strategy consists of stabilizing domestic price and exchange rates; reducing the physical deficit; increasing and mobilizing savings; strengthening financial markets; strengthening mother and child health care; undertaking further civil reform; and implementing privatization.

It is evident that the changes needed for further progress are more difficult as issues surface that confront human resources, institutional, legal framework and other constraints. The availability of capital budget funding from multilateral and bilateral donors has been catalytic to overall economic and sectoral development. The government is now addressing the planning of assistance and the provision of local funding and implementation capabilities to improve the sustainability of the development efforts by applying for international community finance and technical assistance.

Lao People's Democratic Republic can be divided into three main economic regions, namely, the northern region, central region and southern region. These regions have administrative functions and trade relations with neighbouring countries.

B. Overall achievement of water resources development

1. Hydrology

Hydrological and meteorological stations in Lao People's Democratic Republic are part of the overall network supported by the Mekong River Commission (MRC) Secretariat. The network is operated by two main agencies, the Inland Waterways Division, and the Hydro-Meteorological Department. The network comprises those stations which are entirely or partially established with equipment provided by the MRC Secretariat and national budget.

Data collection and monitoring is undertaken by these two main agencies in cooperation with the MRC Secretariat. For major planning of large and medium scale projects, research and management work, the network has been improved, updated and expanded to cover the mountainous region in the northern and eastern part of the country.

The hydrologic measurement of the network is made by the Inland Waterways Division for 48 stations, and are made by the Hydro-Meteorology Department for more than 200 hydro and meteorological stations. These activities are supported by the MRC Secretariat with technical assistance and some funds for improvement and rehabilitation of the network. The computer software for data processing is also provided by MRC. The data is processed, and stored in a computerized data base in the office of national agency concerned and MRC Secretariat. The Yearbook has been published by the MRC and provided to users in different fields.

Data collection in Lao People's Democratic Republic at present is facing difficulties due to lack of advanced equipment, vehicles, technical support, limited budget and skilled technical staff. Moreover, the coordination between the data collecting agency and MRC Secretariat is still not clear and complicated.

2. Water quality

The study of water quality and quantity has not been implemented by the national programme. All the projects are undertaken by MRC Secretariat and sometimes form only part of the hydrology programme.

With respect to water quality, the Mekong River and its upper reaches and tributaries in Lao People's Democratic Republic may be generally categorized as good. This is due to low population density, low level of industrialization, and limitation of agriculture land along the Mekong River and its tributaries. The water quality situation in the central and southern part of the country might be considered poorer.

3. Water quantity

The Mekong River is one of the largest rivers in the world, and may be considered as South-East Asia's most significant water resource. Each year, about 475,000 million m^3 of almost unregulated water flows into the sea. However, the total run off from the catchment in Lao People's Democratic Republic is about 38 per cent of the total run off. Therefore, there is a large potential for hydropower generation, irrigation, navigation, domestic water use etc.

4. Watershed management

For management of forest land use throughout the watershed areas of the republic, the government of Lao People's Democratic Republic has adopted the tenets of the tropical forestry action plan (TFAP). Within the framework of the TFAP, and in planning for the acceleration of integrated rural development, the government of Lao People's Democratic Republic is currently reviewing and formulating various laws related to land and the use of water resources in the catchment areas.

Achieving sustainable land use in watershed implies that the percentage of soil loss from each rainstorm must be minimized, while maximizing the amount of run off to the rivers and reservoirs.

5. Irrigation

Technically there is a very large potential for irrigation development in Lao People's Democratic Republic; Department of Irrigation (DOI) and Water Resources Development Consultants (WADCO) estimated that about 600,000 ha could be irrigated.

However, the schemes as identified by WADCO in its study (1984) are mainly large gravity systems, ranging from 15,000 ha to 70,000 ha and requiring a large investment, which is not appropriate to the present situation of the Lao economy. The large and medium scale projects are mainly situated in the central and southern areas, and micro-irrigation schemes are located in the northern part of the country.

In fact there are a lot of identified projects (about the same size as existing schemes) to be developed, including those associated with major hydropower projects and the resettlement of people from the catchment area. There is also a need to invest quite a large amount of budget to complete the above schemes. But the development policy now has changed. Instead of relying only on the government and foreign assistance, farmers or the people as the community are strongly-motivated to mobilize their own resources or credit money from the agriculture promotion bank, which the government is now strongly supporting.

Until now, the major part of investment in irrigation (especially the medium scale, or the government plus community type) is from the government and foreign donors, and farmer's contributions are limited to only some labour and local materials.

6. Major irrigation schemes

So far there has been no master plan the whole country. As a result, there are no major projects identified for implementation. The two biggest reservoir schemes near the capital city could never be completed. Nam Houm and Nam Xuang barrages were completed in 1979 and 1980, but the canal systems have not yet been completed.

Major irrigation projects as well as the on-going and planned hydropower projects need more funds and man-power (in term of quantity and quality) to be successfully completed. Without irrigated agricultural development, people resettled from hydropower dam sites would not have permanent jobs, and they would practise slash and burn cultivation, causing environment degradation. Table 11 shows the situation and achievements of the irrigation sector in Lao People's Democratic Republic.

Table 11. Incremental irrigation area and flood protection

Year	Wet supplementary (ha)	Dry season (ha)	Flood protection area (ha)
1991	136,000	16,500	7,000
1992	138,000	18,000	10,000
1993	140,000	20,000	12,000
1994	145,000	22,000	20,000
1995	150,000	26,000	23,000

Source: DOI, February 1995

(a)   Community irrigation

This kind of irrigation includes small earth dam, weir, gabion weir, small pond, simple tube well, and small pump irrigation, where the community has made the investment themselves with support from the government (technical and financial). Such irrigation schemes cover more than half of the total irrigated area of the country.

(b)   Permanent small to medium scale irrigation schemes (50-100 ha)

These include weir, reservoir, pumping stations etc.,where the community was assisted by the government (community and government contributions) in the development, either through a grant or loan, or from the government's own budget. This type of scheme can assure water availability more than the community irrigation.

(c)   Government managed irrigation scheme (grant, loan or budget) ranging between 100-1,000 ha

This type of scheme is often built with higher technology and without community participation. However, only a few such schemes have been implemented, namely, Nam Houm reservoir, Nam Xuang reservoir, Pak cheng, Tha Ngone pumping station, Vientiane municipality scheme, Km 6 pumping station, Meuang Cau pump station, Km 35 (Savannakhet) gravity systems, Nam Ngum pump Project, and Sirap Projects.

7. Hydropower

Lao People's Democratic Republic is classified as a country having the highest power potential in the lower Mekong region. The estimated potential amounts to 18,000 MW. The major projects are located in the Mekong river and its tributaries. About 59 tributary projects are estimated as medium to major projects, having capacity ranging from 50 to 900 MW.

The hydropower dams currently under operation are Nam Ngum I, Nam Dng, Xe Xet, and Xelabum. The power generated by the Nam Ngum Power station and Xe Xet power station is exported to Thailand.

Lao People's Democratic Republic is presently developing many hydropower projects, ranging from 100 to 900 MW in the tributaries of Mekong river as joint venture developments.

8. River works and transport

(a)   River works

Under the support of the MRC Secretariat, the government of Netherlands and the government of Australia, the Mekong river morphology of Vientiane and Nong Khai reach was studied during 1987 to 1990. At the same time, various locations of critical bank erosion were identified and classified to be protected. Since 1988 the government of the Lao People's Democratic Republic has received a grant from the Australian government through MRC Secretariat for the Mekong River Bank Protection Project. Until now, several locations of bank protection along the Mekong river in Vientiane municipality have been constructed, namely, Tha Deua phase I, Lao-Thai Mekong Bridge, Hat Dokeo, Tha Wattay, Tha Wat Meuang Wa and Kao Lieo. Reno mattress and gabion lining in combination with geotextile poly felt were used to protect the slope of the river bank from the bottom to the top.

(b)   Transport and navigation development

Lao People's Democratic Republic has an inland waterways network of 4,600 km all within the Mekong river system. The Mekong river flows through the extreme west of Lao from north to south for a distance of 1,886 km. To conform to the natural characteristics of navigation from North to South, the Inland Waterways Division and the Lao National Mekong Committee have made the navigation section delimitation to facilitate socio-economic development planning as follows: Section from Lao-China border to Golden triangle 240 km; Section 2 from Golden triangle to Louang Phrabang 363 km; Section 3 from

Louang Phrabang to Vientiane 430 km; Section 4 from Vientiane to Savannakhet 455 km; Section 5 from Savannakhet to Pakse 256 km; Section 6 from Pakse to Done khong island 146 km.

Each of the above sections of navigation has its own difficulties. For example, in the rainy season, rapids, strong current, waterfalls, and in the dry season, channels are narrow, winding and shallow. Where there are sand banks, navigation channels shift their direction and location every year.

Due to the above problems, boats navigating in the northern and southern section have different shapes, loading and haulage capacity. Many types of motor boats, made of wooden and steel structures varying in capacity from 2 tons to 200 tons ply the section of Mekong river passage through Lao People's Democratic Republic. The boats sailing between Vientiane and Savannakhet are almost all steel boats and larger, equipped with one or two motors. The boats sailing upstream from Vientiane to Houay Sai are 8 to 15 tons wooden boats, with full load draught of 0.5-0.8 m. The boats of 30 tons to 100 tons and 150 tons are also plying in this part of the river, but they must be equipped with powerful engines and skilled pilots.

(c) Navigation aids

Before the sixties, navigational aids consisted of black stupas and red stupas to indicate rocks and other signs, from Don Deth (Lao Cambodia border) to north of Vientiane Ban Khok km 1,634. These were built during the French administration. Bamboo buoys are made during the dry season on the river stretch from Vientiane to Savannakhet and from Pakse to Khinak.

In 1975, Lao People's Democratic Republic received funds through the Mekong River Committee to continue building signs from Vientiane to North Louang Phrabang. Up to the present, 30 per cent of them have been knocked down by the current and boats.

These navigational signs are used during the medium water level only as they are submerged and during the high flood season. For the fiscal year 1995, Lao government allocated 120 million kip[1] for construction of new concrete beacon marks from Vientiane to Oudomxay and large scale Hydrographic survey at 7 rapids. In April 1996, the new album of the

updating of the Hydrographic Atlas of the Lower Mekong have been approved by the Lao-Thai government and the MRC Secretariat. It provided the new navigation chart and the data for implementing navigation aids project and other means.

(d) Port development

On both banks of the Mekong river and its tributaries, there is a total of 26 ports of which 5 are both long haul and cross haul. Ports in Lao People's Democratic Republic can be classified into three categories. In the first category they are equipped with warehousing facilities and unloading machinery. Ports belonging to this category are Keng Kabao (Savannakhet), km 4 river port at Vientiane, and Thadeua port (Xayaboury province). The second category ports are mooring ports built with steel reinforced concrete but without unloading machinery and the third category ports are built with laterite and natural soil.

All the ports are connected to roads linking with the national road network. Ports on the left tributaries of Mekong river, or on Lao People's Democratic Republic territory, or in the region not accessible by roads, are used by the people as nature allows and these are not developed up to the present.

9. Flood control

Flood forecasting and warning level of the Mekong river and its tributaries are predicted by the MRC Secretariat and informed to the agencies concerned. Flood embankment along the Mekong river on the Lao People's Democratic Republic side is available only in Vientiane municipality for a total length of 35 km from Kao Lieo to Xieng Khouan. This project is supported by EU grant. As the flood protection dike is insufficient, the agriculture field, towns and other infrastructure are annually affected by floods.

10. Environment

The objective of the environment programme is to integrate environmental aspects at all steps of the project cycle, in the development of water and related resources, by developing procedures for environmental planning, screening and assessment.

---

[1] US$ 1 = 970 kip

The environment programme in Lao People's Democratic Republic is one part of the Mekong Work Programme as inventory and management of wetland, water quality, control of soil erosion, sedimentation and flood hazard.

11. Fisheries

The actual estimated fish production in 1994 was about 30,000 tons, of which 19,240 tons was from inland capture and 10,760 tons from inland culture (using mainly indigenous fish species). The riverine fisheries is reportedly declining by 20 per cent over the last decade (1984-1994). Production in the reservoir declined by 60 per cent during the past 15 years. The production of pond culture is about 1,200 kg/ha.

The increasing demand of fish and aquatic resources versus the decreasing capture of fishery is due to the deterioration of the environment. As in other parts of the Lower Mekong Basin, fish has traditionally contributed to the major proportion of the animal protein intake of the rural population in Lao People's Democratic Republic. Nevertheless, estimated levels of consumption have remained a very low 7 kg/person/year national average, but the increase of urban population, immigrants and tourists, in Vientiane city require more than 10 kg/person/year, and the deterioration of natural habitats has led to a decline of natural fish stocks.

C. New strategy on water resources development

The government gives high priority to water resources development, especially to hydropower development, and is assisting the project development groups in any way it can. It is also strengthening the cooperation with community, private sector investment, international agency and other organizations related to the water sector. The evaluation and ranking of projects will take account of environmental impacts and cost, and thereby alert all parties to the problems of each site, before any commitment is made.

The strategy of agriculture and irrigation development is to the year 2000. The government is aiming at rice production of at least 2.2 million tons; dry irrigated area to attain 10 per cent of the total rice cultivation; wet, supplementary irrigation area to attain 40 per cent of the total; completing the development of the upper Mekong navigation within agreement of the four countries; and increased production of aquatic resources.

D. Conclusion

Lao People's Democratic Republic is known as one of the least developed and land-locked countries in the world. It has to face many problems and constraints (lack of qualified man-power, shortage of social, physical infrastructure, lack of financial resources, etc.). However, it is fortunate to be endowed with plentiful natural resources, especially water and related resources, which can be developed for socio-economic benefit. Through the New Economic Mechanism, or the principle of renovation policy, the government has committed strongly to proceed further with the implementation of its macro-economic reform policy, to expand its friendship and mutually beneficial cooperation with all countries in the world, especially with its neighbouring countries.

X. WATER AND SUSTAINABLE DEVELOPMENT IN MALAYSIA

Liew Chin Loong
Director of Planning and Evaluation Division
Department of Irrigation and Drainage, Malaysia

Abstract

Malaysia is comparatively rich in water resources with the current per capita water availability of 28,000 m³ per person per year. The main issue challenging sustainable water resources development is the increasing deterioration of the river water quality. About 12 per cent of Malaysian rivers are classified as highly polluted and the trend is increasing in tandem with the rapid pace of industrial development. Water resources projects are generally sustainable because of the strong support by the Federal government and the practice of partial cost recovery. The country is currently short of experienced human resources in the water sector. Only 1.5 per cent of Malaysian engineers have adequate experience in the field of water resources. The Federal government is investing about 9 per cent of it's budget on water resources projects under the Seventh Malaysia Plan period (1996-2000). With the exception of irrigation and flood mitigation, the private sector is expected to invest significantly in the development of water supply, sewerage and hydropower projects. The irrigation sector which consumes about 80 per cent of the total water demand is still being heavily subsidized and subsequently there is little incentive to improve irrigation efficiency. The paper also highlights the institutional setup, the government strategy and policy in the water sector, the status of water supply, water conservation and the impact on the environment.

Introduction

Malaysia is a small country with a population of 20 million and occupies an area of 329,758 km². The country consists of Peninsular Malaysia (13,100 km²), the states of Sabah (73,711 km²), and Sarawak (124,449 km²). The Federation of Malaysia consists of the States of Perlis, Kedah, Federal Territory (Kuala Lumpur and Labuan Island), Pulau Pinang, Perak, Selangor, Negeri Sembilan, Melaka, Johor, Kelantan, Terengganu, Pahang, Sabah and Sarawak. Peninsular Malaysia and East Malaysia is separated by about 540 km of the South China Sea.

A. Environmental sustainability of water resources development

1. Water resources availability

The annual rainfall in Malaysia is about 2,500 mm and this gives an average volumetric precipitation of 990 billion m³ (bcm). Out of this 360 bcm, 36 per cent returns to the atmosphere due to evaporation and transpiration. The rest constitutes surface runoff amounting to 566 bcm (57 per cent) and groundwater recharge which is estimated to be about 64 bcm (7 per cent). With a relatively small population of 20 million, this gives a per capita availability of water of about 28,000 m³ per person per year.

2. Total water demand

Total water demand has risen from 8.7 bcm in 1980 to 11.6 bcm in 1990 and is expected to reach 15.2 bcm by year 2000. Irrigation consumption accounts for the bulk of this demand (78 per cent) followed by domestic and industrial water demand (20 per cent). However, irrigation demand is expected to decline as the government policy places emphasis on improving irrigation efficiency and water demand management.

In 1993, the irrigation water demand and water supply accounted for 10,000 million m³ and 2,300 million m³ per annum respectively. As the population is growing at 2.4 per cent per annum and the manufacturing sector at 11.5 per cent per annum, the water supply sector has to grow at about 6.4 per cent in order to meet the water demand of rapid economic development. The quantity of water supply has increased from 4,162 million litres per day (MLD) in 1985 to 7,766 MLD in 1995. The total treatment plant capacity is normally about 25 per cent above the total supply requirement.

3. National Master Water Plan

A Master Action Plan for water resources development was formulated in 1982 with the completion of the National Water Resources Study. The Master Action Plan recommends an integrated development of water resources projects to solve problems associated with water supply, irrigation, pollution, hydropower and flood mitigation. The estimated cost for implementing all the recommendations was US$16 billion (1980 constant price) to be spent over a 20-year period. The main components are water supply (34 per cent), sewerage (16 per cent), hydropower (16 per cent) and irrigation (10 per cent). The water policy and recommendations as contained in the Master Plan are only accepted in principle by the government. Lack of funding is partially responsible for the late or non-systematic implementation of the recommended projects. Nevertheless, the Master Action Plans has served as a useful guide for the planning of water resources projects for the past two Malaysian development plans as well as the current Seventh Malaysia Plan (1996 - 2000).

4. Environmental impacts

Water resources projects such as water supply, irrigation, sewerage, flood mitigation generally bring benefits to the people. The associated cost to the environment in terms of permanent loss of forest or pollution is minimal. In fact the water supply projects have contributed very significantly to the reduction of water borne diseases and the improvement of the public health in general. The Environmental Quality Act in the country requires most of the large projects (more than 50 ha or certain prescribed activities irrespective of physical sizes) to be subjected to EIA and subsequent monitoring before, during and after the construction of the project. There have been cases where the projects were scrapped or stopped on environmental ground or for non-compliance with EIA requirement. Water pollution is mainly caused by non-water resources projects such as land development, oil palm mills, rubber factories and animal husbandry. Another concern is the occasional discovery of the dumping of toxic waste near water bodies.

The controversial issue is perhaps the construction of large dams. For instance, many environmentalists object to the Bakun Hydropower Dam project. One of the reasons given is that the reservoir would submerge about 700 km^2 of forest land. But on the other hand the government has to protect some 14,000 km^2 of catchment to ensure the long term viability of the project. Many dams have been constructed in the past and so far there is no threat of

water borne diseases associated with snails living in stagnant water of the reservoir. Eutrophication of reservoir is generally not an issue at the moment.

A potential negative effect arising from the privatization of water supply and sewage treatment is that many factories may switch to free groundwater to supplement their water supply. This is to avoid payment for piped water supply and a further payment for the treatment of waste water. At the moment there is no regulation by the Government on the abstraction of groundwater. So far no significant study on the impact of groundwater abstraction on the groundwater hydrology and the ecology of the environment has been carried out. A specific case study in a sensitive region may merit further consideration in the interest of the environment.

5. Institutional and legal framework

(a) Institutional framework

Malaysia practices constitutional monarchy and has two-tiered system of government, namely, the Federal and State Governments. The powers of both Governments are clearly defined in the constitution. Under the constitution matters pertaining to natural resources such as land, mines, forestry and water falls are under the State List, that is under the State jurisdiction.

Water supply only becomes a federal matter if a dispute arises in the case of a river basin which is not wholly within one state. Fortunately, the majority of the State boundaries follow the natural watershed.

Partly because of the constitutional constraint, there is no central authority solely in charge of water resources for water supply and irrigation in Malaysia. Thus the development and management of water resources is fragmented among the various federal ministries as well as amongst the 13 State Governments.

Water supply: The Public Works Department (PWD) under the Ministry of Works is responsible for the overall planning of the national water resources development to meet the domestic and industrial water supply as well as giving technical assistance to the State Water Authorities. The development and operation of water supply schemes can be undertaken directly by PWD or by the State governments through agencies such as the State Water Department, State Water Board, or State Water Authorities or privatized water supply companies.

Irrigation: Unlike water supply, irrigation activity falls under the Concurrent List which means that irrigation is both a Federal and a State function. The Department of Irrigation and Drainage (DID) which is under the Ministry of Agriculture is responsible for the planning, development and operation of irrigation schemes.

(b) Legislative framework

Legislation on matters pertaining to water abstraction and irrigation is confined to two old enactments which are rather inadequate and thus they are seldom enforced. Abstraction of water from watercourses for irrigation or water supply is regulated by the Waters Enactment 1920. This enactment is mainly concerned with the regulation of water abstraction and protection of watercourses against pollution and other human interferences. The Irrigation Areas Act, 1953 is the only legislation that governs irrigation activity and is mainly concerned with the protection of irrigation infrastructures. These two obsolete enactments are silent on institutional setup for water resources management and conservation. There are also several other legislation which deal indirectly with the protection of watershed, namely, the Land Conservation Act, Forestry Act and Mining Enactment. As the enforcement authority for these Acts is assigned to various departments, there is no coordinated effort to manage the watershed. As a result the relevant authority tends to respond to complaints rather than taking pro-active actions.

6. Human resources development in water resources projects

Successful water resources management requires many specialized skills and competence in planning, design, and operation of water development projects. A recent survey by the Institution of Engineers, Malaysia shows that only 422 engineers or 1.5 per cent of a total of 27, 300 registered engineers have at least 5 years of experience in the water resources sector. The 1.5 per cent manpower in water resources is rather small compared to the Federal Government budget for the Seventh Malaysia Plan (1996-2000) in which the water resources sector

accounts for about US$2,470 million or 9 per cent of the Federal budget.

Owing to the rapid socio-economic development in the country, there is a shortage of experienced hydrologists, water resources planners, engineers specializing in water supply, sewerage, hydropower, flood control, water managers and EIA consultants in the water sector. As a stop-gap measure Malaysia has to rely on foreign consultants. For government funded or bilateral aid projects, it is a common practice to insist on technology transfer to train Malaysian nationals in water resources planning, development and management.

7. Overview of water resources development

The general policy for water supply is to make piped water accessible for the whole nation at an affordable price. Towards this objective the government aims to provide piped water supply to all people in urban areas by 2000 and in the rural areas in Peninsular Malaysia by 2005. For the rural areas of Sabah and Sarawak the target is 90 per cent coverage by year 2005.

The strategy of water supply development is to meet the domestic and industrial water requirement, particularly in areas that are identified as new growth centres as well as areas without access to potable water supply. In addition, as part of the Government's effort to promote economic development and improve the quality of life in the rural areas, the development of rural water supply programmes will continue to be given emphasis in order to achieve a balanced development.

Towards this end, the Government has embarked on various new source development programmes such as the development of new storage and treatment plant capacities, laying of new distribution systems and utilizing groundwater.

In addition to the development of new sources, the old treatment plants and distribution systems are also being upgraded to reduce the high unaccounted for water losses which is expected to reduce from 43 per cent in 1988 to 38 per cent in 1995. This strategy requires the replacement of old water meters, replacing old pipelines and refurbishing treatment plants in priority areas. This strategy will not only reduce pressure on new source development but also improve the levels of service to existing users.

The implementation of the rural water supply programme was given greater emphasis under the Fifth Malaysia Plan (1986-1990) and Sixth Malaysia Plan (1991-1995) to enable more rural people to have access to potable water. In addition to the normal rural water supply schemes, the government has embarked on two separate programmes, namely, the Special Rural Water Supply Programme (515 million litres per day) on a turnkey basis and the Rural Water Supply and Sanitation Programme for the remote villages. As a result of the implementation of accelerated water supply programmes, 78.3 per cent of the total population already had access to piped water by 1990. By 1995, the coverage in urban areas was about 98 per cent (9 million) and 79 per cent (8.8 million) for the rural area.

In the case of irrigation both the Federal and State Governments are involved in the development of irrigation schemes to maintain national rice sufficiency level at 65 per cent. The Federal Government provides the capital investment to upgrade the irrigation infrastructures and the completed schemes are maintained by the State Governments. The government's effort is now focused on in-situ development to upgrade the irrigation and drainage infrastructures in eight rice granary areas covering 211,400 hectares. In terms of public expenditure the irrigation sector gets a lower priority compared to the water supply sector.

In the sewerage sector the government has privatized the national sewerage project in Peninsular Malaysia to Indah Water Konsortium (IWK) which will be responsible for upgrading the existing sewerage system, maintenance and to build new facilities. By the end of year 2000, it is envisaged that 79 per cent of the population will be provided with modern sewerage facilities.

In the flood mitigation sector both the Federal and State governments will continue to finance flood mitigation projects especially in the urban areas which are prone to flash flooding. Hydropower development in Malaysia is now the responsibility of the privatized utility companies. The biggest privatized hydropower project currently being implemented is the US$5.4 billion Bakun Hydropower Project which is scheduled for completion by year 2002.

B. Financial sustainability of water development projects

1. Cost recovery, public expenditure, water pricing and rate structure

During the Fifth Malaysia Plan Period (1986-1990), the government spent RM2,467 million for water supply projects and about RM1,700 million for drainage (including flood mitigation) and irrigation. Under the present Seventh Malaysia Plan period (1996-2000), the allocation for water supply is RM3,575 million and for drainage and irrigation is RM 2,500 million.

The domestic and industrial water consumption is metered for each consumer. The main source of revenue for the State Water Authorities is from the sale of water. All States adopt block tariffs, but the range of consumption blocks and the tariffs vary. Table 12 gives an indication of the range of water rates. The water rates vary slightly from state to state depending on the cost and efficiency of water production.

Table 12. Water charges in Malaysia

Type of charge	Consumption (m³/month)	Rate (RM)
Domestic	0 - 9	0.22 - 0.90
	9 - 60	0.40 - 1.15
	> 60	0.60 - 1.15
Industrial	0 - 10	0.52 - 1.40
	10 - 50,000	0.52 - 1.60
	> 50,000	0.70 - 1.80

(US$1.00 = RM 2.50)

In the irrigation sector the farmers pay according to the size of the farm lots they hold and not on volumetric consumption. Like the water tariffs the irrigation water rates also vary from state to state and typically in the range of RM7 to RM35/ha. The revenue from water rates for irrigation covers only about 10-20 per cent of the actual operational cost. It is unlikely for the rice farmers to pay the full economic cost in the near future unless rice planting can be managed on a commercial scale.

In the sewerage sector the Federal government has al located some RM112 million whereas the private sector is expected to spend RM1,760 million during the Seventh Malaysia Plan period. The cost recovery for sewerage would be charged to all water consumers based on the amount of water used.

In the flood mitigation sector the Federal government has allocated about RM900 million for river improvement and flood mitigation works to be implemented by the Department of Irrigation and Drainage. At the moment the government is not imposing any drainage charge to the beneficiaries although the existing law (Building, Street and Drainage Act) permits the local authority to levy drainage charges for drainage improvement works.

C. Sustainable use of water resources

1. Water conservation

Water conservation could be viewed from two perspectives - one from the efficiency point of view and the other from the water source point of view. In Malaysia water use efficiency is rather low. As water is still relatively cheap, the awareness for conservation is generally lacking especially in the irrigation sector which unfortunately is the major consumer of water. The irrigation efficiency in the country is around 50-60 per cent. Water recycling is not widely practiced because of the high pumping cost. In the Muda Irrigation Scheme (98,000 ha) water recycling accounts for about 15 per cent of the total water demand.

From the water source point of view there is a growing concern regarding the shrinking of water catchment areas due to massive land development as well as human encroachment into water catchment areas especially the forested land. Research has shown that deforestation tends to decrease water yield in the long term, particularly the river discharge during the dry period. The condition of existing water catchments is deteriorating due to deforestation and land development which causes the degradation of water quality. Malaysia has 19.4 million ha of forest land which covers 59 per cent of the land mass. Under the National Forest Policy, permanent forest reserve is fixed at 14.1 million ha (43 per cent) which means that another 5.3 million ha will eventually be cleared and replaced probably with tree crops. Only 2.9 million ha (or 9 per cent of the country) is classified as protective forest where no logging is permitted.

2. Water quality protection

The increasing deterioration of water quality is of serious concern in the country. Water quality monitoring is carried out by the Department of Environment (DOE) since 1978 and to a minor extent by the Department of Irrigation and Drainage (DID) even earlier. The 1994 river water quality survey based on 893 samplings covering some 7,599 km of river shows that 12 per cent of the rivers are classified as highly polluted especially those flowing through urban centres and only 33 per cent are clean. The authority which has some allocation to rehabilitate rivers is DID which incidentally has no enforcement authority.

The existing legislation for protection of water quality is generally adequate and the real issue is the lack of enforcement. Without coordinated effort to protect water quality, enforcement becomes a low priority. The relevant department could only spring into action in response to public or negative press report. Through licensing the government can technically impose standards for industrial effluent discharges by polluting industries. Unfortunately, the Environment Quality Act has no provision to license non-point sources of pollution arising from activities such as logging, irrigation, land clearing, etc. Sediments from land development and logging is one of the main reasons why many Malaysian rivers look murky and brownish at the middle and lower reaches. This normally happens when the sediment load exceeds 1,000 mg/l. Domestic sewage which is the main source of organic pollutants can only be resolved through the implementation of modern sewerage system for all households.

3. Wastewater management

The most common form of disposal for wastewater is to discharge the effluents either legally or illegally into the drains, rivers and other watercourses. In order to overcome this problem DOE has imposed stringent conditions which require polluting industries to treat their industrial wastes to the required standards as stipulated in the licensing agreement. Previously toxic waste disposal and management was a problem due to the lack of modern treatment facilities. The government has recently privatized the centralized treatment of toxic wastes.

Malaysian researchers have developed considerable local expertise and technology in the treatment of wastes from palm oil mills and rubber factories which are the major causes of organic pollution in the rivers. In the sewerage sector the implementation of the national sewerage project by the privatized entity is aimed at reducing sewage pollution. The government has imposed an effluent standard of 50 mg/l BOD for out-fall where there is no water supply abstraction downstream. If there is an abstraction, the standard is increased to 30 mg/l. At this point in time it is too early to assess the effectiveness of sewerage privatization. Only a continuous monitoring by DOE in the next few years will show whether there is any significant improvement in the river water quality.

D. Conclusion

In conclusion sustainability water resources development requires the public, government and private sector to play their respective roles to conserve water, minimize wastage, optimize the planning, management, development of water resources projects and preserving the sources of water by proper management of the water catchment. The present water demand is less than 3 per cent of the surface runoff although some parts of the country have water demand

exceeding the water stress level of 10 per cent. The present focus is on the exploitation of surface water in preference to groundwater because surface water is readily available and cheaper to abstract. Water resources projects are generally sustainable because of the strong support by the government and the practice of partial cost recovery. In line with the government's privatization policy the private sector is expected to play a greater role in the development of water supply, sewerage and hydropower projects in the near future. The issue of institutional weakness could not be resolved without a strong action and commitment by the Federal government such as to review the existing laws related to the control of pollution, watershed management and institutional arrangement. With the growing awareness that water is a finite resource and that there is increasing competition among the various sectoral users, both the Federal and State Governments would eventually have to recognize the need to have a sound national water policy to ensure sustainable development of water resources through the implementation of an integrated water resources management plan.

XI. SUSTAINABLE DEVELOPMENT OF WATER RESOURCES IN MYANMAR

Ohn Myint
Director General, Irrigation Department
Ministry of Agriculture and Irrigation, Yangon, Myanmar

Introduction

Myanmar has a total land area of 68 million ha and arable land is 19 million ha or 27 per cent of the total land area of the country. Present cultivated area accounts for 9 million ha or 49 per cent of the arable land. The achieved double cropped area is 13 per cent million ha or 143 per cent of the area under cultivation.

The present population of Myanmar is about 45 million and with an annual growth rate of 1.87 per cent, the annual demand for food is increasing in parallel. The annual rice production of approximately 12 million tons surpasses the domestic demand and such an amount could adequately meet the domestic demand of the expected population of 50 million by the year 2000.

The Government of the Union of Myanmar, is also exerting its efforts in line with the established agro-based economic objectives so as to achieve the planned annual targets of agricultural exports, including rice. Thus, the increased agricultural production of cereal crops, oil crops and industrial crops etc. keeps pace with population demand, meaning that Myanmar will continue to be free from a food shortage problem in the future. The increased production is based on both horizontal and vertical expansion enhanced by the Government's support, such as, addition of more irrigation facilities, intensification of fertilizer use and increasing use of modern farm machineries, introduction of modern agricultural techniques based on better rice varieties, and providing more incentives to the farmers through introduction of market oriented economy principles.

Agriculture is the largest sector of the economy, in terms of contribution to gross domestic product (49.9 per cent) and in the share of total labour force (65 per cent). Paddy remains, by far, the most important crop, accounting for 48.7 per cent of the gross cropped area, followed by oil seeds (21 per cent), pulses (6 per cent), wheat, maize and millet (4.7 per cent), the so-called industrial crops of cotton, jute and rubber (3.1 per cent), sugar cane and tobacco (0.5 per cent) and others (16.7 per cent). In addition, at least two thirds of the manufacturing sector is agro-based.

Although the country is generally blessed with abundant water, this resource is poorly distributed both in space and time. The heavy rains during the south-west monsoon and the torrential downpours associated with sudden storms lead to sustained flooding in the wetter areas and to flash floods in the drier parts or in places where steep mountain torrents overflow. Such floods can cause immense damage, eroding river banks, sometimes washing away whole sections of towns or villages, and at other times forming huge sandbanks that impede navigation. Flash floods may also cause serious erosion of valuable agricultural lands. During the dry season, on the other hand, scarcity of water becomes a problem over much of the country. A depth of as little as 1.2 metres is not uncommon in the nighty Ayeyarwady River during the low water period, and 0.75 metres in the Chindwin, creating considerable difficulties for navigation.

Thus, while in parts of the country the scarcity of water makes it imperative that water is used to its maximum potential, elsewhere flood control and protection of inhabited places and cultivated lands are of vital importance.

Due to the climatic conditions, even the abundant rainfall areas become short of water for crops once the rainy season is over. As a result, irrigation water supply is essentially required in most of the cultivated areas.

Although history of irrigation dates back to more than a thousand years ago in the country, the significant growth of irrigated area has been achieved only in the past three decades, from 0.6 million ha to the present 1.9 million ha, including the Government operated irrigated area of 1.1 million ha. The total irrigated area currently stands for 20.8 per cent of the total cropped area of the country. In line with the second five-year short-term plan of the Government, it is aimed to achieve the total irrigated area of 2.27 million ha, or about 25 per cent of the total cultivated area, by the fiscal year 2000-2001. The irrigation works of both State and private sectors include all types of irrigation works, such as storage dams, run-of river works, pumps, tube wells, dug wells, temporary storage and diversion works and village tanks and crib weirs.

In parallel with accelerated implementation of irrigation works the Government is developing flood protection and reclamation schemes. Presently 1.34 million ha has been brought under such schemes.

The annual surface water resources availability of the country is about 828 km^3 out of which the proportion of water use for irrigation by the year 2000 would not be more than 5 per cent of the total resources. This would leave a large reserve for sharing with the other Government agencies and private sector enterprises.

A. Status of water resources potential

1. Water resources availability

The assessment of water resources availability and water demand in Myanmar is carried out on the basis of planning units corresponding to the regions or river basins indicated below:

Region 1.	Chindwin Basin (tributary of the Ayeyarwady)
Region 2.	Upper Ayeyarwady Basin
Region 3.	Lower Ayeyarwady Basin
Region 4.	Sittoung Basin
Region 5.	Rakhine Basin
Region 6.	Tanintharyi Basin
Region 7	Thanlwin Basin (within Myanmar territory)
Region 8.	Mekong Basin (within Myanmar territory)

There are few lakes in Myanmar. The largest is the Inle Lake, which covers about 259 km^2 located in the Shan Plateau. It is the residue of a much larger body of water that is still shrinking. Drained by a tributary of Thanlwin River, it abounds in fish and is surrounded by very fertile paddies and a cluster of farm villages. It is also a much-favoured recreation spot. Other lakes and ponds are, for the most part, either closed bodies in the courses of former rivers of upper Myanmar or have been formed by reclaiming marshes of the deltas.

There is plenty of groundwater in the non-hilly areas of the country though no accurate and comprehensive data about the depths, locations and sizes of the aquifers have yet been compiled. However, there is a severe shortage of water during the three months from mid-February to mid-May. Even a drought is experienced at the end of May, if the rains do not come on time.

The Rural Water Supply Division (RWSD) of the Agriculture Mechanization Department (AMD) under the Ministry of Agriculture is the responsible government division for the exploration and exploitation of groundwater and the operation and maintenance of tube wells. The number of tube wells drilled between 1952 and 1993 totalled 11,743. Groundwater resources management in Myanmar is at an initial stage of development with the establishment of a water analysis laboratory at RWSD in 1984. Groundwater quality management plays a major role in the sustainable development and use of groundwater resources.

In the recent years, groundwater demand has increased in the country for various uses such as rural and urban domestic use, industrial use, and irrigation use.

The annual surface and groundwater potential of Myanmar is given in table 13.

Table 13. Myanmar's annual average water resources potential by river basin

Region/river basin	Surface water (km^3/yr)	Groundwater (km^3/yr)
Region 1. Chindwin	105	58
Region 2. Upper Ayeyarwady	172	93
Region 3. Lower Ayeyarwady	230	153
Region 4. Sittoung	53	28
Region 5. Rakhine	83	42
Region 6. Tanintharyi	78	39
Region 7. Thanlwin	96	75
Region 8. Mekong	11	7
Total	828	495

2. Surface and groundwater quality

(a)   Surface water

The water quality in the rivers of Myanmar is reported to be deteriorating gradually, particularly with regard to turbidity. The main reason for this is that the suspended solids load of the rivers is increasing progressively as a result of deforestation and other developmental activities in the catchment areas. It has been reported that the country's forests are being denuded at the rate of 2.1 per cent per year, which is adversely affecting water quality as well as the environment. For example, the Pugyi reservoir, which is part of the water supply system for Yangon, is already being affected by the increasing silt inflow into the reservoir and UNDP assistance has been sought to implement appropriate catchment management practices. Soil erosion and resulting sedimentation problem is also affecting some hydraulic structures in the country, including the many irrigation facilities in use. The rates of soil erosion are reported to be highest over the Bago Yoma area, reaching as high as two tons/km^2 per annum.

The effects of agricultural chemicals on water quality have not so far been recognized because of the lack of a monitoring system for chemical parameters. However, it appears that consumption of fertilizers in Myanmar is relatively modest at present, totalling about 165,000 tons in 1990/1991. On the other hand, it has been reported that salinity intrusion has reached well into the inland areas along the tidal lower reaches of the Ayeyarwady River system. A maximum chloride content of 1,000 mg/l has been observed in the river at Pathein, Mawlamyinegyun and Thabawchaung during the dry season.

(b)   *Groundwater*

In the dry-zone, studies of groundwater chemistry indicate that the shallow groundwater is of low to moderate salinity (1,000-2,000 microseimens/cm) mainly of a sodium-bicarbonate type in all areas. Although there is little variation in the degree of salinity in the vertical direction, there is some variation in the horizontal direction.

B. Water use

In Myanmar a number of Government agencies, including the Irrigation Department of the Ministry of Agriculture and Forests, are interested and engaged in surface water use but the extent and type of water use is different from each other.

Government agencies engaged in water use are:

- Irrigation Department - Irrigation
- Inland Water Transport - River navigation
- General Affairs
  Department - Domestic water supply and sanitation (some cases combined with irrigation)
- Myanmar Electric
  Power Enterprise - Hydropower generation (some cases combined with irrigation)
- Ministry of Industry - Industrial use
- Fishery Department - Fishery works
- Water Resources
  Utilization Department - Pump lift irrigation
- Private users - Domestic water, navigation and fisheries.

The above agencies are under different Government Ministries. It is quite evident that surface water is of multisectoral interest and use, all leading towards the socio-economic objectives. Presently, Myanmar Electric Power Enterprise, under the Ministry of Energy is embarking on the implementation of a number of hydropower schemes, most of which are incorporated with irrigation purpose treated as multipurpose projects.

The National Committee on Environmental Affairs (NCEA), generally chaired by the Ministry of Foreign Affairs of Myanmar is addressing the adverse effects on environment and ecology caused by land and water development. However, the criteria for sharing water use among different agencies is to be formulated and coordinated in the future by NCEA or another National Committee, although such coordination work is not immediately required now.

Since the national economic objective is based on agro-based economy, the Irrigation Department plays the major role as the prime water user, mainly for the purpose of supplying water to the irrigated crops. However, the Department is aware of the need for sharing water resources with other Government agencies, and coordinates sharing of available water with these agencies.

1. Agricultural water use

The total area under irrigation is less than 10 per cent of the land under cultivation. Irrigation is undertaken principally in central Myanmar where the annual rainfall falls almost entirely during a five-month period. The largest of the irrigation projects are the Mu Valley, the Sedawgyi Reservoir, Kinywa Reservoir,

Nyaung-kyat Reservoir and the Hanthawaddy on the Sittoung River.

Rice represents half the value of all agricultural output and covers about 5 million hectares of land. Prior to the Second World War, Myanmar was the world's leading exporter of rice. However, the war caused extensive damage to the rice fields and the pre-war levels of acreage and output were not achieved until 1964.

The use of groundwater for irrigation started only recently in Myanmar. In 1989, the Irrigation Department started the groundwater irrigation projects in the Sagaing Division funded by UNDP and IDA. Since 1991, under this project a total area of 8,094 hectares has been irrigated.

In 1992, the Rural Water Supply Division, started the drilling programme for groundwater irrigation, mainly for double paddy cropping in the dry season. During the fiscal year 1992/1993, a total of 93 bored wells in 14 townships irrigated 554 hectares of non-monsoon paddy land in Yangon and Bago Division as a result of this programme and in cooperation with the local farmers. The local farmers have been the expenses of 85 bored wells which irrigate 368 hectares of paddy land in Yezagyo Township, Magway Division. Agriculture Mechanization Department (AMD) provided technical assistance and machinery for this purpose. Further, 264 bored wells for irrigation are under construction in four divisions.

Cropping in Myanmar is controlled by regional and local authorities to meet the needs of the country. Crop irrigation water is liable to some water charges according to the prescribed laws, regulations and instructions.

Irrigation is required mainly for the second crop of paddy cultivation in addition to rainfed paddy. Conventional rainfed paddy yields 50-60 baskets per acre, whereas the second crop yields 70-80 baskets per acre. Additional extension in irrigated paddy cultivation is not only expected to raise the living standards of the rural people but will also meet the increased food requirements of the annual increase in population.

To meet the water requirements of the extension of paddy area by 1.6 million hectares as a second crop, construction of dams, and other works on rivers, and creeks, as well as drilling of tube wells, are now under way. AMD is responsible for constructing boreholes with the cooperation of local farmers. Water-lifting devices will be installed at the boreholes using diesel engines where electricity is not available. In addition, low-lift and high-lift centrifugal and axial flow water pumping devices are to be installed according to the requirements of the local conditions.

Achievement of the national target of rice production of 800 million baskets in 1993/1994 was dependent on the availability of water and water-lifting devices which were required for the double rice cropping in the dry season. Farmers' participation in the operation and maintenance of water-lifting devices has been encouraged, and training courses are being conducted for the farmers by AMD for improved operation and maintenance of water-lifting devices.

2. Domestic water use

The planning, design and construction, and implementation of water and sanitation projects directly involve six ministries and eight departments, with supporting activities provided by five other ministries and six departments. Specifically, urban water matters involve fewer bodies but the number is still large and the responsibilities overlap somewhat.

(a) Urban water use

The task of planning and design of urban water supply is carried out by the Urban Water Supply Department (UWSD) of the Department of Development Affairs of the Ministry of Progress of Border Areas and National Races and Development Affairs. UWSD also undertakes the construction and supervision of water supply facilities and usually carries this out through the town development committees. The jurisdiction of UWSD covers 284 out of 300 towns in Myanmar, excluding Yangon and Mandalay cities, which have special independent administrative arrangements for water supply and sanitation.

Township development committees are responsible for the provision and management of water supply and sanitation services within their respective areas of authority, the exception being the cities of Yangon and Mandalay. Water supply and waste disposal in Yangon and Mandalay are the responsibility of the respective city development committees. All of these development committees function under the Ministry of Home and Religious Affairs.

The Urban Water Supply and Sanitation Division of the Housing Department, Ministry of Construction, together with the Water and Sanitary Division of the Construction Corporation, Ministry of Construction, will in the future be responsible for the planning and construction of water supply and sanitation works in the towns (except Yangon and Mandalay cities).

(b) Rural water use

The Rural Water Supply Division and the Environmental Sanitation Division envisage providing drinking water supply to an additional 2.36 million and sanitary/excreta disposal facilities to 4.2 million in the rural areas. The programme also includes provision of water supply and sanitation facilities to 360 institutions. There is also a programme to motivate and assist people in the construction of a number of sanitary latrines in urban areas.

Rural water supply works were started in Myanmar in 1952. Between 1952 and 1976, RWSD constructed 6,261 tube wells serving some 4.5 million rural people. These works were funded by the Government. Negotiations initiated in 1976 with external agencies resulted in the formulation of a tube well programme for the dry zone which comprised the construction of 3,100 tube wells for the three divisions of Sagaing, Mandalay and Magway. This programme was implemented in 1997/1978 with the combined resources of the Government and external agencies, namely, WHO, UNICEF and ADB. Based on the current rate of progress, 1,900 tube wells are expected to be completed by the end of the current fiscal year. These wells will provide water for an additional population of 2.34 million. However, the survey which was conducted in 1979 to assess the condition of the existing tube wells in lower Myanmar revealed that some 2,000 tube wells were not in operation and needed rehabilitation. Taking this into consideration, it is estimated that only 5.5 million rural people had safe water supply facilities by the end of the year 1981/1982. This represents 20 per cent of the rural population.

3. Industrial water use

Industry contributes 9.3 per cent to the country's gross domestic product while employing 10 per cent of the labour force. Its annual growth rate from 1973 to 1983 was 7.7 per cent. Value added in manufacturing was $86 million, of which the share of agricultural products was 31 per cent, the share of textiles and clothing 14.1 per cent, machinery 1 per cent, chemicals 4 per cent and other manufacturing 50 per cent. From 1973 to 1983, the manufacturing grew by 6.1 per cent.

The major industrial area is in Bago and Yangon divisions. Of the 29,202 manufacturing establishments 27,393 are privately owned, accounting for 50 per cent of the value added and 1,476 are state-owned. Establishments with fewer than 10 workers account for 80 per cent of the output. The main industrial products are textiles and cement.

In 1984, the Government announced the formation of a joint venture company with a German firm to produce heavy industrial equipment. The Government invested K8.15 billion (US$1.35 billion) in the state sector in 1983/1984.

Industrial credit is provided by the Myanmar Industrial Bank and the Myanmar Economic Development Corporation.

Myanmar's total production of energy in 1984 was equivalent to 3.02 million metric tons of coal and consumption equivalent to 2.50 million metric tons of coal, or 68 kg per capita. The annual rate of growth of energy production from 1973 to 1983 was 7.2 per cent; the corresponding figure for energy consumption was 5.7 per cent. Apparent consumption of gasoline per capita was six gallons.

The total output of petroleum in 1983 was 11 million barrels and consumption 10 million barrels. Reserves of natural gas were estimated at 5 billion m^3 and production in 1984 was 476 million m^3. Myanmar has excess crude which it cannot process. In 1979, the Government contracted to sell one million barrels to Japan. Myanmar is also an exporter of paraffin was, petroleum coke and furnace oil; nearly 135,000 tons of these items are exported annually.

Total electric power production in 1984 was 1.71 million kWh (60.1 per cent hydropower and 39.9 per cent fossil fuel) and per capita consumption 47 kWh.

The Myanmar Electric Power Enterprise increased its yearly generation during the third five-year plan from 931 million kWh in 1977/1978 to 1,405 million kWh in 1981/1982. Power consumption also increased correspondingly from 677 million kWh in 1977/1978 to 1,012 million kWh in 1981/1982 representing an annual average growth rate of 10.6 per cent during the plan period.

Work on Kinda and Sedawgyi large-scale hydroelectric and irrigation projects was completed in 1985 and 1989 respectively. The aim was to meet long-term power requirements at minimum cost.

4. Non-consumptive water use

It has been estimated that a hydroelectric potential of 4,000 MW could become available with full development of the power sites. In order to expand electric power generation, mini-hydro schemes and thermal generation are being carried out as a short-term measure. As a long-term development programme, large hydroelectric projects are being implemented as separate entities and also in conjunction with multi-purpose dam projects.

According to 1992/1993 data, the total installed capacity in Myanmar was 1,151 MW. Of the total hydroelectric power potential of 4,000 MW, only 288 MW, or 7 per cent, has been exploited up to now.

C. Strategies for sustainable development

The Ministry of Agriculture and Irrigation, composed of thirteen Government agencies, is responsible for the agricultural sector development of the country. In line with the national objectives, the Ministry has oriented and laid down agricultural policies and guidelines to be manipulated by the agencies concerned. Such orientation is also aimed at promoting greater reliance on the private sector through massive participation of farmers.

As for the Irrigation Department the guidelines which are set by the Ministry for achieving sufficient and timely irrigation water are:

-   Implementation of new irrigation projects.
-   Rehabilitation and renovation of existing irrigation facilities.
-   Construction of flood storage tanks along the river banks.
-   Pump lifting from rivers and other water bodies.

-   More use of ground water.

In accordance with such guidelines the Irrigation Department has laid down its own plans and strategies for the development and expansion of irrigated agriculture during the past 7 years.

All other agencies, belonging to the same Ministry have been performing in line with the set guidelines resulting in the following achievements:

-   the acceptance by farmers of multiple cropping including paddy as the main crop;
-   the adaptation of farmers to modern farming techniques, including use of farm machineries and realization of increased use of fertilizers;
-   increased incomes and raised living standards of the farmers;
-   area development and infrastructure improvement;
-   self sufficiency in food at some rice deficit areas;
-   boosting up of the agricultural produce;
-   participation of private sector with large scale ownership of cultivation allowed and encouraged and achieved up to certain extent; and
-   increased export earning for the country.

D. Problems, issues and constraints

The policies and guidelines of the Ministry for agricultural sector are directed towards achieving sustainable development of water resources. Some problems, issues and constraints that are encountered in the implementation of these policies and guidelines can be classified as institutional, technical and sectoral in nature as follows:

1. Institutional problems

(a)   The Government agencies in exercising the agricultural strategies and guidelines need to emphasize more contact with farmers through grass root level employees, who in turn need to do extension and demonstration services to farmers and report back to the agencies concerned about the difficulties encountered;

(b)   Shortage of manpower at the grass root levels;

(c)   Insufficient supply of agricultural inputs due to changing and increasing cropping intensities;

(d)   Lack of flexibility for more decentralization of authority so as to respond better to farmers' needs;

(e)   Absence of a well defined coordination framework comprising water users and authorities concerned for putting more emphasis on the proper use of inputs, including irrigation water and other logistic support;

(f)   Socio-economic problems faced by the farmers in the implementation of agricultural policies which should be clearly understood by the organizations concerned so that certain flexibilities could be allowed by the Ministry;

(g)   Recovery of the subsidized costs of agricultural services, including irrigation projects, should be considered more in line with the socio-economic situation of the farmers and in line also with the policies and guidelines. Such recovery in some cases should be extended over a longer period.

(h)   Irrigation maintenance engineers should be trained to achieve proper system management for better system performance, administration, financial and participatory management. This requirement applies also to other grass-root level workers of other organizations having day to day contact with farmers;

(i)   Improvement should be made to the feed-back system by the grass - root level employees;

(j)   More emphasis should be placed on proper and efficient use of operation and maintenance funds for the canal systems with involvement and participation of farmers in operation and maintenance of field ditches and on farm irrigation facilities;

(k)   System performance monitoring and evaluation needs to be improved;

(l)   Lack of role of farmers in integrated agriculture due to their lack of interest in the planned crops. Crop policies should be adjusted according to market prospects for both farmers and the authorities as well.

2. Technical problems

These include:

(a)   Incomplete irrigation systems implementation leading to incomplete command area;

(b)   Poor construction and supervision of canal systems;

(c)   Generally, water distribution in the command area is not timely, adequate and equitable;

(d)   Lack of planning and monitoring in water distribution;

(e)   Maintenance difficulties resulting from technical and non-technical problems;

(f)   Tendency of the Irrigation Department to expand the service area by new project implementation rather than improving and managing the existing systems properly;

(g)   The collection of water charges or water tax is minimal and no longer suitable and relevant to prevailing prices.   Operation and Maintenance is heavily supported and subsidized by the Government;

(h)   Timely maintenance can not be carried out due to incessant irrigation for multiple cropping;

(i)   Inadequate coordination among the agencies concerned, including local authorities as well as water users; and

(j)   An overview of the system performance and maintenance as well as the assessment of cropping policies and market prospects should be made periodically to assist in reviewing and improving the agricultural policies and guidelines.

3. Sectoral problems

These include:

(a)   Lack of revision and improvement of policies. The policies and guidelines should be amended whenever necessary to adjust to the socio-economic situation taking in account the concerns and interest of the farmers who are the key input to the agricultural sector;

(b)   Tendency to expand services without adequate capability.   Horizontal   expansion   and   vertical expansion should be planned and formulated relevant to and within supporting agricultural services capacity of the sector;

(c) Lack of motivation by farmers. Incentives should be given to the organizations and to the farming communities;

(d) Lack of cost sharing by beneficiaries of the operation and maintenance cost. Cost sharing by the beneficiaries in maintenance works of the systems should be promoted and encouraged.

(e) Complex system of agricultural support services. Supporting services to the farmers including agricultural loans should be based on more simplified and straight formulations;

(f) Lack of flexibility of policies and regulations: Rigid decision making should be reduced in certain areas such as recovery of subsidized costs by fixed quota buy-backs of agricultural produce. Flexibility in the recovery of agricultural produce according to prevailing socio-economic and agro-economic situations is necessary;

(g) Lack of understanding by the farmers of Government policies. Better understanding with the beneficiaries should be reached instead of rigidly exercising departmental plans and procedures;

(h) Poor working environment. Attractive and prospective working conditions should be created for the staff to get better performance and increased productivity from the farmers; and

(i) Inadequate coordination, cooperation and understanding among the agencies. Concerted efforts are required to create better understanding with the farming communities to solve the problems of farmers.

E. Conclusions

According to the statistics of the Myanmar Economy, agricultural exports accounted for nearly 46 per cent of the total export in 1994/1995, thus highlighting the important role of agriculture in the economy of the country.

As a result of heavy reliance on the agriculture and in line with the Government Economic Objectives based on agriculture, it is imperative to improve the agricultural sector performance by all governmental and non-governmental agencies concerned including farmers.

For achieving better performance, innovative and practical ways and means must be explored and adopted on sectoral, subsectoral, and communal basis. Regional and international cooperation and understanding supported by suggestions, comments and guidelines in line with the socio-economic and agro-economic situation of Myanmar are of crucial importance.

Emphasis is being given to the rehabilitation and rescheduling of existing systems as well as planning and implementation of new irrigation projects, some combined with hydropower generation to achieve the sustainability in agriculture.

With the liberalization and opening up of the Government's policy on trade, agriculture and investment some problems and constraints have become less severe. Some of the decontrolled and reformed measures have allowed farmers to decide what crops to cultivate according to agro - economic conditions and market prospects.

Positive and massive response of farmers is expected in the future by new Government policies and remedial measures in agricultural sector.

To alleviate poverty and to achieve sustainability of agriculture timely and effective measures should be explored and applied taking into consideration technical, socio-economic and socio-political factors as well.

At present the adverse effects of the implementation of new irrigation projects on environment are still insignificant. However, with the rapid and expanded development of irrigation works in the future, every effort should be made to alleviate and mitigate the environmental impacts likely to be caused by such a development.

XII. CURRENT STATUS AND FUTURE TRENDS OF WATER AND SUSTAINABLE DEVELOPMENT IN NEPAL*

Introduction

Nepal being a landlocked mountainous country, two third of its territory is covered by Himalayan ranges, mountains and hills and only one third of its territory is flat land. It has a total area of 147,181 km^2. Present population of the country is estimated to be about 20 million with an estimated growth rate of 2.08 percent per annum.

The lower flat and fertile southern frontier of the country is Terai that borders India. The northern elevated part comprises the medium-sized Mahabharat mountains and the panoramic Himalayas that separate the country from the Tibetan plateau of China. The average annual rainfall is 1,500 mm. The climate varies from alpine to tropical depending upon the altitude.

There are five administrative regional divisions, namely the far western, western, mid-western, central and the eastern. The country has been further divided into 14 zones and 75 districts.

Agriculture is the main economy of Nepal which contributes 42 percent of the nation's GDP and employs over 80 per cent of its population. Rice, maize and wheat are the main agricultural products. Seasonal produces include varieties of fruits, oil seeds, jute and sugarcane. Livestock keeping is popular among the people all over the country.

The country is rich in water resources possessing about 2.27 per cent of the world's water resources. The major sources of water are glaciers, snow-melt from Himalayas, rainfall and groundwater. About eight per cent of the county's area is estimated to be under permanent snow cover. It is estimated that there are altogether 6,000 rivers totaling about 45,000

km in length. Koshi, Gandaki, Karnali and Mahakali are the four main river systems receiving a major part of their water supply from snow-melt, glaciers and small tributaries. Other important rivers are Kankai, Kamala, Bagmati and Babai.

To many observers, harnessing the immense water resources of Nepal is the key to achieving rapid economic development in Nepal. This view is reflected in the Water Resources Development Policy of the Eighth Plan as well.

The total annual discharge of these river systems is approximately 225 billion m^3 which can be utilized both to generate electricity and irrigate the cultivable land. However, just 254 MW of hydroelectricity have been harnessed out of a potential of 83,000 MW and just about 30 per cent of the cultivable land have been brought under some form of irrigation. There have been insignificant developments in drinking water supply, navigation, fisheries and industrial uses.

A. Environmental sustainability of water resources development

1. Overview of water resources availability

(a) Surface water

In Nepal, rainfall occurs due to south west monsoon which lasts between the months of June to September. The humid monsoon air stream moving from the Bay of Bengal is forced to rise as it meets the Himalayas. As a result, heavy rainfall occurs on some sections of the Southern Himalayan slopes. Rainfall is also high along the Churia range. Nepal can be divided into four ecological zones ranging from the Terai, the Churia, the Middle Mountains and the Himalayan region. Regions close to the Indian border receive about 1,500 mm rain in a year, while at the foot hills of the Churia the annual rainfall reaches up to 2,000 mm. The average rainfall in Nepal is about 1,500 mm. As 75 per cent of this annual rainfall occurs from June to September, the period from October to May is dry with sporadic rainfall.

---

* Consolidated by ESCAP from papers presented by Mr. Dev Raj Regmi, Joint Secretary, Ministry of Water Resources, Nepal, at the Seminar on the Establishment of Guidelines on Water and Sustainable Development, Bangkok, 9-12 December 1996 and Mr. Murari Lal Chaudhary, Deputy Director General, Department of Water Supply and Sewerage, Nepal, at the Ad Hoc Expert Group meeting on Sustainable Development of Water Resources, Bangkok, 10-12 July 1996.

In the northern Himalayan region precipitation occurs in the from the snow. Glaciers and snow contribute significantly to the run-off of the major rivers of Nepal and dominantly influence the hydrological behaviour. Accumulated snow acts as reservoir which releases water after melting. Snowfall is estimated to account for about 10 per cent of the total precipitation in the country.

Rivers in Nepal can be classified into three categories in terms of their sources of dry season discharge. The first group of rivers have their sources in snow and glaciers. The Mahakali, the Karnali, the Gandaki and the Saptakoshi are the four rivers in the first category,. The second group of rivers originate in the middle mountains which are mostly rain fed. Bagmati, West Rapti, Mechi, Kamala and Babai are in this category. Rivers in the third category, originate in the Churia, the southern face of the Mahabharat in the Terai. In the dry season the discharge of these rivers become nominal and several even dry up. Sirsia, Dodhara, Jalad, Rato, Bishi, Banganga, Sunsari are some of the rivers in this group.

The storage available in lakes is estimated to be about 2 per cent of the annual run-off. Phewa, Rupa, Begnas, Rara, Phoksinndo and Gosaikunda are some of the major lakes. Major glaciers in the Himalayan region are Chorolpa, Khumbo, Lamtang, Kanchanjunga, Yolung, Ramitang and Barun. The proportion of flow annually contributed by glaciers has not yet been accurately established.

The annual water input over the Nepalese territory is estimated to be in the order of 147 billion m^3. The total annual run off is out flowing from Nepal is estimated to be 225 billion m^3.

(b)   Groundwater

Groundwater is available in the southern region of the Terai as well as in the inner Terai valleys. The Terai is underlain by sediments that wedge out towards the north along the foot hills of the Churia. The sediment layers thicken towards the south to the Indo-Gangetic plain. Static water tables of the Terai normally lie between 3 and 10 m from the ground surface in the eastern and central Terai with yields of 100 to 300 m^3/hour under the draw-down of 7 m to 15 m. Groundwater occurring in artesian conditions yields between 2,000 and 3,000 m^3/day. A broad assessment of groundwater potential, undertaken by geo-hydrologists, indicated a reserve of about 12 billion m^3.

2. Overview of water resources use

(a)   Present uses

Domestic: Water resources are used for drinking, cooking, washing clothes and cleaning purposes, etc. sources of which are mainly streams, springs and groundwater. At a few places rivers, lakes and ponds are also used. Water for domestic uses is supplied through different types of large and small water supply schemes and projects.

In the hills and mountains mostly gravity flow type water supply systems are being constructed. Generally springs and streams are tapped by simple intakes and water is transmitted to ground reservoirs through pipes and then distributed to consumers mostly via public stand posts. If there is sufficient water in the source, reservoirs are not constructed, and water is supplied directly from the source. In the Terai region, groundwater is the main source. Water is pumped from deep tube wells to overhead tanks and then supplied through pipes via private connections or public stand posts in urban or semi-urban areas whereas in rural areas, shallow hand pumps or dugwells are constructed to supply water. So far 51 per cent of the country's population have access to safe drinking water from drinking water supply schemes constructed by the Government. The rest of the population either use traditional water sources, such as, springs, stone spouts, private shallow wells or dugwells.

Municipal: In Nepal there are 36 municipalities, of which the capital city Kathmandu has recently been declared as a metropolitan city and Biratnagar as an industrial city. Pokhara tourist centre and Lalitpur historical city have been declared as sub metropolitan cities. Nepal Water Supply Corporation (NWSC) is looking after the management of water supply for 13 municipalities including the above-mentioned four cities. Water supply is managed by the Department of Water Supply and Sewerage (DWSS) for the rest of 23 municipalities.

Surface as well as groundwater sources are used to meet the municipal demand of Kathmandu and Lalitpur. In the Terai towns, groundwater is being used.

Industrial: There are a few industries in Nepal and the industries such as cement factories, jute, sugar, paper and leather factories. The factories of beverages, textiles and carpet mainly use groundwater by making water supply systems on their own. Some big hotels in Kathmandu and Lalitpur are also using groundwater from their own tubewells as the municipal water supply systems do not provide adequate water covering only partial demand of hotels and factories.

Irrigation: Agriculture is the most dominant sector in the Nepalese economy. About 94 per cent of the country's population is engaged in agriculture, which is the main income source of the country. Rainfall is the major water resource for land cultivation in Nepal, but as rainfall alone is not sufficient for higher crop production, irrigation plays a vital role in agriculture.

Although the ultimate theoretical potential for irrigation development in the country has been roughly estimated at 5 million ha of land, due to existing topography and other constraints, the maximum economically viable potential irrigable area has been estimated at about 1.9 million ha. Out of that about 1 million ha is already being irrigated by the government managed irrigation systems as well as by farmer managed irrigation systems. There are many completed river irrigation projects in Nepal, among which, Kankai, Koshi, Kamala, Narayani, Mahakali and Bangaga are the main projects. Similarly, major river irrigation projects under construction include Sunsari-Morang, Bagmati, Babai etc. Besides river irrigation projects there are some groundwater irrigation projects, of which, Bhairwa-Lumbini groundwater irrigation project is the main project. There are many small irrigation projects already completed and under construction in the hills and Terai areas.

Power generation: Hydropower is Nepal's major resource endowment. Numerous attractive run-of-river and multi purpose hydro-schemes have been identified but remain undeveloped. Small and micro-hydro potential remains virtually unused in the hill and mountain areas. The theoretical hydropower potential is estimated at 83,300 MW based on the average flow, out of which the technical and economic hydropower potentials are currently estimated at about 45,600 MW and 42,100 MW respectively. Existing installed capacity of hydropower is only 254 MW which constitutes 0.6 per cent of the economic hydropower potential.

Other purposes: Some lakes, such as, Phewa, Rupa and Begnas are used for fishery development. Such activities are being carried out in ponds and in other small lakes in 60 out of 75 districts in Nepal. Some rivers like Narayani are used for breeding and development of crocodiles. In Chitawan district wetlands are being used for wildlife preservation, such as, ducks and the one-horned rhinoceros. Fewa lake in Pokhara is being used for boating, and some rivers like Trisuli and Narayani are being used for white water rafting.

(b)   Future uses

As Nepal is a land locked country, rivers like Koshi, Karnali and Gandaki (Narayani) may be used for navigation from the Ganga river of India and thus may provide cheap transport means, to import and export goods to and from Nepal. Many hydro projects may be constructed and power may be sold to India, Pakistan, Bangladesh and even to China, thus boosting the country's economy.

3. Incidences of overexploitation and overuse and measures to prevent such incidences

As already mentioned, Nepal is rich in water resources, and the surface water resources have not yet been fully harnessed and utilized for irrigation, hydropower generation and even for drinking purposes. Therefore there are very few incidences of over exploitation and overuse of water resources. However, over-exploitation of groundwater in the Kathmandu valley presents an alarming situation. Due to rapid urbanization and migration of people, as well as increase of industries, existing surface water resources around the Kathmandu valley are not adequate to meet the domestic and industrial demands in the valley. At present, the average daily demand of Kathmandu and Lalitpur is 130 million litres per day (MLD) but the actual supply, with a 40 per cent leakage in the system, is only 60 MLD in the dry season. Thus, to meet the demand in full, there is no option but to exploit groundwater resources. As a result, traditional stone spouts flowing excellently one decade ago, are now completely dry. Even the historical "Rani Pokhari" in the centre of Kathmandu city is in the process of drying up.

Where there are no systematic irrigation facilities, farmers mostly rely on rain-water or they construct small irrigation systems on their own, using springs, streams or pumping groundwater. But as rainfall is becoming irregular, springs and streams are drying up and people are being compelled to exploit more groundwater resources in some areas.

To prevent the incidence of over-exploitation and overuse of water resources, especially in the Kathmandu valley, carpet and garment industries which require much water, as well as other industries need to be shifted to other parts of the country, and the urbanization need to be undertaken in a planned way. Furthermore, the proposed Melamchi Water Supply Project, considered to be the only solution to meet the increasing water demand of Kathmandu Valley, need to be implemented. Strong measures also need to be taken to check deforestation. Big or small rivers could be harnessed and utilized for irrigation, and for generating power to minimize the use of wood as fuel.

4. National master plan on water resources

An integrated national water resources master plan is yet to be prepared in Nepal. However, institutions involved in developing and using of water resources have their own plans, programmes and strategies. Hence, the Government has set out plans for irrigation, hydropower and drinking water, as follows:

Irrigation: As per the available data the total area of irrigated land at the end of 7th five year development plan (end of 1991) was about 0.8 million ha and during the 8th. five year development plan as additional 0.3 million ha of land was planned to be provided with irrigation systems utilizing governmental, agricultural development bank and NGOs resources.

Hydropower: As mentioned earlier, the existing installed capacity of hydropower is about 254 MW. There are five major hydropower and two small-hydro projects under construction, which will provide an additional 244 MW by the year 2000. There are 22 major and 5 small-hydro projects, planned and proposed, which will provide about 16,401 MW when realized. In the construction of these hydro projects, resources will be sought from donor countries, international banks, financial agencies and the private sector as well.

Drinking Water: Since about 51 per cent of the country 's population have access to safe drinking water at present, the government has put a target of providing safe drinking water by the end of the year 2002. To meet the target, the government is seeking financial and technical assistance in the form of loans and grants to construct water supply projects. Besides, many NGOs are also involved in the construction of water supply schemes. To have sustainable projects, community based approach is being adopted, by involving beneficiaries in all stages of the projects and seeking voluntary labour from the user groups. Such projects, after completion, are handed over to communities for operation and maintenance.

There is no central authority responsible for integrated water resources planning and development for the country. Hence, a suitable government agency could be made responsible for overall water resource development planning. This agency should have adequate capability in terms of equipment, upgraded skills of national staff in water resources development planning and also in creating a scientific basis for planning. Such basis could include a data base, and a water plan providing practical ways and means for the most economic utilization of water resources, and the most profitable allocation of water to various users. A procedure for periodic revision of the plan depending on changes in water availability and demand also needs to be established.

5. Environmental impacts of water development projects

Although, Environmental Impact Assessment is a fairly new concept for Nepal, it has been made mandatory for medium and larger sized water development projects. This concept has been well introduced in the feasibility studies of projects such as Arun III Hydro-Power (402 MW), the Karnali Chisapani Multipurpose (10,800 MW), Kali Gandaki A Hydro-Power (144 MW), Kodkhu Water Supply and the Greater Kathmandu Water Supply (Melamchi Project Supplying Water to the Kathmandu Valley from outside the valley source) and scores of others.

Environmental Protection Act, 1996, has been promulgated. Besides, the National Environmental Impact Assessment Guidelines which were formulated by the National Planning Commission (NPC) with assistance from International Union for the Conservation of Nature and Natural Resources (IUCN) was gazetted in 1993. The Ministry of Water Resources (MWR) has also published a manual on "Environment Protection Measure for Hill Irrigation Schemes in

Nepal, 1992". Sectoral Guidelines on EIA have already been prepared.

Some other positive developments in the environmental area have been the formation of the Environmental Protection Council (EPC) under the chairmanship of the Prime Minister in October 1992. The EPC is an apex body to think, execute, monitor and coordinate the activities of ministries and agencies related to environment.

In Nepal, the environmental impacts of water development projects may be soil erosion, land slides, loss of vegetation, water use conflicts, changes in demographic patterns, inundation or damage of historical/cultural monuments, etc. In the study of Arun III Hydro-Project, a study on glacier lake outburst floods (GLOFs) was carried out and measures to eliminate the threat of GLOFs by monitoring, and possible draining of those lakes which may adversely affect Arun III Hydro-Project were identified. Likewise, the environmental impact on involuntary resettlement of indigenous people was carried out and specific remedial measures were also proposed.

For example, in Kodkhu Water Supply Project, about 100 ha of land will be submerged after the construction of the dam and about Rs 60 million[1] will be required to pay for the compensation of land.

Since the importance of assessing the environmental impact of water development projects has been acknowledged by all, Nepal Electricity Authority (NEA) has set up an Environmental Division which is involved in Environmental Impact Studies for Upper and Lower Arun, Kali Gandaki, Modikhola, Chilime and Upper Bhote Koshi, etc.

6. Institutional and legal framework

The government makes decisions regarding the responsibility and authority of institutions in the water resources development sector. The water sector management responsibility and authority are spread over several institutions. They are National Water Resources Development Council (NWRDC), NPC, MWR, NEA, Water Energy Commission Secretariat (WECS), Department of Hydrology and Meteorology (DHM), Department of Irrigation (DOI), Ministry of Housing and Physical Planning (MHPP), Department

of Water Supply and Sewerage (DWSS) and Department of Soil Conservation and Watershed Management (DSCWM). In Nepal there are some legislative Acts which are directly or indirectly related to the water resources development. These are:

- The Water Resources Act, 1992, prohibits any act that may pollute water resources and maintains that the utilization of the resources should be made without causing any considerable damage to the environment through soil erosion, floods, landslides or any other similar reason (Art 19 & 20). The Act declares that the state owns the water resources. The Act prescribes that a person willing to utilize water resources has to obtain license. However, it makes an exception in regard to domestic uses of water. For domestic use, no licenses are required. A license from the competent authority is required for irrigation on an institutional basis and no license is required for the irrigation of one's own land on an individual or collective basis. Persons wishing to make use of water resources for collective benefits on an institutional basis may form a Water User's Association (WUA).

- The Electricity Act, 1992, stipulates that electricity generation, extension or distribution shall be carried out without causing any considerable adverse impact on the environment through soil erosion, floods, land slides or air pollution, etc. (Art 24). Under the provision of this act, generation, transmission and distribution of electricity up to 1 MW does not require a license.

- The Soil Conservation and Watershed Management Act, 1982, has laid down provisions for the proper protection and utilization of land, natural resources and watersheds.

- The Nepal Water Supply Corporation Act, 1989, has empowered the Nepal Water Supply Corporation to take necessary steps to control water pollution. Similarly, there is a legal provision to penalize anyone

---

[1] US$ 1 = Nepal Rs. 50.

found contaminating the drinking water (Art 5.1.19; 18.1.2 and 19.2.1).

7. Human resource development

Human resource development (HRD) is one of the prerequisites of national capacity building. Nepal occupies 22nd position from the bottom, ranked by Human Development Index (HDI). The sustainable (financially, physically, socially and environmentally) development of water sector depends on the quality and dimension of this capacity. The water sector and other relevant institutions, at present, lack the capacity for comprehensive management of this sector. As the past efforts in HRD for water sector were guided by fragmental approach and basically concentrated on sub-sectoral capacity building, there is an urgent need for creating new, additional capacity capable of facing new challenges. The present capacity seems to be inadequate for efficiently executing the present government policy of cost recovery, users' participation, resource mobilization and environmental impact assessment of water sector.

In hydropower, NEA's Human Resource Department is responsible for making assessment of human resources for NEA and conducting training, seminars and other similar skill oriented programmes. At present, two in-house training facilities are available: (i) NEA Training Centre, established with the assistance of International Development Association (IDA), provides training to NEA technicians in the field of operation and management of the system, and (ii) Water Induced Disaster Prevention Training Centre, established under MWR with the assistance of Japan, trains technicians of MWR, NEA, Department of Roads (DOR), DOI, and the Department of Soil Conservation and Watershed Management (DSCWM). NEA and Electricité de France (EDF) had training arrangements for nearly two and half years. Under this agreement, EDF experts were stationed in Nepal to help NEA in preparing corporate planning, establishing office, preparing operation and maintenance (O&M) manuals and modernizing financial management.

NEA's present capacity is limited in constructing small hydro and preparation of feasibility studies for medium size projects. However, NEA operates and maintains all hydropower plants built so far. As the NEA is facing new challenges such as commercialization, private sector development, and

users' participation - HRD needs to be directed towards these areas as follows:

In irrigation, major projects with strong HRD focus are: (i) Irrigation Management Project (IMP) assisted by United States Agency for International Development (USAID) and designed to enhance the capability of DOI in management of the irrigation system and institutionalize the training and research capabilities required to support government agencies and WUGs in management of irrigation system; (ii) Planning and Design Strengthening Project financed by UNDP which is designed mainly to prepare the Master Plan and the design manuals for irrigation development (iii) Irrigation Sector Project (ISP) assisted by the World Bank and ADB and designed to develop and strengthen Farmers' Managed Irrigation System (FMIS); and (iv) Irrigation Sector Support Project (ISSP) funded by UNDP and executed by the World Bank and ADB aimed at strengthening the capacity of DOI in implementing ISP and institutionalizing the farmer participatory approach in DOI. There is a HRD branch within DOI. Regular training activities are carried out by this branch for both irrigation technical staff as well as user farmers.

Present capacity of DOI is largely limited to construction works. The efficiency in managing feasibility studies and preparing project proposals has yet to be strengthened. The capacity is even more inadequate in mobilizing local resources for investment and O&M cost, promoting FMIS and managing larger irrigation Projects. There is a need felt for the institutionalized training programme targeted at the new technical recruits, establishment of comprehensive in-service training and continuation of projects like IMP and ISSP.

In water supply and sanitation, fellowships for post graduate studies have been made available on a regular basis. In-country short term training courses, observation tours, seminars, workshops and conferences are being organized by various donors. In country training programmes have also been conducted through a UNDP/WHO project and as components of UNICEF and ADB assisted projects. Technical training, trainers' training are being given to junior staffs by Central Human Resources Development Unit (CHRDU) funded by UNDP and UNICEF. Similarly for high ranking staffs administrative and management training are also conducted by Nepal Administrative

Staff College sponsored by CHRDU. At present, community based approach has been adopted in the implementation of water supply and sanitation schemes or projects. Hence, pre-construction and post-construction trainings are given to Water Users' Committee (WUC) members of various projects. It is necessary to conduct more training aimed at promoting users' participation, achieving cost recovery and developing an effective service delivery system. Hence CHRDU needs to be well equipped with all logistics and its mandate should be broadened to include provision of comprehensive training.

8. Assistance required

Following several decades of isolated and narrow sub-sectoral development approach, the government has felt a need for capacity building in overall management of water resources and their sustainable development. Nepal being one of the poorest countries in the world cannot develop its water resources without the capital and technical assistance from donor countries, agencies and organizations. Hence, the government is seeking external assistance to set up a machinery for comprehensive water resources planning and for national management of the resources in order to meet the requirements of all water users in an optimal way and on a sustainable basis with due regard to national economic, social and environmental objectives.

Capital and technical assistance during the period 1975 to 1991 in water supply, irrigation and hydropower constituted about 42, 55 and 83 per cent of their respective total development expenditure. The shares of loan in the total external assistance in water supply, irrigation and hydropower were 65,77 and 67 percent respectively. It appears that this trend will continue during the current 8th plan (1992-1997) and for future also. For instance, in the irrigation sector the total amount required for the construction of on-going and new irrigation projects will be Rs 12 billion[1] out of which Rs 7.2 billion will be borne by external assistance which is about 57 per cent of the total cost.

In the water supply sector, table 14 indicates the assistance fund allocations between the years 1991-1997.

---

[1] US$ 1 = Nepal Rs. 50.

Table 14. Government and assistance funds allocations for 1991-1997

Fiscal Year	Budget in Nrs				
	Total	HMG/N	Percentage	Assistance	Percentage
1991/92	1,054.2	502.72	47.7	551.5	52.3
1993/94	1,139.2	444.1	38.7	695.1	61.3
1994/95	1,157.6	417	36	740.6	64
1995/96	1,302.7	683.5	52.5	619.2	47.5
1996/97	1,312.8	775.5	59	537.3	41

Similarly, for the construction of a almost all hydro projects a major part of the cost has been and will be borne through external capital assistance.

In other water resources development projects, such as watershed development and flood control projects, the major part of the cost is also covered through external assistance.

In irrigation, technical assistance (TA) is needed for the planning and management of irrigation system, providing support to FMIS, promoting private sector participation and carrying out feasibility studies. In water supply and sanitation, TA is required for technical training, financial management and establishment of pipe testing and water quality testing laboratories. In hydropower, TA is required for reviewing all river basin master plans, updating small hydro master plan and rural electrification master plan, establishment of hydraulic laboratory, commercialization study of NEA, and operational planning and training.

TA has been a necessary component for the development of the water sector. However, the following factors should be given due consideration to make the TA more productive: (i) cost effectiveness of TA activities; (ii) proper coordination between the government and the donors; (iii) transparency of TA policy; (iv) promotion of local resources and technology; (v) motivation of counterpart staff; (vi) coordination and monitoring of TA; and (vii) effective design and implementation of TA.

B.   Financial sustainability of water development projects

1.   Overview of social and economic conditions and their relationship with water resources development

Out of the total population of 20 million only about 40 per cent is economically active. The Nepalese society is culturally diverse with several ethnic groups, languages and religions. More than 90 per cent of the population lives in rural areas. Agriculture provides employment to over 80 per cent of the labour force. Literacy rate is 40 per cent. Infant mortality rate is 102 per 1000 and life expectancy is 55 years.

The total GDP for Fiscal year 1994/95 was Rs. 210,532 million and this was divided into Rs. 87,072 and Rs. 123,532 million for agricultural and non-agricultural production respectively. The per capita GDP was estimated to be Rs. 10,527 in nominal form. The GDP growth rate at constant price (at 1984/85 price) was 2.3 per cent in 1994/95 but GDP growth rate was 7.1 per cent in 1993/94. Average GDP growth rate for the last 10 years has been about 4.8 per cent per annum.

Nepal is heavily dependent on external assistance. According to 1995/96 budget estimates 34.5 per cent of total expenditure of Rs. 51.6 billion and 62 per cent of the development expenditure was planned to be financed from external assistance in the form of grants and loans. Loan payment and interest consumes 27 per cent of the total government revenue.

2. Cost recovery from water development projects in the country

With a recent increase in tariff NEA has improved its cost recovery situation. The profit and loss account of NEA for the last four years from 1992 to 1995 showed that net loss of Rs. 50.4 million in 1992 was changing into profit of Rs. 106.2 million from 1993 to Rs. 762.9 million in 1995. However, the increase in tariff is not the only alterative left to NEA to improve cost recovery situation. High investment cost, delay in commissioning the projects, large electricity losses (ranging from 25 to 30 per cent of total generation), over staffing, low level efficiency and delays in revenue collection have increased the operation costs in NEA.

The government has granted subsidy to the private sector through Agricultural Development Bank of Nepal (ADB/N) to set up mini hydro plants with a view to promoting rural electrification and lessen pressure on forests for domestic fuel. According to this policy the private sector has to bear 30 to 50 per cent of the investment cost depending upon the project location.

In irrigation even the fraction of O&M costs are not recovered in Agency Managed Irrigation System (AMIS). The major reasons behind poor cost recovery under AMIS are: (a) low incentive for agency staff to increase collection or improve services to farmers; (b) lack of relationship between collections and O&M budgets; and (c) little support from the budget for O&M activities. The prevailing average tariff rate in AMIS is Rs.60 per ha which is totally inadequate to cover the actual expenditure which is about Rs. 300-600 per ha for surface irrigation schemes and more than Rs. 2,000 per ha for lift irrigation or ground water irrigation schemes.

Under FMIS, certain percentage of the total investment cost has been raised through farmers' participation in terms of labour and cash. But money for maintenance cost raised by farmers is insufficient. In some districts of Far Western, Mid Western and Western regions, pilot programmes introducing Irrigation Land of Credit (ILC) are underway. In these programmes farmers have to deposit 0.5 per cent of the total cost of the project, which will be spent for O&M. Besides farmers have to contribute 15 per cent of cost of the project in the form of labour. The government has set a policy to hand over the irrigation projects which can irrigate lands up to 2,000 ha to users' group (farmers) for O&M.

In water supply projects cost recovery situation is not improving. Income from water tariff is not even adequate to meet the O&M cost. There are four categories of tap connections (a) private; (b) industrial; (c) Government; and (d) public stand posts.

Present water rates for the first 8,000 litres are Rs 20.00 and Rs 26.25 for private or government, and industries respectively. Additional Rs 5.00 or Rs 8.00 is charged, respectively for each 1,000 litres of water beyond 8,000 litres. Now the government has adopted a community based approach in the implementation of water supply projects, especially in the rural areas in order to have sustainable projects. Community is involved in every stage of the projects and the completed projects are being handed over to Water Users' Committees (WUCs) for O&M. Now cost recovery is also being done in the form of free labour contribution which constitutes about 10 per cent of total cost of the project. Also a Rs 500 cash contribution for each public stand post and Rs 300 for each shallow handpump is being collected in the Terai region. Cash contributions are being used for O&M works.

The Nepal Water Supply Corporation (NWSC) is raising water tariff rates from time to time to cover the O&M costs, depreciation and working capital. The Government Policy requires a 5 per cent annual increase in tariff to cover inflation, but that rate does not take into account higher actual inflation rates. NWSC management contemplates that improvements in operating efficiency such as reduction in water leakage (about 40 per cent), reduction in excess manpower and control of administrative overhead cost could reduce the deficit that is not offset by the tariff increase.

The water sector (irrigation, hydropower and water supply) contribution to the government revenue is about 0.05 per cent only which does not represent the true picture of water sector contribution to Nepalese economy. It is so because it does not take into account the whole incremental benefits which are enjoyed by the users and consumers of water and water products. No study has yet been conducted at macro level to quantify this contribution.

3. Natural disasters and water development projects

In Nepal there are many instance of water related natural disasters caused by both nature and water development projects. The heavy rainfall on 19-21 July 1993 produced catastrophic floods in several rivers of central and eastern Nepal. Consequently, the flood waters in Bagmati river exceeded the design discharge at the Barrage site at Mangalpur, overflowed both banks, and caused great damage to canal intakes, inundated several hundred hectares of lands, washed out a few villages including hundreds of people and livestock. Due to the siltation problems in front of the Koshi Barrage, the river bed level is rising. Consequently, the 40 km embankment along the eastern bank of the Koshi river also gets damaged at

places due to floods in the rainy season. Similarly, quite often, parts of the western embankment of the Koshi river gets washed away by floods, causing heavy loss of lives and property.

To mitigate such disasters watershed management needs to be carried out in a planned way and deforestation has to be stopped so that minimum siltation of river bed occurs. Again, if there is adequate vegetation cover over the watershed area, rainwater will be partly infiltrated into the ground the remaining overland flow will slowly reach the dam sites and may not exceed the design discharge as it had happened at the Bagmati Barrage. Some parts of dykes and embankments prone to damage by flooding, need to be better constructed. Some appropriate action also needs to be taken to remove the silt from the upstream of Koshi Barrage.

C. Sustainable use of water resources

1. Water conservation and wastage prevention through demand management

(a) Water allocation system and procedures

To conserve water through rational use, water allocation system and procedures in Nepal are as follows:

Domestic use: Drinking Water supply systems are designed allocating 45 litres per capita per day (lpcd) for rural areas and 65 lpcd and 110 lpcd for partially and fully plumbed connections in urban areas, respectively.

Hydropower: Water is allocated as per the necessity of how much power is needed to be generated and how much water is needed in the downstream for the survival of aquatic life. In Nepal, Kulekhani I hydro project of 60 MW installed capacity stores the rain water with the construction of a rock fill dam, and uses stored water in the dry season to generate power. Marsyangdi hydro project of 69 MW capacity, diverts whole of the river flow to generate power in dry season rendering dry few kilometres downstream.

Irrigation: In Nepal canals are designed generally allocating 1 to 31/sec of water per ha of land depending on temperature, land, topography (Terai or hills), cropping patterns, etc.

(b) *Use of water saving devices*

Water meters are used to avoid the misuse of drinking water. For the rational use of water, Water User Committees (WUCs) have been made responsible for O&M in drinking water projects and irrigation projects as well. Repairs of leakages and replacement of old pipes are under way in Nepal Water Supply Corporation (NWSC) in Kathmandu. Irrigation of land is being done after sunset to avoid evaporation loss. In hills pipes are used in several portions of the canal. Timely repairs of canals are being done where WUC has taken O&M responsibility. Wherever possible, farmers are growing crops demanding less water and people are being encouraged for that.

(c) *Water pricing policies and structure*

Though water pricing is not a new concern in Nepal, yet in the past it remained as a futile exercise because of the public opinion that water resources like other natural resources is abundant and a free God-gift coupled with a religious belief that the providing water is a sacred activity. Therefore there is a need to develop an awareness programme to promote the concept that water is not a free commodity.

As the water pricing policies are determined based on equity, health, administrative, fiscal and institutional, cost recovery and O&M cost considerations, NWSC is adjusting the water tariff from time to time. The concept of opportunity cost of water is also yet to be stressed in Nepal.

2. Water quality protection

In Nepal, recycling or reuse of water for the purpose of water quality protection is not currently in practice. Similarly, regulations concerning wastewater disposal and their enforcement are also not so effective due to many reasons. In Kathmandu valley there are only two sewage treatment plants (lagoons), one for Kathmandu and another for Lalitpur city. These two lagoons are not adequate to treat all sewage of Kathmandu and Lalitpur, hence untreated sewage are directly discharged into Bagmati, Bishnumati and Tukucha rivers, turning them virtually into sewers.

Watershed management practices, to reduce erosion and sedimentation problems are now underway at some regions. In Nepal, watershed management programmes have been undertaken in all the eco-belts but mainly have been concentrated in the midlands. The nature of activities include (i) stabilization of landslides; (ii) rehabilitation of degraded terrain; (iii) terrace development; (iv) conservation plantation; (v) trail improvement; and (vi) provision of irrigation.

Currently Bagmati Watershed Project under the technical and capital assistance (91 per cent) of European Union (EU) is underway with an objective to bring about changes in land use and management within the catchment area of the Bagmati River so that the productivity of the land can be sustained and erosion reduced. Similarly Phewa, Begnas Lakes (in Pokhara) watershed management projects are under way to reduce the sedimentation problems of these lakes which are very important for tourism.

3. Monitoring and enforcement of the quality of wastewater for disposal into water bodies

In Nepal there are several Acts to prevent wastewater disposal into water bodies and polluting water resources. For example:

(i) The Industrial Resources Act, 1992, has provision for a licensing system for the establishment and operation of cigarette, leather, beer, sugar, paper, textile, cement, carpet washing, soap, stone crushing and forestry based medium and large scale industries as they affect public health and environment (Act 9);

(ii) The Water Resources Act, 1992, prohibits any act that may pollute water resources (Acts 19 and 20);

(iii) The Nepal Water Supply Corporation Act, 1989, has empowered the NWSC to take necessary steps to control water pollution;

(iv) The Pashupati Area Development Trust Act, 1987, aims to save the Bagmati river against pollution.

However, monitoring and enforcement aspects appear to be very weak. Consequently rivers and rivulets and water bodies have been polluted due to indiscriminate disposal of wastewater into them. The situation in Kathmandu valley is particularly alarming where the Bagmati, Bishnumati and Tukucha rivers have been converted into open sewers. The reason for this is that the oldest drain in the core area of Kathmandu and Lalitpur were built during Mala period some 200 years ago and was extended in the Rana period (1888-1905). The purpose of the drain was to drain the storm water from the city core area to nearby rivers and rivulets. This system, exclusively designed for storm water, have lately been abused extensively by connecting to it foul sewers from adjoining households.

In developing the fringe area of the Greater Kathmandu people often build costly septic tanks for safe disposal of the sewage. After some time the city dwellers demand the installation of storm water drains. As soon as the drain pipes are laid, often with community participation, these city dwellers switch over from the septic tank system to the piped drain meant for storm drain only.

At present there are only two sewage treatment ponds, one for Kathmandu in Dobighat and another for Lalitpur in Kodaku. These sewage treatment ponds are on 31 ha of land and can treat the sewage for 200,000 population in maximum, that is, the capacity of these sewage treatment ponds is limited to about 5 per cent of the required capacity. The treated sewage with the effluent standard containing not more than 30 mg/1 BOD is then disposed into the Bagmati river. With a view to make Bagmati pollution free, a Bagmati area sewage construction project has been launched. Under this project a sewage treatment plant will be constructed at the bank of the Bagmati river upstream of the Pashupati temple. Sewage coming to Bagmati river will be intercepted and diverted to sewage treatment plant and the effluent will be conveyed through 530 m long tunnel to a location downstream of the temple. This will help to keep clean the portion of Bagmati river near Pashupati temple. This project will take all the necessary measures to keep the Bagmati river pollution free near Pashupati Temple. Similarly other rivers and rivulets will be made pollution free under the Greater Kathmandu Drainage Master Plan, but this will require time and money which of course will be met through loans, grants from donor agencies as well as mobilizing resources of Kathmandu metropolitan and Lalitpur sub metropolitan cities.

XIII. WATER AND SUSTAINABLE DEVELOPMENT IN PAKISTAN

Zubair M. Pirzada
Vice President, National Engineering Services Pakistan Ltd.
Lahore, Pakistan

Introduction

Pakistan may be divided into three hydrologic units out of which only the Indus river basin produces dependable surface flow. Surface water supplies available to the Indus basin are the sum of the rainfall and inflow to the Indus river system. Annual average inflow into the Indus basin of Pakistan has been estimated to be about 144 million acre-feet (MAF)[1] of which 85 per cent occurs during the monsoonal rainy season. A substantial part of the surface flow in rivers and canal system finds its way into the underground aquifer spread over some 25 million acres from where it is pumped by tubewells for agricultural use.

Presently 74 per cent of the total river inflows are diverted into canals for irrigation while urban, rural domestic, commercial, industrial and livestock use only about 3 per cent. Around 22 per cent is still lost to the sea due to insufficient storage facilities.

Agriculture is at the centre of socioeconomic development and irrigation is the lifeblood of agriculture. Irrigation history of Pakistan dates back to 14th century. Presently the Indus Basin Irrigation System has grown to comprise 3 major reservoirs, 19 barrages, 12 link canals, 43 canal commands with irrigation system length of 58,000 km.

Groundwater development began in the sixties, first for waterlogging control and then for supplementing irrigation. Presently some 300,000 private tubewells pump 43 MAF of water for irrigation.

Hydropower development could not keep pace with the national power demand. At present three major hydel projects produce around 4,700 MW and one under construction would add another about 1,500 MW. Several small projects are under investigation. Lately thermal generation, though expensive, is being promoted to meet the pressing national power demand.

A. Water resources availability

Pakistan may be divided into three hydrologic units: the Indus Basin covering 70 per cent of the country's area; the Kharan desert (15 per cent); and the arid Makran coast (15 per cent) along the Arabian Sea. The later two lie in the highly dry zone where rainfall is too small to produce any dependable surface water flow.

The Indus river, together with its six main tributaries, the Kabul on the right bank and the five Punjab rivers - Jhelum, Chenab, Ravi, Beas and Sutlej - on the left bank has a total drainage area of 942,800 km[2], of which some 56 per cent lies in Pakistan and the remaining in India, China and Afghanistan.

Surface water supplies available to the Indus basin are the sum of the rainfall and the inflow derived from snowmelt and rainfall primarily outside the Indus Plain. A review of the post Tarbela Dam (1976) operation of the Indus system shows that the mean annual inflow from the western rivers (Indus, Jhelum, and Chenab), including direct tributaries, amounted to about 144 MAF. Given the seasonal nature of the Himalayan runoff, 85 per cent of the total inflow occurs during the kharif season (April-September) and 15 per cent during rabi season (October-March).

Groundwater in Pakistan is an important resource for agricultural, domestic and industrial water supplies. The Indus Basin has been formed as a result of alluvium deposits by rivers from the mountain ranges in the north. The alluvials consist principally of fine and medium grained sands and silts. Their depth ranges from over 300 m in the Punjab to 60 m in the Lower Sindh. There is a vast unconfined aquifer of around 25 million acres covering most of this area. The hydro-geological conditions are mostly favourable for pumping by tubewells. The quality of groundwater ranges from fresh near the major rivers to highly saline further away. About 79 per cent of the area in Punjab Province and 28 per cent of the area in Sindh province has fresh groundwater.

---

[1] 1 MAF = 1.234 billion m[3].

1. Surface water potential

The flow of the Indus River and its tributaries constitutes the main source of surface water for the country. Under the Indus Water Treaty 1960, the flows of three eastern rivers, the Sutlej, Beas and Ravi, have been allocated to India. Various storage reservoirs have already been constructed on these rivers. Bhakra on the Sutlej in 1964; Pong and Pandoh on the Beas in 1972 and 1977 respectively; and Thein dam is under construction on the Ravi. Once this is completed, there will be no significant flow from the eastern rivers into Pakistan, except for occasional flood flows towards the end of the monsoon season.

Water from the three western rivers, the Indus, Jhelum and Chenab - except for specified limited use in occupied Kashmir and India - is available to Pakistan. The flow is measured at three rim stations; at Kalabagh on the Indus which includes the flow of the Kabul River and its tributaries), at Mangla on the Jhelum, and at Marala on the Chenab. These rim stations include most of the tributary inflows and are above the existing canal system except for the Swat, Kabul and Kurram River canals in the North West Frontier Province (NWFP).

Based on 64 years of historic data, from 1922-1986, the average annual inflow of the western rivers at the rim stations amounted to 137.27 MAF. The flow varies from year to year: the maximum was 186.79 MAF (36 per cent above the average) in 1959-1960 and the minimum 100.31 MAF (26.9 per cent below average) in 1974-1975. The flow varies markedly during the Kharif and Rabi seasons also. Kharif inflows average 115.18 MAF or over five times the Rabi inflows of 22.06 MAF. The characteristics of river inflows are shown in table 15. Of the three western rivers, the largest flow is contributed by the Indus with an annual mean of 89.22 MAF. The

Table 15. Western rivers inflow (million acre-feet)

Item	Kharif	Rabi	Annual
Mean	115.24	22.03	137.27
Median	116.20	21.66	137.64
Minimum	80.64	15.74	100.31
Maximum	154.74	34.09	186.79
3 out of 5 years	110.10	20.38	132.22
4 out of 5 years	101.28	18.76	123.59

Source: Water Resources Management Directorate, Pakistan Water and Power Development Authority (WAPDA).

corresponding values for the Jhelum and the Chenab rivers are 22.55 MAF and 25.48 MAF respectively.

After estimating inflows from hill torrents and other water sources below the rim stations, average surface water flow of the western rivers available for development is 130 MAF, as shown in table 16.

Table 16. Estimate of water availability in the Indus Basin (million acre-feet)

	Description	Mean	In 4 of 5 years 80 per cent probability
1.	Western rivers: rim station inflows	137.27	123.59
2.	Eastern rivers: contribution	2.0	1.5
3.	Used above rim stations	5.5	5.5
4.	Total inflow (1 + 2 + 3)	144.77	130.59
5.	Losses & gains below rim stations (inclusive of inflows)	- 10.0	- 8.0
6.		- 5.0	- 3.0
7.	Outflow to sea	129.77	119.59
8.	Net Available for utilization (4-5) Average post-Tarbela canal withdrawals Current (1986-87)	107.79	103.44
9.	Balance available (7-8)	21.98	16.15
10.	Authorized use by India out of the western rivers	- 2.0	- 2.0
11.	Actual potential available	19.98	14.15

Source: Water Resources Management Directorate, WAPDA.

2. Groundwater potential

Pakistan's groundwater resources have been extensively investigated during the last 25 years. The investigations have established the existence of a vast aquifer underlying the Indus plain, recharged in the past by natural precipitation and river flow, and more recently by seepage from the canal system. Other small aquifers have also been identified in the inter-montane valley alluviums.

The estimated usable potential (up to 3,000 ppm) is about 43 MAF of groundwater of which 33 MAF is in the canal command area and 10 MAF in riverine and other areas. The annual groundwater potential of areas outside the Indus Basin, established so far, is estimated at 1.41 MAF.

Although groundwater is a supplementary source of irrigation water, the quality of the pumped water is inferior to river water due to the absence of silt and the presence of dissolved salts. Unrestricted groundwater use is a potential hazard, leading to water quality degradation. Groundwater pumpage also adds significantly to the farmer's cost of productions.

3. Water requirements in the future

Estimation of future water needs depends on how irrigated agricultural areas are to be expanded to meet national requirements. The historical expansion of irrigated areas in the last three decades is given in table 17.

Table 17. Growth of irrigated areas (million acres)

Year	Pakistan	Punjab	Sindh	Balochistan	NWFP
1960-61	25.71	-	-	-	-
1965-66	28.36	-	-	-	-
1970-71	26.16	-	-	-	-
1976-76	33.39	22.98	7.79	1.03	1.59
1980-81	36.50	25.87	7.52	1.30	1.81
1985-86	38.68	27.95	7.47	1.26	2.00
1990-91	41.61	29.62	8.57	1.32	2.10

Source: Ministry of Food and Agriculture. N.d. Agricultural Statistics of Pakistan, 1987-88, Islamabad: Government of Pakistan.

The future food and fibre requirements of the country can be met partly through increased yields per acre and partly through an expansion in irrigated areas. It is estimated that a 1 per cent compound growth would be acceptable. Keeping this in view and assuming 2.75 feet per acre as water requirement at the farmgate, the cropped area and water requirement for the year 2000 would be 45.96 million acres and 126.40 MAF respectively, as given in table 18.

B. Water use

The flows into the Indus are from glacier and snow melt, as well as from rainfall outside the Indus Plain (table 19).

1. Water use in agriculture

The agricultural sector is the major user of water and its consumption will continue to dominate water requirements. Direct rainfall contributes less than 15 per cent of the water supplied to crops. The major source of water for irrigation is the Indus Basin

Table 18. Estimates of future irrigated areas and their water requirement (million acre-feet)

Province	Period		
	1990-91	1995-96	2000-01
Punjab			
Irrigated area (million acres)	29.62	31.14	32.72
Water requirement at farmgate (MAF)	81.46	85.64	89.98
Sindh			
Irrigated area (million acres)	8.57	9.01	9.46
Water requirement at farmgate (MAF)	23.57	24.78	26.02
Balochistan			
Irrigated area (million acres)	1.32	1.39	1.46
Water requirement at farmgate (MAF)	5.78	3.82	4.02
NWFP			
Irrigated area (million acres)	2.10	2.21	2.32
Water requirement at farmgate (MAF)	5.78	6.08	6.38
Pakistan			
Irrigated area (million acres)	41.61 (16.84)	43.75 (17.70)	45.96 (18.60)
Water requirement at farmgate (MAF)	114.44	120.32	126.40

Source: Ministry of Food and Agriculture. N.d. Agricultural Statistics of Pakistan, 1987-88, Islamabad; Government of Pakistan

Table 19. Average annual inflows and water use in the Indus Basin*

Inflows at rim stations	Millon acre-ft	Billon m³
Western rivers	130.8	161.4
Eastern rivers	5.1	6.3
Tributary inflows		
Western rivers	6.1	7.5
Eastern rivers	2.0	2.5
Total inflow	144.0	177.7
Canal withdrawals	106.2	131.0
Outflow to sea	32.7	40.4
Net system losses (including gains, unmeasured inflows, and water uses)	5.1	6.3
Total use and losses	144.0	177.7

*Period of record: Indus, 1936-1988, Jhelum and Chenab, 1922-1988, Ravi and Sutlej, 1966-1988 other inflows 1966-1976, Canal diversions and Outflow to sea, 1978-1991. According to the Indus Water Treaty of 1960 flows of Eastern rivers are allocated to India.

Irrigation system (IBIS), to which is diverted 106 MAF of water annually (at the canal heads); around 43 MAF or so is pumped from groundwater. Surface irrigation systems are the main source of recharge to the groundwater.

2. Urban and rural sector water use

These use less than 3 per cent of average river inflows and about 4 per cent of surface water diverted for irrigated agriculture (about 4.3 MAF in total). Most urban and rural water is supplied from groundwater except for metropolitan Karachi. In saline groundwater areas, irrigation canals are the main source for domestic water. Over 50 per cent of village water supply is through hand pumps installed by private households. Total requirements for urban and rural domestic, commercial, industrial and livestock use are estimated at 10.2 MAF by the year 2010 and 15.9 MAF by 2020, that is 10-15 per cent of present surface water diversions. Importantly, more than 80 per cent of the domestic, municipal, and industrial diversions usually return back to the system however, with degraded quality. Net consumption here will be about 2 MAF (2 per cent) by the year 2010 and 3.1 MAF (2.9 per cent) by 2020.

Average annual freshwater lost to area is presently 32.7 MAF which occurs during the monsoon (July-September) season.

3. Irrigation development

Agriculture supplies most of the country's food, accounts for 20 per cent of GDP, and employs 54 per cent of labour force. It is also the source of raw materials for major domestic industries, particularly cotton which accounts for 80 per cent of the value of exports. The health of the agriculture sector has important implications for poverty relief. Irrigation is the lifeblood of agriculture and thus irrigation development has a direct bearing on the socioeconomic uplift of the country.

Irrigation in the subcontinent started as early as 14th century with the construction of an inundation canal from river Jumna by King Feroz Shah Tughlaq. The later period saw construction of several other canals. By the end of 19th century, the rivers were controlled by headwords and canals carried water for long distances to areas opened for agricultural development. At the time of Independence (1947) the

irrigation network of Pakistan consisted mainly of old established canal systems with total average canal head withdrawals of 64 MAF excluding 4 MAF taken from the Kabul, Swat and Kurram rivers in the North West Frontier Province (NWFP). Of this, over 10 MAF was being drawn from the three eastern rivers, the Sutlej, Seas and Ravi, whose headwords were located in Indian territory.

During the period 1947-1960 Pakistan undertook the construction of three inter-river link canals to ensure continuous supply of water when eastern river sources were cut off by India. These were the Bomdanwala Ravi Bedian Dipalpur link, the Balloki Sulemanki link and the Marala Ravi link canal. These canals ultimately became part of the Indus Basin Replacement Plan. Under the Indus Water Treaty 1960, three eastern rivers namely Ravi, Sutlej and Beas were awarded to India and certain replacement works were agreed upon to provide alternative water supplies to canals offtaking from these rivers.

The Indus Basin Irrigation System, which has steadily grown since independence, presently comprises three major reservoirs (Tarbela 9.3 MAF, Mangla 5.9 MAF and Chashma 0.7 MAF), 19 barrages, 12 link canals and 43 canal commands with over 100,000 watercourses. The canal systems total about 58,000 km in length. The communal watercourses (WC) and farm ditches run up to more than 1.6 million km. River water is diverted by barrages and weirs into the main canals and subsequently into branch canals, distributaries and minors. Open flume and orifice type of outlets (moghas) are generally in use for passing supplies from distributaries and minors into the WCs. WC command area (chak) is a complex system of farmers plots and ditches. Farmers take water from the watercourse on weekly time rotation (warabandi) in proportion to their land holdings.

There is about 4.5 million acres (1.82 Mha[1]) of irrigated land outside the Indus canal commanded area. This is scattered in relatively small parcels irrigated from open wells, tubewells, lift pumps, karezes, springs and small stream diversions. The water supply from these sources remains uncertain and varies with location and the seasonal precipitation. These systems developed by communities are generally self-managed.

---

[1] 1 Mha = million hectares.

During the 10-year period 1959-1960, prior to the signing of the Indus Water Treaty, canal head withdrawals had increased to an average of 78.6 MAF - an increase of about 23 per cent over the 64 MAF withdrawn at the time of Independence. In the seven-year period ending, 1967, that is, prior to the completion of the Mangla Dam, withdrawals had further increased to an average of 87.7 MAF. After the completion of Mangla and prior to the commissioning of the Tarbela Dam in 1976, average canal withdrawals rose to 98.9 MAF. In recent years, withdrawals have averaged 100 MAF. Thus, since Independence overall canal head withdrawals have risen by 36 MAF or 56 per cent. Average canal head withdrawals province wise and by season (kharif or rabi) from 1 967 to 1 987 are shown in table 20.

4. Development of groundwater

Development of groundwater for irrigation began with the Governments' effort to control waterlogging and salinity under Salinity Control and Reclamation Projects (SCARPS) aimed at lowering the watertable through vertical drainage. Large capacity electrically driven public tubewells were installed in fresh groundwater areas as well as in saline groundwater areas. About 1 4,000 tubewells in the Public Sector were installed in the past three decades (1960-1990) of which 75 per cent were in Punjab, 8,000 tubewells in fresh groundwater areas and 1,800 in saline groundwater areas. In fresh groundwater areas water from tubewells was pumped into watercourses to be mixed with canal water for irrigation use. in saline groundwater areas the tubewells pumped water into drains or large canals. The public tubewells generally served their purpose of lowering groundwater tables and providing supplementary irrigation. However their performance could not be sustained due to inadequate O&M funding and poor management. Most of the tubewells are worn out resulting in frequent breakdowns. The present utilization of these tubewells is considerably low due to mechanical faults and prolonged power supply cuts.

5. Private tubewell development

There had been a virtual explosion in the private tubewells (PTWs) development following the Public Sector tubewells (PSTW). Currently there are some 300,000 private tubewells (PTWs) installed for irrigation purposes, of which 80 per cent are in Punjab, and they supply 40 per cent of total irrigation water. PTWs are generally small (average capacity 1 cubic feet per second) and shallow employing locally produced diesel engine and pump. PTWs play an important role of reducing the risk of crop failure during times of peak demand and canal water fluctuations. However the utilization rates remain low. Farmers owning area of more than 5.0 ha generally install their own tubewell.

Considering the role of both public and private tubewells, groundwater pumpage in the Indus Plains increased from 3.34 MAF in 1959-1960 to 43.2 MAF in 1990-1991. The present number of tubewells in public and private sector along with their pumpage is shown in table 21.

6. Hydropower development

Hydropower development is considered very important for economic development of the country. The present peak demand of about 6,500 MW is expected to grow to 1,5000 MW by the turn of the century, whereas, planned additions to the system amount to 4,065 MW only. The rest of the generation requirement will have to be met by the environmentally hazardous thermal power units, most of them consuming imported fuel implying a higher cost of energy generation. The only way to flatten the steep continuous rise in the cost of energy is to better utilize the existing hydropower projects and develop additional projects to the maximum extent possible. The existing major hydropower projects of the country are Wasak Dam (160 MW), Mangla Dam (1,000 MW), and Tarbela Dam (3,478 MW).

At present the Ghazi Brotha Hydro-power Project with 1,425 MW installed capacity is under construction and is expected to be completed in 1998.

Planned hydropower projects include Kalabagh Dam with an installed capacity of 3,600 MW (Project Planning studies for the project were completed in 1984 and tender documents were finalized by the end of 1988). Basha Dam with an installed capacity of 3,360 MW; Munda Multipurpose Dam with an installed capacity of 400 MW; Kurram Tangi Multipurpose Dam with a power potential of 40 MW; Hingol Multipurpose Dam with a power potential of 2.5 MW; and Mirani Multipurpose Dam with a power potential of 1.8 MW.

Table 20. Average canal head withdrawals by season (million acre-feet)

Period	Punjab		Sindh/Balochistan		NWFP		Total		Withdrawal
	Kharif	Rabi	Kharif	Rabi	Kharif	Rabi	Kharif	Rabi	total
1967-1972	33.14	15.91	27.63	12.17	3.29	1.82	64.06	29.90	93.96
1972-1977	31.98	18.75	29.70	12.73	3.43	1.96	65.02	33.44	98.46
1977-1982	34.66	19.84	29.40	15.76	3.56	2.00	67.62	37.60	105.22
1982-1987	32.59	19.57	19.57	15.48	3.56	2.09	65.68	37.14	102.82

Source: Water Resources Management Directorate, WAPDA

Table 21. Number of public and private tubewells and their pumpages

Province	Tubewells (Number)			Pumpage MAF		
	Public	Private	Total	Public	Private	Total
Punjab	11 030	290 091	301 121	4.34	33.54	37.28
Sindh	4 555	17 409	21 964	1.32	2.01	3.33
NWFP	491	6 065	6 556	0.13	0.70	0.83
Balochistan	-	15 163	15 163	-	1.75	1.75
Total			344 804			43.19

Source: Agricultural Statistics of Pakistan 1990-1991.

C. Environmental impact of water resources development

Irrigation development in the past has not been without its effect on environment. Some environmental impacts of concern are given below.

1. Rise in the groundwater table

When agriculture was limited to the barani (rainfed) and sailaba (riverine) areas, and to some extent to land irrigated by Persian-wheel wells, the watertable was in a state of dynamic equilibrium. But with the development of an extensive irrigation system, thousands of mites of unlined conveyance channels were dug. A new and extensive source of groundwater recharge was introduced through infiltration of water from the conveyance system.

But failure to develop discharge channels, to balance the new recharge, has disturbed the hydrological balance and set in motion the problem of a rising water table. The water table has risen at different rates varying from 0.15 m to over 0.6 m per year, depending upon the imbalance between recharge and discharge.

2. Waterlogging and salinity

A rising water table, in the absence of drainage channels, discharged excess water through evaporation from the soil surface and transpiration from plants. Uneven land surfaces were affected by patchy waterlogging when acted as sinks. Where evaporation was less than recharge, swamps appeared which gradually grew larger to provide enough surface area to attain a new hydrological balance. Slightly higher areas became shallow swamps choking root aeration. As mineralized water evaporated, salts accumulated in the soil profile and on the surface.

The water table exhibits an annual cycle of rise and fall. It is at its lowest point in the period prior to the monsoons (April-June). Recharged through Kharif season irrigation and the rains, it rises to its highest point in October, when it is closest to the land surface before declining again. High water table conditions after the monsoon, though transitory, interfere with the cultivation of Rabi crops. Its position in April-June is particularly critical, as this level persists throughout the year and is used as an index for waterlogging. The extent of waterlogged area, where the water table remains within 1.5 m of the land surface throughout the year has been estimated at 15 per cent.

3. Salt balance

Extensive canal irrigation together with waterlogging and salinity has effected the salt balance of the Indus Basin. The average annual salinity of the western rivers at the rim stations is about 131 ppm, and at outflow near Kotri, 243 ppm. Assuming 138 MAF as inflow and 5 MAF as outflow to the sea under complete development of water resources, the salt retained in the basin would be around 20 million metric tons per year.

A programme of drainage and reclamation was started by WAPDA in 1958. Non-saline groundwater drainage projects were implemented first. Nearly 6 MAF groundwater is being pumped by public tubewells. The demonstrative effect of these projects triggered private tubewell development, that now pumps up 38 MAF of groundwater per year.

The use of groundwater for irrigation has increased the amount of salt infiltrating the soil to far more than what was being dumped by canal water. A study for PSTW indicated that nearly 2 tons of salt per acre per year was being dumped. Part of this salt is accumulating in the soil and in the long run is likely to endanger the productivity of agricultural land.

4. Disposal of saline effluent

Saline effluent can be disposed of in three ways: through drains and rivers; through evaporation ponds; and through canals.

All these methods have been used in Pakistan, subject to their technical and economic feasibility. However, they all have long-term adverse effects on the environment. Water discharged into rivers and canals is ultimately going to find its way, through headworks, into downstream canals leading to further salt accumulation. Ponds are a short-term measure also, as they fill up with salt and become unusable. Besides this, ponds pollute the groundwater reservoir; and land under the pond is permanently lost to agriculture and other uses.

5. Surface water pollution

Water supply and sewer systems are neither efficient nor adequate in any of the industrial cities. Sewerage, in most cases is carried by open surface-flow drains which ultimately discharge in to a stream, a river or the sea, affecting surface water.

Both small industries (mechanical and auto workshops, hosiery and carpet looms, spice and grain-grinding mills) scattered within residential areas, and medium and large scale industries located in planned industrial estates, do not pretreat their effluent. it is simply discharged into a nearby channel. But the waste waters of the textile, plastic, tanning, food and metal-processing industries contain toxic chemicals used in processing the raw material that need different treatment from municipal discharges.

6. Impact of dams and reservoirs

The major impact of dam/reservoir development can be described with reference to the existing projects.

Fisheries development: Commercial fisheries have been developed at reservoirs after their construction. However due to drastic fluctuation in reservoirs because of large draw downs, highly productive fisheries cannot be supported. In the downstream river channel, the fish is generally destroyed due to Nitrogen supersaturation and water impact.

Public health: Vector borne and water borne diseases appear due to creation of reservoirs in the nearby settlements. Particularly incidence of Malaria is very common. A well financed malaria eradication programme is necessary to check the onslaught of these diseases.

Effects of sediment trapping on the Indus delta: A continual supply of silt is necessary in the Indus delta to prevent deterioration of its mangrove ecosystem. The scientific community expressed this concern in a resolution at the November 1982 oceanographic conference which blamed the deterioration of the delta on trapping of silt by upstream dams and barrages. Tarbela dam is mainly credited with substantially reducing the sediment load of the Indus, currently trapping more than 80 per cent of the sediment entering it.

D. Strategies for sustainable use of water resources

Water must remain available in adequate quantity and quality to sustain agricultural development on a permanent basis. On the other hand sustainability of large investments in the existing irrigation system is equally important. Pakistan's irrigation system which is considered as the largest contiguous irrigation systems of the world, is not yielding its full potential because of lack of resources and several other problems. A number of problems relate to management. Insufficient funding for O&M coupled with lack of financial discipline has rendered the systems inefficient. Deterioration has set in and is fast progressing. This system has not only to be saved from total collapse but restored to good condition for its sustained utility. It is therefore imperative that as a first step towards achieving sustainable use of water the problems faced by the existing system must have to be tackled, and the system managed to its optimal utility. Major areas needing attention are discussed below.

1. System management

Funding for operation and maintenance has generally received low priority in the national spending. Water charges from beneficiaries offset most of the financial needs of the system but they are not adequate. Periodically these have been raised but still fall short of the requirement. The Government is planning to introduce initially on pilot basis a system by which irrigation sector becomes self financing, and the beneficiaries gradually take over the management. First step in this direction is the creation of semi-autonomous irrigation and drainage authorities in the provinces. These authorities would have powers to increase water charges to meet the system needs. Being autonomous, the authorities would be free from political interference considered as a major reason for lack of financial discipline.

2. Reliable supplies

The natural wear and tear of the canal banks need regular maintenance. In the absence of such maintenance canals breach and cause not only loss of precious water but also damage crops and property. Unreliable supplies discourage the water users from investing in non-water inputs for maximum gain. All canals must be rehabilitated periodically to restore their bank heights and free boards.

3. Equitable distribution

Periodic desiltation of irrigation channels is part of maintenance. Silt clearance should be carried out during canal closures. Silt deposit can affect the hydraulic performance of channel causing inequitable distribution of water into outlets. The head water users get away with bigger share of supply while the tail enders receive less than their share. Another reasons for inequitable distribution is illegal tampering of outlets due to absence of discipline in the management agencies. Inequitable distribution breeds discontent amongst the sufferers to the detriment of agricultural output.

4. Control of system losses

Losses in the canal system are estimated to be as much as 25 to 30 per cent, a major part of which goes to groundwater recharge. Lining the canals would be valuable, especially in areas underlain by saline groundwater, as this would perform the twin functions of expanding the water supply and reducing system losses, particularly where the canal traverses highly permeable soils. However, it is unlikely that cost-effective methods would be available in the near future. A start can be made by lining the smaller canals, that is, the minors and distributaries using conventional techniques; enact laws and regulations requiring future canal system in the country to be lined; and make efforts to line the existing system wherever possible.

Efforts to control conveyance losses in the watercourses have already been undertaken through the on-farm water management programmes, for example, lining of 10-30 per cent length of the main watercourse and improvements of its remaining part. It has not been possible, so far. to shift the entire financial burden of this improvement onto the private sector. It is therefore necessary to shift the entire burden of improvement and maintenance onto the private sector through legislation, namely, the Canal Act; and to make Water User's Associations more effective.

5. Conjunctive use of surface and groundwater

Irrigation in Pakistan works on a system of constant fixed supply delivered through the outlets irrespective of the crop water requirement at different stages of growth. Ideally the systems should be flexible in supply to suit the crop needs. This requires physical modification of the system as well as sophisticated management. However, with the presence of tubewells in the canal irrigated area some flexibility of supplies has been achieved. During times of peak demand tubewells are operated at maximum capacity to sustain the crops. Farmers have realized the advantage of tubewells.

More and more tubewells are being installed in the canal irrigated areas. Nearly 44 MAF of groundwater is being pumped to be used in conjunction with surface water. This uncontrolled development may deplete the groundwater. In several canal commands the watertable is declining indicating overuse. Such large scale movement of groundwater may result in brackish groundwater moving laterally into less saline groundwater zones. There is a need to monitor the depth and quality of groundwater regularly and extensively. Where aquifers are endangered by brackish water intrusion, further installation of tubewells should be stopped through suitable legislation.

6. Watershed management

Storage reservoirs are created to regulate river water supply. Since river deposits silt in the reservoir, the storage capacity decreases over time, reducing the dam's ability to ensure a sustained supply of water on a predetermined basis. In order to maintain a continuous supply, two measures need to be undertaken, namely, watershed management to reduce silt inflow and make up for lost capacity by continuously adding new storage facilities.

The original cumulative live capacity of Tarbela and Mangla reservoirs (15.20 MAF) has been reduced by about 2.0 MAF in 20 years. In the next 50 to 70 years, the capacity may theoretically be reduced to nil. In the almost 20 years that have passed since Tarbela was constructed, no additional storage capacity has been added.

7. Drainage of irrigation areas

Due to flat topography and lack of adequate drainage, irrigated areas are subject to flooding in the rainy season. The situation is worsened with the increase in infrastructural development like roads, railways, canals, embankments etc. Agriculture yields are substantially affected by flooding of crop lands. Existing drainage system has been made ineffective through poor maintenance. The importance of draining irrigated lands has been lately realized. The Government is embarking on an ambitious and urgently needed project of National Drainage Programme (NDP). It would comprise physical works, institutional reforms and motivation of beneficiaries; and initiating farmers and private sector participation in O&M of the drainage systems. Farm drainage will be implemented by the farmers as a first step. The programme, one of the largest drainage works ever taken up in Pakistan is estimated to cost over US $ 800 million and is expected to be implemented in a six year period (1997-2003).

8. Monitoring water quality

With the provision of drainage, the effluent from the irrigated lands is not only going to be increased in qualitative, but its quality also would be further downgraded. Industrial waste effluent will also find its way in the newly created channels. Increased toxicity can seriously damage the environment downstream causing health hazard and irrigated land degradation to the overall detriment of agriculture. It is therefore of utmost importance to carefully plan and implement a system of water quality monitoring for the existing and planned drainage systems. This work would best be carried out by the provincial agencies responsible for the O&M of the drainage systems under the guidance of a central organization such as WAPDA.

9. Land conservation

Land is an important natural resource which must be protected against the adverse effects of development activities. Though water is the source of life, its careless or improper use may result in the deterioration of the land.

Water development efforts in Pakistan since the turn of the century have resulted in waterlogging and salinity in millions of acres of fertile land. This does not mean that water use must be abandoned, but that there is need to ensure that drains do exist and efficiently carry away excess water. Because of Pakistan's flat topography, a surface drainage system is not efficient. It is therefore proposed that special agencies, equipped with adequate machinery, be created to maintain and operate surface and sub-surface drainage systems. Pumped drainage should also be gradually introduced in the design of surface drainage for steeper slopes.

Construction of "diversion structures" such as barrages and weirs on river have constricted waterways and raised the bed level of rivers. Similarly, construction of reservoirs have stopped certain river channels, constricting flow and encouraging encroachments. The result is that flood waters play havoc with both agriculture and human life. Control measures being undertaken to date to control flooding have been inadequate. It is, therefore, proposed that national flood protection plans be prepared and implemented in a systematic manner for sufficiently long reaches of the river. All constrictions and encroachments should also be removed through legislation. All communication lines such as roads and railways should be provided with cross-drainage works to allow the unobstructed passage of water. Besides, riverine forests must be encouraged to stabilize river channels.

The drainage of lands affected by saline groundwater is a serious problem. This water cannot be discharged into the existing drainage system as it will eventually degrade the quality of river water. Presently, it is being dumped in evaporation ponds covering thousands of acres of land. Not only is this land permanently lost, but the saline water gradually affects adjoining land. In addition, these ponds are temporary in nature, as the accumulating salt raises the bed level and makes gravity flow into the pond difficult. These ponds need to be connected to the sea through drains and disposal channels.

E. Strategies for sustainable development of water resources

1. Environmental checks

Pakistan, at this juncture is at the very initial stages of developing strategies for promoting sustainable and environmentally sound land and water development mainly at macro level. It was as late as 1983 that the Environmental Protection Ordinance was promulgated in Pakistan for the establishment of a national agency (Pakistan Environmental Protection Agency) which, inter alia, would establish National Environmental Quality standards co-ordinate environmental programmes nationally and internationally, and establish systems for surveys, monitoring and inspection. Environmental Protection Agencies (EPA) were also required, under the Ordinance, to be set up at provincial level for supplementing the efforts of the EPA at federal level and for developing public awareness programmes.

At present, the Ordinance specifically covers industrial activities only. A proposed amendment extends the EIA requirement to cover developments in all sectors of the economy, including physical and social infrastructure, and also requires an assessment of beneficial as well as adverse impact. Under this ordinance, the Environmental and Urban Division of the Government of Pakistan has published guidelines for various kinds of development projects including dams and reservoirs which are similar to the World Bank guidelines for this type of projects. Irrigation and drainage projects being important in the context of Pakistan could be specially included in the guidelines in the line with the World Bank requirements.

The Federal Environmental Protection Agency: A Federal EPA has been created in accordance with the requirements of the Environmental Protection Ordinance but is not yet fully functional. Its duties are currently undertaken directly by the Environmental and Urban Affairs Division of the Ministry of Housing and Works, which is monitoring all public sector projects, without waiting for the proposed amendments to the Environmental Protection Ordinance to be formally enacted into law. This enactment is expected in the near future. A handbook setting out EIA guidelines has been prepared and was issued in June 1986. Four provincial EPAs have also been set up in Punjab, Sindh, Northwest Frontier Province and Balochistan which corroborate the work of the federal EPA and develop programs for environmental awareness.

2. National conservation strategy

The National Conservation Strategy Secretariat (NCSS) has been set up by the Environment and Urban Affairs Division. It is charged with developing a conservation strategy for Pakistan in co-operation with the International Union for Conservation of Nature (IUCN). Its members are keenly aware of the principal environmental issues associated with water sector development, and are greatly concerned that environmental issues should be identified at the earliest possible stage in the planning process for major projects. A National Conservation Strategy Plan is being prepared, which is expected to include projects affecting issues of major environmental concern and for which foreign or international financing could be sought.

3. Strategies for sustainability

One of the key measures to mitigate adverse effects in water resources development is in Pakistan to provide adequate and appropriate drainage. Drainage has both advantages and disadvantages for each area, depending on which aspect of environment it is being examined. Strategies adopted to suit specific problems of drainage and irrigation are as follows.

(a)   National drainage programme

In 1991, the Government of Pakistan undertook an environmental assessment of the irrigated related drainage in the country, which culminated in the preparation of a framework for a National Drainage Programme (NDP).

The National Drainage Programme is a mix of physical works, institutional and policy reforms, communication, education and motivation of beneficiaries, research and studies in drainage, and initiating changes in the legal and regulatory framework to allow farmers and private sector participation. The first phase of the programme which will be taken up simultaneously in the four provinces of the country will consist of the following main components:

- Rehabilitation and remodelling of main and branch drains
- Extension/construction of new drains
- Operation and maintenance of drainage systems through performance contract under private agencies
- Construction of subsurface tile drains in acute saline areas to replace old public tubewells
- Implementation of farm drains by beneficiaries
- Institutional development, WUAs etc.
- Research and studies

The project is aimed to provide adequate sustainable surface and subsurface drainage to check environmental damage and degradation of irrigated lands.

(b)   National irrigation programme

Consideration is being given to formulate a National Irrigation Programme on the same lines as National Drainage Programme (NDP) to systematically cover rehabilitation of existing irrigation systems which have grown inefficient over time due to accumulated maintenance. This has resulted either due to lack of

O&M funds or lack of financial discipline by the public agencies managing these systems. Due to general financial constraints schemes where beneficiaries are willing to share the O&M responsibility will be given priority for taking up the scheme in the programme. The aim is to transfer, in stages, responsibility of these systems from public to the private sector (beneficiaries), starting with lower level systems first. It is also proposed to evolve a system by which schemes can be managed by a self financing mechanism under a separate governing body for each of the canal commands. This programme is expected to go a long way in efficiently maintaining the largest contiguous irrigation system of the world and help in sustaining the precious irrigation water for most optimal use.

(c)   On-farm water management and canal lining

The need for drainage will diminish as the canal and watercourse losses and the quantity of water applied per acre reduces; and also as the salinity of the irrigation water fails. Improved water management will also reduce the need for drainage. The On-Farm Water Management programme of Pakistan has gone a long way to achieving this. However, to make significant improvements in water management that will result in a need for lesser drainage is a substantial task, particularly as canal systems are rather long and there is little storage available. Obviously, improved water management is a desirable objective, which is being emphasized by international experts.

(d)   Biological methods

A good deal of thought and research has been going on in Pakistan (especially at the University in Faisalabad and at Islamabad in the Bio-Science Department of Pakistan Atomic Energy Commission and also at the University of Karachi) and elsewhere on use of plants which can tolerate higher water tables and/or salinity in an effort to develop a biological alternative to "engineering" drainage. Both salt- and water-tolerant trees and crops have been considered, with some useful results but as yet there have been really no major trials on a field scale in Pakistan. Sindh Arid Zone Development Authority (SAZDA) is also studying the possibility of using drainage effluents for raising salt tolerant crops and trees in the Thar Desert. A salt-tolerant wheat has been developed by the Plant-Breeding Institute at Cambridge, UK, and has had promising trials in Canada. Some of this material has also been supplied to the University of Faisalabad.

Salt-tolerant fodder crops are also being considered. The use of trees such as Eucalids, as biological pumps to lower the watertable is also a potential biological control method but pilot studies are required to confirm the effectiveness of such an approach.

F. Policy guidelines

Compatible with the country's resources and priorities there is a need to set policy guidelines for future development in the water sector as the projected water requirements of the country cannot be met on a sustained basis. These could be based on the following criteria.

-   Other water uses like domestic urban and rural water supply and industrial demands are going to compete with the agricultural needs in the near future. With limited availability of water future requirements need to be regulated to keep a check on limited resources use.

-   Availability of water on demand basis need to be enhanced by way of further storages so that extra flood water available during rainy season is not wasted.

-   In order to cope with the growing demand for water for agriculture due to rapid growth in population, rationalizing the efficient use of all available water through improved water use efficiency by accelerating on-farm and command area management programmes is required.

-   Cropping patterns needs to be made compatible with the availability of water in specific zones to optimize the limited water available.

-   As agriculture is going to be the major user for a long time provisional allocation for other uses need to be targeted now.

Ultimately agriculture has to compete with other users contributing to national economy. Economic price of water needs to be realistically assessed and promoted to be charged to agricultural users.

G. Conclusions

Although Pakistan is blessed with an abundance of water and land, the key resources for an agriculture economy, these resources are finite and limited. With the population growing at an alarming rate (doubling in 20 years) it is imperative that in order to sustain the need for the food and fibre a well planned strategy is required. The following actions are suggested to be undertaken if sustainability in the water resources development is to be achieved.

-   Policy guidelines for judicious use of the water resources should be finalized and backed with legislation.

-   A balance should be struck between the future water resource development and environmental issues so that none suffers at the cost of other.

-   Loss of water through perpetual floods and wastage to the sea should be minimized to save every drop of this precious resource.

-   National Drainage Programme should be implemented to save and reclaim agriculture lands.

-   National Irrigation Programme should be finalized and implemented to rehabilitate the country's largest irrigation system and save it from any further deterioration.

-   Use of modern techniques for irrigation, research in optimal use of water for various crops and on-farm water management should be accelerated.

References

Khalid Mohtadullah and et al 1992. Water for the 21st Century. A Pakistan National Conservation Strategy Sector Paper.

Ministry of Food and Agriculture, Government of Pakistan 1 988. Report on National Commission on Agriculture.

Mott MacDonald, Harza Engg. Co., National Engineering Service Pakistan, 1990. Water Sector Investment Planning study. Lahore WAPDA, UNDP, The World Bank.

NESPAK-Mott MacDonald 1995, Feasibility Study National Drainage Programme.

Rashid A. Chaudhry 1991. Country Paper on Environmental issue in Water Development in Pakistan.

World Bank 1994. Pakistan Irrigation and Drainage. Issues & Options

XIV. CURRENT STATUS AND FUTURE TRENDS ON WATER AND SUSTAINABLE DEVELOPMENT IN THE PHILIPPINES

Luis M. Sosa, Executive Director
National Water Resources Board, Metro Manila, Philippines

Introduction

The Philippines is an archipelago of some 7,100 islands southeast of the Asian mainland, with a total land area of about 300,000 km². Its population as of 1995 is about 69 million with an estimated growth rate of about 2.3 per cent per year. The country's annual rainfall amounts to 2,360 mm of which 1,000 to 2,000 mm are collected as runoff by a natural topography of more than 400 principal river basins, 59 natural lakes and numerous small streams. It has extensive groundwater reservoir with an estimated aggregate area of about 50,000 km².

However, the distribution of these water resources varies widely in time and place, due to the variances in the geographical and climatic conditions in the different parts of the country. Although nationally abundant, water shortages occur almost regularly in some areas, particularly during the dry season. Moreover, as the use of water has grown steadily, due to rapid population growth and increasing economic activities, the quality of water resources has become increasingly vulnerable to pollution, which threatens its availability for sustainable development.

A. Institutional and legal framework

There are 30 government agencies and departments dealing with water resources activities in the country. The major water service providers and users are the National Irrigation Administration (NIA) for irrigation and drainage; Local Water Utilities Administration/Water Districts (LWUA/WDs), Metropolitan Water Supply and Sewerage System (MWSS), Department of Public Works and Highways (DPWH) and the Department of Interior and Local Government/ Local Government Units (DILG/LGUs) for municipal and industrial supply. The DPWH is also involved in flood control and small water impounding projects.

The Water Code of 1976 (P.D.1067) provides the legal framework for the water resources management. The responsibility for administering and enforcing the Water Code lies with the National Water Resources Board (NWRB), which is vested by the Code with broad powers for coordinating and regulating the development, utilization and protection of water resources in the country.

Another important institution in the water resources sector is the Department of Environmental and Natural Resources (DENR), which is responsible for watershed management and monitoring of water quality. The issues of pollution prevention and control are the primary concern of the DENR, with the cooperative efforts from various regulatory agencies, particularly Department of Health (DOH) for sanitation and country-wide surveillance of drinking water sources to protect public health.

B. Water resources assessment

In order to have a manageable unit for comprehensive planning of water resources development, the country is divided into twelve (12) water resources regions, namely, Ilocos, Cagayan Valley, Central Luzon, Southern Tagalog, Bicol, Western Visayas, Central Visayas, Eastern Visayas, Southwestern Mindanao, Northern Mindanao, Southeastern Mindanao and Southern Mindanao. The major considerations taken into account in the regionalization are hydrological boundaries as defined by physiographic features and homogeneity of climate.

The water resources regions generally corresponds to the existing political regions of the country. Minor deviations from political regional divisions affect only the Ilocos, Cagayan Valley, Central Luzon and Northern Mindanao Regions.

Based on this regionalization, assessment of the water supply and demand situations have been made based on readily available data. The study approaches the issues basically on a quantitative dimension, by comparing water supply with current and projected requirements, using 1990 as the base year projected up to year 2000.

1. National water picture

From a national perspective, the total demand of the major water users, namely, irrigation, domestic/municipal and industrial uses is expected to increase from 288 million cubic metres per day (MCM/day) in 1990 to 504 MCM/day in the year 2000. The available water supply, on the other hand, aggregates to 975 MCM/day based on dependable surface runoff and groundwater safe yield. Using the average surface runoff, the total water resources available would amount to 1,456 MCM/ day. Comparison of water demand to available water supply indicates that there appears to be no problem, as the projected demand in the year 2000 is still well below the dependable supply. Existing and projected water demand by regions is given in table 22 and the dependable regional water availability is given in table 23.

Table 22. Existing and projected use by regions (MCM/day)

Region		1990	2000
I	Ilocos	13	24
II	Cagayan Valley	23	47
III	Cental Luzon	41	72
IV	Southern Tagalog	45	81
V	Bicol	24	36
VI	Western Visayas	23	33
VII	Central Visayas	11	21
VIII	Eastern Visayas	17	25
IX	SW Mindanao	17	22
X	N. Mindanao	22	41
XI	SE Mindanao	28	48
XII	Southern Mindanao	24	54
	Total	288	504

2. Regional comparison

The estimated water use by regions have been calculated to show the available water supply in each region based on dependable surface runoff and average surface runoff. Comparison of the supply and demand indicates that Region III in Luzon and some regions in Visayas and Mindanao will probably have long-term water problems in the future, as the projected demand rapidly catches up with the dependable water supply in these regions.

3. Water resources development programme

The thrusts of the government efforts on water resources development have focused mainly on the sectoral areas of water supply and sanitation, irrigation, hydropower, flood control, water pollution abatement and related environmental concerns.

Table 23. Regional water availability (MCM/day)

	Region	Dependable surface runoff*	Ground-water	Total
I	Ilocos	42	7	49
II	Cagayan Valley	130	28	158
III	Cental Luzon	5	16	68
IV	Southern Tagalog	139	15	154
V	Bicol	46	9	55
VI	Western Visayas	33	11	44
VII	Central Visayas	28	3	31
VIII	Eastern Visayas	101	13	114
IX	SW Mindanao	53	5	58
X	N. Mindanao	74	16	90
XI	SE Mindanao	63	10	73
XII	Southern Mindanao	72	9	81
	Total	833	142	975

* 80 per cent occurrence frequency

Among the major sectoral uses, irrigation is the biggest water user, accounting for about 80 per cent, followed by industrial and domestic/municipal uses which account for about 15 per cent and 5 per cent, respectively. Water use for hydropower generation is non-consumptive but the pattern of water releases has to meet the power demands. To maintain instream aquatic life, water quality control and related environmental concerns, a minimum of about 10 per cent dependable flow needs to be maintained in the river, as a matter of policy.

C. Sustainable development issues

1. Resource sustainability

(a)   Water quality

Of the country's more than 400 principal rivers, between 30 and 40 have been classified as polluted, some of which are affected to a degree of critical concern. The primary sources of pollution include domestic sewage, industrial effluents and agricultural runoff, as well as solid wastes. Other threats to water quality are sedimentation due to watershed denudation and mining operations, and salt-water intrusion of coastal aquifers due to groundwater overpumping.

Records from DENR show that of the 74 designated water quality monitoring stations in various parts of the country, 65 per cent show that water quality has already deteriorated beyond official beneficial use classification of the water at that station, while 47 per cent of river stations and 60 per cent of coastal stations show water quality lower than the lowest level use classification. Examples are the Pasig River in the National Capital Region, where the actual count of BOD ranges from 20 to 120 mg/l, far exceeding the safe limit BOD level of 7 mg/1 for category "C" water use classification; and the Iloilo Coast in Region VI as well as Yasay Beach in Region X, where the coliform counts are recorded at 12,500 mPN/dl and 300,000 mPN/dl, respectively which are way beyond the safe limit of 1,000 mPN/dl.

This pollution problem, which has become a critical resource issue in just over two decades, will continue and probably worsen due to population and industrial growth, if appropriate prevention and control measures are not implemented. Water use classification in the Philippines is given in table 24.

Table 24. Philippine water use classification

Beneficial uses	Classification	
	Freshwater	Coastal Water
Public water supply requiring disinfection only	AA	-
Public water supply following complete treatment	A	-
Commercial shellfish rowing, tourist zones, marine parks and reserves	-	SA
Contact recreation, fish spawning	B	SB
Non-contact recreation, commercial and sustenance fishing, industrial water supply following treatment	C	SC
Irrigation and livestock watering, industrial water supply	D	-
Industrial water supply	-	SD
Net classified	NC	NC

(b)   Groundwater overexploitation

Due to the insufficiency of surface water supply, and deficiency of distribution facilities to provide the means for such supplies to reach the intended beneficiaries, groundwater overpumping is being resorted to in Metro Manila as well as in other coastal cities of the Philippines by private individuals,

business and industries. Water tables in Metro Manila are being drawn down at a rate of 612 metres per year, which has caused saline water intrusion along the coastal areas.

In the Visayas, particularly in Negros Occidental and Cebu, where prawns are being raised for export, over-exploitation of groundwater is causing saltwater intrusion in the coastal aquifers and causing deepwells for domestic water supply to run dry in nearby communities.

(c)   Watershed degradation

Excessive logging and shifting cultivation are common practice in the watersheds, triggering widespread degradation of watersheds and consequent accelerated erosion and siltation of and decrease inflows in rivers, lakes and reservoirs. Such is the effect of increasing density of upland population, wanton mining, rapid urban growth, industrialization, use and abuse of the country's watersheds.

With the recurrence of water shortages, limiting the amount of water fit for human consumption coming from the watersheds, the government recognized the need to mitigate the occurrence, or address the looming water crisis to ensure adequate, affordable, safe and sustainable water supply.

(d)   Water use conflicts

In view of the increasing overall demands brought about by the rapid population growth and expanded agricultural and industrial activities, satisfying the needs of all concerned requires efficient allocation of the limited water resources among competing users.

For example, at the outset when the Angat Reservoir was completed, water was plentiful and could easily supply the needs of the farmers within the project irrigation service area and the needs of Metro Manila for domestic and industrial uses. However, with the rapid increase of Metro Manila's population, the reservoir is stretched to satisfy the demand of all users, especially during summer. With domestic and industrial water supply and irrigation competing for limited water available in the reservoir, there is bound to be a conflict.

2. Financial sustainability of water development projects

(a)   Inadequate public investment

The apparent lack of financial resources is noted to be a major constraint to water resources development which is capital-intensive. All the agencies depend on loans or external grants to finance their respective programmes and projects. Without adequate budgetary allocation and continued dependence on external assistance, long-term development of the nation's water resources cannot be sustained.

There is an increasing concern on how to raise the capital needed in the face of financial constraints so much so that there is now a tendency to a policy of full cost recovery of projects, or for beneficiaries to pay a larger share of the cost of the project for sustainability, with regard to operation and maintenance, expanded coverage and reliable service.

(b)   Low recovery of project cost

In general, government agencies exist primarily to provide service to the people and as such, funds for the construction and operation and maintenance of facilities come entirely from the annual budget provided by the national government. On the other hand, other government organizations, like the government-owned and controlled corporations, are motivated by profit and thus practice a policy of cost recovery of their water development projects. However, bill collection efficiency is generally low.

The financing scheme for the construction, operation and maintenance varies with the organizational structure as well as mandate of the agency involved. The same is true with the policy on the recovery of costs. Government corporations operate as self-liquidating entities while other agencies perform purely proprietary government functions.

In the case of Metropolitan Waterworks and Sewerage System (MWSS), capital outlays for the construction of projects come from various sources such as the national government's subscription to its authorized capital stock, system's revenues, and domestic and foreign borrowings. The MWSS follows a policy of full cost recovery for its projects. Water rates charged are such that sufficient funds can be generated to recover operation and maintenance costs as well as debt service of loans and bond fund obligations.

For the Local Water Utilities Administration (LWUA), funds for the projects come from the national government's subscription to its authorized capital stock as well as from domestic borrowings and foreign loans. When LWUA grants loan to a local water utility (Water District), it gives the entire funding requirement to assure completion of the project for which the loan is granted. The water utility (Water District) recovers the entire amount of the loan plus interest from the water consumers. The operation and maintenance of the utility is the concern of the Water District and as such it imposes and collects revenues at such rates sufficient to cover the administration costs plus reserves for expansion and contingencies.

In the case of the National Irrigation Administration (NIA), the selection of projects based on the criteria that the project must have an economic internal rate of return of at least 15 per cent similar to the rate used by the National Economic and Development Authority (NEDA) in evaluating project proposals of other government agencies. Irrigation Service Fees (ISF) are imposed by NIA on farmer-beneficiaries of national irrigation systems (NIS) and are the primary source of funds or income of NIA. The operation and maintenance of NIS are funded mainly from these funds. Current rates of ISF/hectare depending on the type of system and cropping season (in cavans of unmilled rice) are:

National Irrigation   : 2.5 cavans (wet season),
  System (Reservoir Type)   3.5 cavans (dry season)

Diversion Systems   : 2 cavans (wet season),
                          3 cavans (dry season)

Pump-lift   : 6 to 8 cavans (wet season),
                          6 to 10 cavans (dry season)

Note: About 2 cavans of unmilled rice is approximately 50 kilograms of milled rice.

Farmer beneficiaries (Irrigation Associations) of communal irrigation systems enter into agreement with NIA for them to amortize costs incurred by NIA in constructing their systems within a period not to exceed 50 years. Not all costs incurred by NIA are chargeable or recoverable from the Irrigation Associations. Only direct costs can be recovered.

(c)   Inadequate pricing of water

Pricing of water does not consider the economic cost of water as an input. The value of the most valuable opportunity foregone (scarcity value or "opportunity cost") constitutes a legitimate element of the total production cost of water.

Furthermore, there is currently no operative system for incorporating the cost of maintaining the sources of the water (e.g. watershed and groundwater recharge areas). Water utilities do not pay an appropriate "resource maintenance cost" for the water that it delivers to its customers, hence it does not reflect such cost in what it charges to the consumers.

D. Sustainable use of water resources

1.   Water conservation and wastage prevention through demand management

(a)   Water allocation system and procedures

Water allocation is a powerful tool for managing the demand for water for whatever purpose. P.D. 1067 otherwise known as the Philippine Water Code, is the basic law that governs the ownership, appropriation, utilization, exploitation, development, conservation and protection of the water resources of the country. This is based on the principle that all waters belong to the State and as such, cannot be the subject of acquisitive prescription. Except as otherwise provided in the Code, no person, including government-owned or controlled corporation, shall appropriate water without a water right. All water rights granted are subject to the conditions of beneficial use, adequate standards of design and construction and such other conditions and terms imposed by the Board. Beneficial use is the utilization of water in the right amount during the period that the water is needed for producing the benefits for which the water is appropriated.

The basic principle of water appropriation is " first in time, first in right". When priority in time of appropriation from a certain source of supply cannot be determined, the order of preference in the use of water is: domestic and municipal use; irrigation; power generation; fisheries; livestock raising; industrial use; other uses.

However, Article 22 of the Code states... "except in times of emergency, the issue of water for domestic and municipal purposes shall have a better right over all other uses; provided, that where water shortage is recurrent and the appropriator for municipal use has a lower priority in time of appropriation, then it shall be his duty to find an alternative source of supply in accordance with conditions prescribed by the Board." There is also a mechanism to alter priorities as Article 23 states ..." Priorities may be altered on grounds of greater beneficial use, multi-purpose use and other similar grounds after due notice and hearing, subject to payment of compensation in proper cases."

(b)   Use of water saving devices

Water saving devices are gadgets or attachment that reduces the amount of water to accomplish the same amount of work. Use of such devices are rarely found in households, even in the urban areas for lack of information dissemination by manufacturers, unlike power saving devices to reduce electric consumption in households. However, Article 21 of the Water Code states ... "excepting those for domestic use, every appropriator of water shall maintain water control and measuring devices, and keep records of water withdrawal. When required by the Council (now Board), all appropriators of water shall furnish information on water use. This, however, is more widely enforced on water rights grantees for irrigation purposes.

(c)   Enhancing water use efficiency

The agricultural sector as a whole is the greatest consumer of water. It is therefore in this sector where increase in efficiency in water use means more water can be saved for other uses.

The problem in the irrigation subsector is low water use efficiency due to technical and institutional deficiencies, flooding in the wet season and inadequate water availability during the dry season. Irrigation efficiencies have also decreased due to lahar flows in Region 3 and decreasing water supply due to watershed denudation. As a result, the irrigated cropping intensity in national irrigation systems is only 140 per cent. The dilapidated state of canal structures in the systems and the low water use efficiencies result in water loss which goes back to the stream draining the system. The target irrigation efficiency in the NIA service areas like the Angat ranges from 50 per cent in the wet season to 55 per cent in the dry season.

Some of the possible responses to enhancement of irrigation efficiency in the NIA systems are changing the cropping schedule to reduce the demand for irrigation at the end of the dry season; change in the crops; canal lining to reduce water losses; use of shallow well pumps in submerged areas; merger of irrigation associations instead of individuals; training of beneficiaries on better farm management. NIA's programme to maximize the use of available water also includes the construction of reservoir-type projects and redesign of irrigation facilities to reuse return flows.

(d) Water pricing policies and structures

In the Philippines, water has traditionally been treated as a public good and as such, the government is expected to bear the cost of making accessible the supply to the population. With the increasing scarcity of water especially in Metro Manila and constraints in financial resources, there is now an increasing tendency to shift to a commodity focus in which water users should bear the full cost of being supplied with water. The MWSS has just raised its tariff rates by about 37 per cent as a demand management intervention to reduce the demand as well as improve the system and reduce system leakages.

(e) Recycling (re-use) of water

Water conservation through recycling or reuse of water, as a concept, is a valuable and useful tool for water resources management especially in critically water-short areas. In view of the recurrent shortage of water, the policy of the government is to encourage re-use of effluent in agriculture and industry. Industries are encouraged to save water and adopt measures to renovate their effluents for other secondary uses.

In the case of irrigation systems, drainage water reuse is another possibility of extending the supply of water. Installation of drainage reuse systems are now being encouraged by NIA and the farmers to supply water to areas which cannot be reached by water supply from canals. NIA's programme as stated above include the redesign of irrigation facilities to reuse return flows.

Water used for power generation as in multi-purpose reservoirs like the Angat is reused for domestic water supply and irrigation.

In times of water shortage, households are encouraged to reuse laundry water for flushing and cleaning toilets and driveways as well as watering garden plants.

2. Water quality protection

(a) Wastewater disposal regulations

Wastewater disposal is an essential part of the environmental management programme of the government. The Department of Environmental and Natural Resources (DENR), the primary agency responsible for the sustainable development of the country's natural resources and ecosystems, together with the Environmental Management Bureau (EMB) and the Regional Offices of the DENR, regulate the discharges of industrial firms into bodies of water through the Environmental Impact Statement (EIS) system.

The Department of Health (DOH) on the other hand, implements the Sanitation Code of the Philippines, thereby, promulgates rules and regulation for the control and prevention of pollution of agricultural products through the use of chemical fertilizers and plant pesticides containing toxic chemical substances and unsanitary agricultural practices. It has also supervision over the discharge of untreated effluents of septic tanks or sewage treatment plants to bodies of water. Effluent standards for discharging into receiving water bodies are given in tables 25, 26, 27 and 28.

(b) Watershed management

About 70 per cent of the total land area of the country of about 30 million hectares is categorized as a watershed area. This is owned by the government and the Department of Environment and Natural Resources (DENR) manages it. The Forest Management Bureau (FMB) under the DENR is mandated to formulate and recommend policies and programmes for the effective protection, development, management and conservation of forest lands and watersheds.

Table 25. Effluent standards: conventional and other pollutants in protected waters category I & II and in inland water Class C[a]

| Parameter | Unit | Protected waters | | | | Inland waters | |
| | | Category I (Class AA and SA) | | Category II (Class AB and SB) | | Class C | |
		OEI	N.I.	OEI	NPI	OEI	NPI
Colour	PCU	(b)	(b)	150	100	200[c]	150[c]
Temperature °C rise (max rise in °C in RBW)		(b)	(b)	3	3	3	
pH (range)		(b)	(b)	6.0-9.0	6.0-9.0	6.0-9.0	6.5-9.0
COD	mg/L	(b)	(b)	100	60	150	100
Settleable Solids (1 hour)	mg/L	(b)	(b)	0.3	0.3	0.5	0.5
5-day 20 °C BOD	mg/L	(b)	(b)	50	30	80	50
Total Suspended Solids	mg/L	(b)	(b)	70	50	90	70
Total Dissolved Solids	mg/L	(b)	(b)	1,200	1,000	----	----
Surfactants (MBAS)	mg/L	(b)	(b)	5.0	2.0	7.0	5.0
Oil/Grease (Petroleum Ether Extract)	mg/L	(b)	(b)	5.0	5.0	10.0	5.0
Phenolic Substances as Phenols	mg/L	(b)	(b)	0.1	0.05	0.5	0.1
Total Coliforms	MPN/dL	(b)	(b)	5,000	3,000	15,000	10,000

Table 26. Effluent standards: conventional and other pollutants in inland waters Class D, coastal waters Class SC and SD and other coastal waters not yet classified

| Parameter | Unit | Inland waters (Class D) | | Coastal waters (Class SC) | | Class SD & other not classified | |
		OEI	NPI	OEI	NPI	OEI	NPI
Colour	PCU	----	----	(c)	(c)	(c)	(c)
Temperature °C rise (max rise in °C in RBW)	°C rise	3	3	3	3	(3)	3
pH (range)	mg/L	5.0-9.0	6.0-9.0	6.0-9.0	6.0-9.0	5.0-9.0	5.0-9.0
COD	mg/L	250	200	250	200	300	200
5-day 20 °C BOD	mg/L	150[d]	120	120[d]	100	150[d]	120
Total Suspended Solids	mg/L	200	150	200	150	(g)	(f)
Total Dissolved Solids	mg/L	2,000[h]	1,500[h]	----	----	----	----
Surfactants (MBAS)	mg/L	----	----	15	10	----	----
Oil/Grease (Petroleum Ether Extract)	mg/L	----	----	15	10	15	15
Phenolic Substances as Phenols	mg/L	----	----	1.0[i]	0.5[i]	5.0	1.0
Total Coliforms	MPN/dL	(j)	(j)	----	----	----	----

Notes for Tables 25 and 26:

1. In cases where the background level of Total Dissolved Solids (TDS) in freshwater, rivers, lakes, reservoirs, and similar bodies of water is higher than the Water Quality Criteria, the discharge should not increase the level of TDS in the receiving body of water by more than ten percent of the background level.

2. The COD limits in Tables 25 and 26 generally apply to domestic wastewater treatment plant effluent. For industrial discharges, the effluent standards for COD should be on a case to case basis considering the COD-BOD ratio after treatment. In the interim period that this ratio is not yet established by each discharger, the BOD requirement shall be enforced.

3. There are no effluent standards for chloride except for industries using brine and discharging into inland waters, in which case the chloride content should not exceed 500 mg/L

4. The effluents standards apply to industrial manufacturing plants and municipal treatment plants discharging more than thirty (30) cubic metres per day.

Legend for Tables 25 and 26:

(a) Except as otherwise indicated, all limiting values in Tables 25 and 26 are 90th percentile values. This is applicable only when the discharger undertakes daily monitoring of its effluent quality, otherwise, the numerical values in the tables represent maximum values not to be exceeded once a year.

(b) Discharging of sewage and/or trade effluents is prohibited or not allowed.

(c) Discharge shall not cause abnormal discolouration in the receiving waters outside of the mixing zone.

(d) For wastewaters with initial BOD concentration over 1,000 mg/L but less than 3,000 mg/L, the limit may be exceeded up to a maximum of 200 mg/L or a treatment reduction of ninety (90) per cent, whichever is more strict. Applicable to both old and new industries.

(e) The parameters Total Suspended Solids (TSS) should not increase the TSS of the receiving water by more than thirty (30) per cent during the dry season.

(f) Not more than 30 mg/L increase (dry season).

(g) Not more than 60 mg/L increase (dry season).

(h) If effluent is the sole source of supply for irrigation, the maximum limits are 1,500 mg/L and 1,000 mg/L, respectively, for old industries and new industries.

(i) Not present in concentration to affect fish flavour or taste or tainting.

(j) If effluent is used to irrigate vegetable and fruit crops which may be eaten raw, Faecal Coliforms should be less than 500 MPN/100 mL.

Table 27. Interim effluent standards for BOD applicable to old or existing industries producing strong industrial wastes (1990-1994)

Industry classification based on raw wastewaters produced	Maximum allowable limits in mg/L*, according to time period and receiving body of water			
	Effectivity date: Dec. 31, 1991		Jan. 1, 1992 - Dec. 31, 1994	
	Inland waters	Coastal waters	Inland waters	Coastal waters
	(Class C & D)	(CI, SC and SD)	(Class C & D)	(CI, SC & SD)
1. Industries producing BOD within 3,000 to 10,000 mg/L	320 or 95% removal	650 or 90% removal	200 or 97% removal	320 or 95% removal
2. Industries producing BOD within 10,000 to 30,000 mg/L	1,000 or 95% removal	2,000 or 90% removal	600 or 97% removal	1,000 or 95% removal
3. Industries producing more than or 30,000 mg/L	1,500 or 95% removal	3,000 or 90% removal	900 or 97% removal	1,500 or 95% removal

Note : *Including old or existing industries producing strong waste whose wastewater treatment plants are still to be considered.

1. Use either the numerical limit or percentage removal whichever is lower (or whichever is more strict)
2. Starting 1 January 1995, the applicable effluent requirements for old or existing industries are indicated in Table 28.
3. For parameters other than BOD, Table 25 and Table 26 both shall apply.

**Table 28. Effluent standards for new* industries producing strong wastes
upon effectivity of these regulations, and for all industries
producing strong wastes starting 1 January 1995**

Industry classification based	Maximum allowable limits in mg/L based on receiving body of water	
	Inland waters (Class C and D)	Coastal waters (Class SC and SD)
1. Industries producing within 3,000 to 10,000 mg BOD/L	130 or 98% removal	200 or 97% removal
2. Industries producing within 10,000 to 30,000 mg/BOD/L	200 or 99% removal	600 or 97% removal
3. Industries producing more Than 30,000 mg BOD/L	300 or 99% removal	900 or 97% removal

Note : *Including old or existing industries producing strong waste whose wastewater treatment plants are still to be considered.

1. Use either numerical limits or percentage removal whichever is lower (or whichever is more strict).
2. For parameters other than BOD, Tables 25 and 26 shall apply.

Among the objectives of the DENR watershed protection and management banner programme for 1996, the construction of impounding structures in critical watersheds and water scarce areas as well as the protection and rehabilitation of critical watersheds are considered as important measures to reduce erosion and sedimentation problems in the country's river basins.

The chronic shortage of water supply in Metro Manila and the countryside in the past years has increased recognition of the adverse effects of man's activities in the watersheds which have caused erosion and siltation problems in the country's rivers, lakes and reservoirs. One particular concern is deforestation, leading to siltation of dams and waters stored in inland lakes, such as the Laguna Lake near Metro Manila and the Ambuklao Reservoir in the north.

The approval of R.A. 8041, otherwise known as the National Water Crisis Act of 1995, paved the way for the creation of a Joint Executive-Legislative Water Crisis Commission to address among other things, the problems in the nation's watersheds. Recently, it promulgated a resolution approving and adopting a criteria for the identification and prioritization of watershed areas where developmental undertakings are to be suspended. Consistent with the criteria a list of priority watershed areas supporting domestic water supply was prepared and recommended for suspension of developmental undertakings within the watersheds. The developmental undertakings to be suspended are road constructions; residential, commercial and industrial subdivision, garbage dumpsites; logging; farming utilizing inorganic fertilizers; all other land and resources uses/ infrastructure projects incompatible with uses of the area as a watershed.

(c) Application of clean technologies

Researches related to environmental management being done presently by the DENR cover industrial processes involving clean technologies and waste minimization. However, the resources available for environmental research activities are very limited and little has been accomplished with regard to the commercialization of research so far completed.

3. Water quality monitoring

(a) Wastewater quality monitoring

The DENR/EMB establishes and monitors water quality standards and criteria for the purpose of meeting environmental objectives. One of the major tasks of DENR down to its Regional Offices, is the monitoring of water quality including quantity in the effluent and in the receiving body of water with the objective of controlling pollution.

(b) Enforcement of effluent standards

The Environmental Management Bureau is responsible for managing the Environmental Impact Assessment (EIA) system in the Philippines.

It also classifies freshwater and coastal water bodies for various beneficial uses and prescribes effluent standards for conventional and other pollutants in various water bodies.

E. Conclusions and recommendations

The country is confronted with formidable water and sustainable development problems including recurrent water supply shortages and increasing conflicts in the allocation of water among competing users; inadequate water infrastructures that have lagged behind levels needed to keep up with rapidly increasing demand; severe water pollution particularly near urban centres; and watersheds and environmental degradation, which threatens the health of population (especially the poor) and aquatic life.

The problem is not the shortage of water itself, as the current demand for water is far less than the renewable water available nationally. The problem arises from supply-demand mismatches caused by inadequate water infrastructure to regulate flood flows and store water in the rainy season for consumption in the dry season. The problem is compounded by limited financial resources for source development and expansion of water distribution facilities; wasteful use of water; and weakness of regulatory agencies in the enforcement and monitoring activities primarily due to inadequate man-power resources and logistic support facilities.

Some of the above issues maybe resolved through larger public investment for developing new water infrastructures; institutional strengthening of concerned water utilities and regulatory agencies to improve efficiency in service delivery and water use; economic pricing of water and higher recovery of project costs; greater participation by beneficiaries in the planning and implementation of projects; and increased participation by the private sector in water service delivery.

The government has taken several initiatives in this regard as part of its overall action plan towards sustainable water resources management. A draft action plan for overall water resources management has been prepared, covering six key areas, namely, water resources management at national and regional levels; water resources planning at national and regional levels; regulatory and coordination systems enforcement; investment needs in the sector; watershed management; and water resources sectoral reform.

XV. WATER AND SUSTAINABLE DEVELOPMENT IN THE REPUBLIC OF KOREA

Gee Bong Han, Senior Officer and Researcher
Water and Wastewater Engineering Division, Water Quality Research Department
National Institute of Environmental Research, Republic of Korea

A. Current status of water and the environment

1. General features

Major mountains in the Republic of Korea are developed along east side of the peninsular and running from north to south to divide the country into east and west regions. The eastern part of major mountain range declines steeply to the east coast which faces the Pacific ocean. On the contrary, the western part of the peninsular has a gentle slope and contains various wide plains. Agricultural lands are mostly located in the western part of the peninsular in which 65 per cent is covered with mountainous regions.

There are four seasons in a year and more than 60 per cent of annual precipitation occurs during the rainy period in summer. This causes a wide disparity of available water resources during different seasons. There are about 3,900 rivers in the peninsular. Of these, four major rivers, namely, Han River, Nakdong River, Keum River, and Youngsan River, provide the bulk of water supply to the country.

2. Water resources

The total annual water resources availability is estimated at 70 km^3 and the total water use 29 km^3. In order to effectively manage water resources and secure a reliable water supply, the government has constructed many multi-purpose dams. About 34.8 per cent of the annual water consumed in the country is supplied from these dams and 21 per cent of total water consumed is used for domestic purposes, 50 per cent for agricultural purposes, 8 per cent for industrial purposes, and 21 per cent for nature preservation. About 82 per cent of the total population are beneficiaries of the public water supply system.

3. Water quality

Water quality of large reservoirs is fairly good because they are located in the relatively clean areas upstream of rivers. The quality of water in the middle and lower reaches of the Han River is relatively fair with a BOD level of 1-2 ppm. Water at the middle and lower reaches of the Nakdong River shows a BOD level of 3-4 ppm after the establishment of industrial complexes in the middle reaches of the river. Water at the lower reaches of the Keum River and the Youngsan River, due to the existence of large metropolitan areas in their upper and middle reaches had a BOD level of 3-4 ppm in 1994. Since the water supply of the country is highly dependent on the rivers, the government has placed a high priority on the protection of fresh water resources.

4. Water pollution

Any discharge of pollutants into natural waters such as rivers, lakes, reservoirs, and coastal regions, etc. cause water pollution when it exceeds their self-purification capacities. If water gets contaminated, it is no longer useful for drinking, industrial supply, leisure, sports etc.

The aggregate volume of sewage generated in the Republic of Korea can be estimated on the basis of daily per capita water consumption. Assuming that 91 per cent of the urban water supply and 86 per cent of the non-urban water supply are ultimately disposed as wastewater, the volume of country's daily sewerage is about 14.6 million m^3. The domestic sewerage generation is given in table 29.

Unlike sewage effluents, industrial wastewater is more toxic and contains higher concentration of contaminants. The water quality protection agencies

Table 29. Domestic sewage generation (1994)

Region	Population (1,000 persons)	Water supply (l/person/day)	Wastewater generation (l/person/day)	Wastewater Volume (1,000 m³/day)
Major cities	21,693	433	394	8,548
Urban areas	12,882	334	303.3	3,913
Country centres	3,391	254	235.3	798
Non-urban areas	7,110	227	194	1,380
Total	45,076			14,638

maintain databases on the volume of industrial effluents discharged from the approved industrial facilities which generate large volume of wastewater. It has been observed that wastewater generated increased annually at the average rate of 13.1 per cent from 2,731,000 m³/day in 1986 to 8,741,000 m³/day in 1995. It has increased 3.2 times during the period but there was 20.4 per cent increase of 7,259,000 m³/day in 1994. The wastewater discharge rate has also increased annually at an average rate of 8.4 per cent from 1,165,000 m³/day in 1986 to 2,375,000 m³/day in 1995.

5. Standards for water quality

(a) Water quality standards

Standards have been established for water bodies and specific water quality parameters. Water bodies are classified into rivers, lakes, and off shores. Specific water quality parameters are set by 8 indicators, namely, pH, BOD, COD, SS, DO, E-coli count, total nitrogen, and total phosphorus for aquatic life and by 9 indicators, namely, Cd, As, CN, Hg, organic phosphorus, Pb, Cr^{+6}, PCB, and ABS for human health. Rivers and lakes are divided into 5 classes (I-V) by their clarity, and class I denotes the best quality. Off shores are managed by dividing those into 3 classes (I-III).

(b) Water regulation standards

Water regulation standards are regulating tools to maintain acceptable environmental standards. They

are composed of wastewater emission standards and effluent quality standards.

Wastewater emission standards are established to regulate wastewater discharge at individual working place in accordance with environmental standards and self-purification capacity of water bodies. Chapter 8 of the Water Quality Preservation Act and the eight provisions of it set 28 parameters which are applied to 4 different regions designated as either Clean zones, A zones, B zones, or Special zones for wastewater emission standards.

Effluent quality standards are applied to the terminal wastewater treatment plants to treat sewage, wastewater, and night-soil and are usually determined by 5 parameters, namely, BOD, COD, SS, total nitrogen, and total phosphorus.

B. Future trends and plans

The ultimate purpose of water resources development is to supply water of acceptable quality to various users. To achieve water conservation, ensure adequate water supply and sustainable development, the Ministry of Environment and other seven ministries, including the Ministry of Construction and Transportation and the Ministry of Home Affairs, launched a new 5 year project (1993-1997) called the Comprehensive Plan for Clean Water Supply. It calls for investment in facilities totalling 15.1 trillion won (US$ 1 = 789 won) during the period to construct and renovate 597 sewage treatment facilities to increase the treatment efficiency to more than 73 per cent, and to construct 8 multi-purpose dams and 21 large-scale water supply networks. The population served with treated water is expected to increase from the current 82 per cent to 86 per cent by replacing 20,000 km of old water mains.

To promote water and sustainable development the government has plans to implement the following 4 programmes.

1. Comprehensive water resources development and management

The programme for comprehensive water resources development envisages constructing dams, expanding water supply networks, developing groundwater resources, and improving water quality of rivers and other surface waters. It also envisages the establishment of an effective water resource management system.

To effectively implement its plans, the government endeavours to secure an additional amount of water supply through the construction of new multi-purpose dams and expansion of water supply networks. It has also plans to establish a comprehensive management system for dams, rivers, and groundwater reservoirs, to centralize water management authority, to conduct research to develop new technologies concerning development of various water management models and desalinization of sea water.

2. Development, and management of groundwater resources

Efficient groundwater management and systematic development of groundwater resources are expected to be achieved through careful research and administrative planning. The action plans of the

government in this regard include conducting a survey of current groundwater use, groundwater resources availability and the status of their quality. There are also plans to build a monitoring network for recording groundwater levels and quality, and to establish framework for preservation and utilization of groundwater resources.

3. Improvement and restoration of the quality of freshwater resources

It is envisaged to improve the water quality of five major rivers to the level suitable for use as drinking water supply sources or at least to the level suitable for recreational use.

The government will gradually enforce wastewater emission standards and require industries to reduce wastewater discharges. It has plans also to repair public sewage systems to promote treatment efficiency for domestic sewage. Terminal wastewater treatment plants will also be constructed for treatment of industrial wastewater. It is currently investigating the sources of nutrient leaching into major lakes and plans to regulate the discharge of nitrogen and phosphorus.

4. Promotion of water conservation policies

The government has plans to supplement the existing water supply through saving of water by promoting water demand management. Consequently, it is encouraging the installation of water-saving equipment in new buildings and promoting the use of reclaimed water by enterprises consuming large quantities of water. Industrial wastewater reuse will be required by the government's new policy. It will revise the water pricing system to charge progressive rates according to actual water consumption, so that the public are motivated to undertake water saving measures.

XVI. SUSTAINABLE DEVELOPMENT OF WATER RESOURCES OF SRI LANKA

Lionel D Wijendra
Director-Policy and Planning (Public Utilities)
Ministry of Housing, Construction and Public Utilities,"Sethsiripaya" Battaramulla

A. Introduction

1. Background

Sri Lanka is an island covering a land area of 65,610 km^2 located in the Indian Ocean. It is predominantly an agricultural country with a rural population making up almost 80 per cent of the total of 18 million. The average per capita GNP is US$ 700. The country is endowed with water resources through inter-monsoonal climatic directions from the South-West and North-East during two seasons of the year. The total amount of water available for use in the country is approximately 127,000 Mcm/year, while the surface water runoff is estimated as 50,000 Mcm/year. The major uses of surface water are irrigated agriculture, hydro-power and domestic supplies, while groundwater resources are extensively used for industry and conjunctive use in commercial agriculture. Economic development, population pressure, growing demands for electric power, and adequate water and sanitation services are placing increasing pressure on water resources. There is competition between alternative uses of water in some catchments, where requirements for irrigated agriculture, electricity generation and urban water supply must be rationally allocated to optimize the resulting benefits.

There is also evidence of stream sedimentation, resulting from upland soil erosion and deterioration of aquatic ecosystems caused by excessive water abstraction. Environmental concerns relating to water include restraining encroachment of agriculture onto hydrologically sensitive areas, alleviating problems related to water quality, the impacts of irrigation, wetland conservation, management of urban wetlands, stormwater detention areas and industrial pollution. Creating awareness among the public on environmental issues including those connected to water issues has become an important consideration in environmental management.

In this paper, attempts have been made to highlight five major constraints faced by Sri Lanka for sustainable water resources management and development, while five policy directions have also been recommended to overcome the constraining factors and to improve water resources development and management. The paper also provides an outline of some of the examples to demonstrate application possibilities of the four Dublin principles that have been recognized globally in the formulation of strategies and projects.

2. Country status

The mean annual rainfall varies from 900 mm to 5,500 mm with an overall average of about 2,000 mm. About 2,800 mm/year of rainfall occurs in the coastal south west Wet Zone, reducing to 130 mm/year in the Northern areas, and 200 mm/year in the Eastern province. Annual variation of rainfall is significant, and in some years it affects the agricultural production, hydro-power generation and domestic water supplies.

Sri Lanka is endowed with approximately 4,500 km of rivers, 2,400 km of irrigation canals, and 3,500 deep water tanks, reservoirs and artificial and natural wetlands. The inland fisheries and aquaculture potential is estimated to include 175,000 ha of freshwater, and 120,000 ha of brackish water bodies such as lagoons, mangroves and estuaries.

The irrigation schemes in Sri Lanka are categorized into three main groups, namely, major, medium and minor. A major irrigation scheme provides water for agricultural land extending over and above 400 ha, while a medium scheme services between 80 ha and 400 ha of land. A minor scheme provides water for up to 80 ha of land. There are 98 major schemes (out of which 16 are provincially based), 282 medium schemes (out of which 90 are provincially based) and over 20,000 minor schemes in operational level in Sri Lanka. The extent of land supported for irrigated agriculture by major, medium and minor schemes is 351,000 ha, 45,000 ha and 140,000 ha respectively, with a total of 536,000 ha. Out of the major irrigation schemes, over 35 are inter-provincial schemes running across the boundaries of two or three provinces.

In the water supply sub-sector, a number of water supply schemes were operated by the principal national agency for domestic water supply, namely, National Water Supply and Drainage Board (NWS & DB). Piped water is supplied to a population of over 4.8 million (26 per cent) while tube wells have been provided to a population of over 1.4 million (8 per cent). In addition, 27 per cent of the population living in rural areas has been provided with safe drinking water through dug wells. Accordingly, 90 per cent of the urban population, and 57 per cent of the rural population are provided with safe drinking water facilities. The industrial water requirements are independently met from dug wells, while tourist hotels depend on tube wells in meeting their water requirements.

The total installed capacity of the hydropower generation systems is in the order of 1135 MW, which is approximately 80 per cent of the total electricity production. The hydropower network installed under the Mahaweli Development Program caters for over 50 per cent of the production.

The projected water deficit for the year 2000 varies from about 200 Mcm/year in the Mahaweli development region, to about 1,400 Mcm/year in the northern dry zone. The piped water supply to Colombo meets an estimated demand of 97 Mcm/year, which is expected to double by the year 2000. Opportunities for development of further major schemes are limited to Kalu, Walawe and Kelani river basins. Accordingly, future irrigation expansion will depend on small-scale tank restoration, scheme rehabilitation, use of groundwater and improved water management practices. In addition, certain minimum flows will have to be retained in the rivers to meet the in-stream demand for wildlife and ecological systems, including inland freshwater fish.

In hydropower generation, most natural flow sites are fully developed, and dependence on mini and micro-projects are promoted, along with energy-saving devices. The improvement in efficiency has been targeted for future potential, in addition to implementing thermal power plants.

Most of the large irrigation, hydro-power and water supply projects have been implemented with the assistance of the World Bank, Asian Development Bank, USAID, JICA/OECF, and other bilateral sources.

B. Major constraints on sustainable development of water resources

The following five constraints have been identified as critical for sustainable development and management of water resources:

1. Inadequate measures for watershed management, resulting in soil erosion, silting reservoirs, loss of fertility and land degradation, flooding etc.

Significant land degradation has been influenced by the large-scale conversion of the hill country lands to plantation crops, and deforestation due to increasing population pressure. The rate of soil loss has varied between 0.24 tons/ha/year in well-managed tea estates, to 200 tons/ha/year on steep, poorly-managed seasonal crop lands in mid-country uplands. Highest rates occur in tobacco, vegetable, chena (shifting cultivation) and poorly-managed tea land. Soil loss in Mahaweli catchment (which is the largest and longest river in Sri Lanka) in the form of sediment transport, has filled almost half of the effective capacity of one of the main reservoirs within a period of 12 years of its commissioning.

Estimates indicate that, the majority of small minor tanks have silted up to 50 per cent of their capacity in recent years, due to their location in valley bottoms. Rapidly-increasing population has led to clearance of the catchment areas for cultivation and encroachment on to the tank reservations. Government policy to regularize encroachments by illegal farmers engaged in shifting cultivation has also led to rapid deterioration of the watershed areas. The traditional conservation practices have also been abandoned due to lack of promotion of farmer groups towards this end. The watershed management, in terms of conservation objectives, has been constrained due to short-term interests of subsistence farmers, insecure land tenure, and non-enforcement of regulations relating to land clearance. Although legislative provision has been made in the Soil Conservation Act, Forest Ordinance and Land Ordinances for water and land management, there has been problems of enforcement capacity and poor understanding of the legal provisions among resource users.

The information available on watershed conditions and of its effect upon water resources is limited to a few conservation related issues. The new method adopted for watershed conservation is to focus on watersheds with linkages established between upstream and downstream users, to resolve conflicting interests of the resource user groups, and to develop and adopt a strategy of production with protection, to enable conservation measures to be established for catchment areas. The examination of the possibility of granting user rights, especially the riparian rights, to cultivators of state lands, and to have them conform to acceptable conservation and environmental-friendly cultivation practices, is being pursued for sustainable resource use. Soil conservation programmes are currently being practiced by the Natural Resources Management Center of the Department of Agriculture, Forestry and Environment Unit of Mahaweli Authority (MWA) of Sri Lanka, through its Share Control of Resources (SCOR) Project that is being implemented by the International Irrigation Management Institute (IIMI) with USAID assistance, Irrigation Management Division of the Ministry of Irrigation, Power and Energy, Forest Department and few NGOs. In particular, MWA/SCOR Project emphasizes achieving a balance between production and protection of water sources with the involvement of resource users.

The most important types of information relating to watershed management should not be limited to conservation needs but also on water balance, demand and supply of water within the watershed, water quality parameters, types of uses and competing demands, potential for development etc., to enhance decision-making for rational management and development of the water resources. However, the current efforts initiated by the government agencies for watershed management have to be supported by national policy and regulatory framework, and committing resources by recognizing their importance in water resources development and management. The research results would also need to be disseminated among the community resource user groups for ensuring long term sustainable use of water resources and related infrastructure facilities that have been developed in the country.

2. Reduction of quality of water arising from industrial pollution, excessive use of fertilizer and agro-chemicals

There are several state agencies involved in monitoring of water quality from different sources, such as reservoirs, piped water, well water, rivers and streams used for bathing, washing and waste disposal from industries and households. Chemical and physical water quality is generally within WHO recommended limits, while BOD values that measure the presence of organic matter, nutrients and biological activity, extend beyond the recommended upper limit of 5 mg/1 in many water bodies. Water pollution is of growing concern in Sri Lanka. Degradation of surface water quality is occurring in the urban as well as rural areas, depending on the intensity of water flow along streams and rivers, quantity and the frequency of effluent discharges at different periods of time. Principal causes have been identified as excessive rates of fertilizer and pesticide application by farmers; dumping of solid and liquid waste derived from agro-processing units and heavy polluting industries located in sub-urban areas in adjacent water bodies; contamination of human waste with groundwater etc. Groundwater quality is affected mainly by over-pumping, which leads to saltwater intrusion into coastal aquifers, nitrate pollution by excessive rates of fertilized application and disposal of sewage effluent from pit latrines and septic tanks.

The most severe water quality degradation is in the urban and industrial areas around suburbs of Colombo, Kandy and other principal towns. Colombo is the only urban area served with piped sewerage covering only 19 per cent of its population. None of Colombo's domestic sewage is treated before discharging into water bodies. 10-15 per cent of the population discharges waste directly into watercourses. These factors are partly responsible for frequent outbreaks of water-borne diseases.

Environmental regulations have recently been introduced by the government requiring an Environmental Impact Assessment (EIA)/ Environmental Protection License (EPL) to resolve the water quality problems arising from point sources, such as polluting industry locations, while non-point source problems arising from unplanned farm management need to be settled through creating awareness among farmers.

The implementation of the EPL/EIA regulations will have to be supported by improving the knowledge base of the existing technical units attached to the environmental regulatory agencies, government extension service agencies, the private sector, and among the NGOs at national, provincial and local levels. Their services should not only be used for monitoring of the water quality, but also to advise the industries on waste treatment, waste management and pollution control mechanisms, while engaged in creating a strong awareness among the public and the potential polluters. However, the impact of water quality in rivers, streams and other water bodies depends on the frequency and intensity of effluent discharges and the rate of water flow during different periods. Hence the standards for water quality should be formulated for different sources of water bodies taking the above factors into consideration.

3. Lack of management measures for extraction of groundwater resources

There is evidence to show that large volumes of groundwater resources are being exploited for coastal aquaculture projects along North Western Coastal belt of Sri Lanka, causing salt water intrusion into coastal aquifers, which is affecting agricultural lands. In the North Central Province (NCP), groundwater resources are utilized by conjunctive use for irrigated agriculture during water short periods. However, there are no regular programmes for continuous assessment of availability of the resource which can supplement agricultural production. There is evidence to indicate the presence of over 20,000 deep wells installed in the NCP for agricultural purposes, without much concern to the sustainable use of the resource. Hence there is a need to introduce legislation to manage the groundwater resources.

Scientific investigations have been conducted by the Water Resource Board in several locations in Northern and North Western provinces to assess the potential of the resource. The wealth of information that has been gathered by the state agencies using scientific investigations is not fully utilized for management purposes, due to lack of regulations for groundwater exploitation. The National Water Supply and Drainage Board also carries out extraction of groundwater resources to provide drinking water to the rural population in remote villages. Several NGOs have also been actively engaged in providing water in remote villages using tube wells, which has created the need for the authorities to take management intervention.

4. Poor sustainability of operation and maintenance of the irrigation and water supply infrastructure

The impact of land degradation from excessive soil erosion, saline intrusion into aquifers due to over-pumping, particularly in the limestone aquifers of the North-Western coastal belt and Southern areas etc., are due to the way in which people use and abuse land and water resources. These factors have led to accelerated siltation of reservoirs, tanks and water courses. Hence there is a need to pay extra attention to operation and maintenance of irrigation, water supply, sanitation and waste water treatment infrastructure, both at the source and at its irrigation command areas. Much of the irrigation infrastructure is inadequately maintained, and cannot continue to achieve its designed rate of water delivery, without addressing rehabilitation needs after a few years of use. During the past, most of the rehabilitation projects have focused on rehabilitation of canal structures in command areas, without paying much attention to management of sources of siltation and sedimentation effects. Similar problems have surfaced in the operation and maintenance of piped water supplies, industrial waste treatment plants and other rural water supply schemes.

A number of measures have been taken to increase physical and financial sustainability of the water supply and sanitation infrastructure including devolution of management structure of the NWS & DB and through extensive management development programmes. Introduction of water user associations has been encouraged, with a view to reducing the cost of O&M to the government and to share the cost among the water users. A water tariff has been introduced to beneficiaries of piped water to cover the full O&M cost and 50 per cent of debt servicing, but there is a large subsidy component for new investment for which no financial return can be attributed. A significant cross-subsidy to small domestic users is provided from the commercial, industrial and hotel sectors.

The non-sustainability of the irrigation sub-sector in terms of financial performance is principally due to inadequate expenditure on O&M and the inability to recover costs from the users, thus leading to high investment on rehabilitation of infrastructure for which no return or repayment can be expected.

Beneficiary involvement in water management has been a traditional concept since ancient times, with full control over water use by the farmers in minor irrigation systems (covering land holdings of less than 80 ha). The concept was extended to major irrigation systems in 1980s and includes joint system management and involvement in rehabilitation.

Participatory management as policy was approved by the government in 1989, and joint management of major systems is now extensively used to achieve partial sustainability through a series of participatory management programmes involving beneficiary farmers in system operation, maintenance and management. Farmer Organizations have been established at distributory canal level and field channels, while project management committees are operational at system level. Different approaches have been adopted in the formation of water user organizations for system management, operation and maintenance by the Irrigation Department (ID), Irrigation Management Division (IMD) and Mahaweli Economic Agency (MEA). Turnover of systems to Field Office (FO) has been carried out by the IMD and MEA. Since 1980s there has been a government commitment to the concept of beneficiary participation in all phases of irrigation project designs, construction and operations and maintenance. The process of implementation of the policies has been slow and difficult, particularly due to insufficient training of farmers, lack of interest shown by some who would be directly affected, and limited availability of resources and capabilities of agencies to promote participatory management approaches.

5. Unclear policy direction and poor coordination mechanisms for development and management of water resources for multiple users

There are no clear policy directions that are being applied directly to water resources development and management.

Policy statements have been reflected in the Public Investment Programme, Budget speech, President's Annual Address to Parliament etc. However, there is no specific national policy for the water sector, and there are many instances where policies and activities in one part of the water sector are not integrated with those in other parts. There are a number of major schemes for water supply, drainage, waste disposal and swampland reclamation in the city of Colombo, which are individually implemented and not well coordinated. Sri Lanka's irrigation schemes consist of two types: those that cover more than one province are called inter-provincial, and are managed by the central government, while those entirely falling within the province are managed by provincial authorities for which there is no consistent policy for participatory management of irrigation infrastructure.

The policy analysis is undertaken to a limited extent by the water related Ministries in response to changing needs of the irrigated agriculture sub-sector, which are inadequately incorporated in the policy formulation process. There are a few standing committees for policy formulation and review, namely, Central Coordinating Committee on Irrigation Management (CCCIM), National Water Supply Sector Coordination Committee (NSCC), National Environmental Steering Committee (NESC), National Development Council (NDC), Cabinet Sub-Committee on Economic Development, and Committee of Secretaries.

Very recently, a Water Resources Council (WRC) has been established as an interim arrangement, with responsibilities to cover formulation of a national water policy, water allocation principles, management information systems, consolidation of water related legislation to a new water code, and administration of water management programmes through provision of water rights and operation of water permits to use and discharge water. It will also make recommendations for a permanent institutional arrangement for future water sector coordination. Assistance of ADB and Netherlands/FAO has already been provided under a Technical Assistance project to carry out the above tasks within a period of three years.

There have been instances of problems relating to water allocation among competing users, such as irrigation, hydropower, water supply for domestic and industrial purposes, which has been settled through ad-hoc administrative mechanisms adopted through government administrative machinery.

The required policy direction and legal framework for extraction and use of groundwater resources are non-existent, while policy for management of wetlands is unclear and responsibility is spread over many agencies for implementation of related legislation.

In many instances the existing legislation is inadequate to meet the changing circumstances of the environment in managing natural resources. The adequacy of the level of implementation of the policies and legislation are yet to be ascertained. In some agencies, the legislation that is amended does not consider the impact on other sub-sectors within the water sector and other sectors, due to lack of coordination and collaboration.

Policy formulation process for the water sector has not taken into consideration other sectoral policy interventions, thus creating a situation where resource allocation has not reached optimal levels. These factors would have to be taken into account when national water policy is developed.

Hence actions are needed to introduce a better coordination mechanism within the water sector agencies and interaction among other sectors of the economy, with due consideration of all stakeholders in public sector, private sector, NGOs and water user associations.

C. Recommended policy directions

1. Promotion of participatory management approaches to achieve economic and financial sustainability

Participatory management approaches have been promoted in Sri Lanka for water management over the past decade in the area of irrigation and domestic water supply. The need for management of the natural resources, has now been identified as equally important, to ensure long-term utilization of the infrastructure and to reduce soil erosion while retaining land fertility. Hence policy directions have been introduced based on action research results, to introduce participatory management approaches to water source areas, while improving the linkages among beneficiary user groups in command areas, as well as source areas. The resource users exploiting the watersheds in water source areas have been encouraged to participate in conservation agriculture and participatory forestry activities.

Similarly, greater involvement of the water users (formed into groups) in different economical activities has been promoted to ensure continuation of the group efforts in management of the irrigation infrastructure, while gaining economic advantages through group actions.

There is a need to ascertain the factors that have contributed to the successful functioning of some of the strong Farmer Organizations (FOs) and promote weak FOs to follow the principles and methods adopted by strong FOs to enable them to perform better in achieving participatory management objectives.

The water user association that has been established by the NWS & DB to manage stand posts for piped water should be encouraged to participate in other activities, such as improving the sanitary conditions, family planning and low cost housing projects, while encouraging them to maintain group cohesiveness to engage in socio-economic development activities.

The government should encourage the community to participate in identification, designing, implementation and management of water projects and programmes, as in the case of village water supply projects. The government should limit itself to regulatory and technical support functions wherever required, while allowing beneficiaries to take management decisions and share ownership of such investments.

2. Consideration of existing water legislation and introducing new legislation to effectively manage surface and groundwater resources for sustainable use

Several acts provide legal authority to manage water resources. However, there are many overlaps, gaps and provisions that have little relevance to current environmental changes. Administration of the laws are carried out by a large number of institutions which have conflicting jurisdictions. Legal arrangements for rights to use water for alternative uses have been found to be inadequate. Allocation among competing uses has become an issue, wherever the available water is insufficient for both hydro-power and irrigation in Mahaweli catchment, especially when frequency of demand fluctuates over different times of the year. There has also been conflicts among maintaining water supply for Colombo, preventing salt water intrusion in lower stretches of the Kelani river, meeting drainage and flood control requirements and operating the hydro-electric power stations in up-stream Kelani river.

Irrigated agriculture has a priority over generation of hydro-power in the Mahaweli system. A Water Management Panel supported by a Water Management Secretariat attached to Mahaweli Authority of Sri Lanka is set up to determine water allocations among different sub-sectors in Mahaweli and Kelani river basins. Legal arrangements for rights to use water are found to be inadequate, as administrative mechanisms adopted by the government, particularly to resolve issues relating to demand for domestic water against irrigation needs, have constrained the urban-rural population linkages.

The NWS & DB has been authorized by legal enactment to take water from any source for distribution among domestic water users after treatment. Legal authority granted to this agency, to take and use water from any source, has created precedence over other sub-sectors. Enforcement of water related laws, such as Soil Conservation Act, Environmental Protection Licenses, Irrigation Ordinance and Agrarian Services Act etc., is weak, in that the state agencies are more geared for development work, rather than management of the resources. Provisions for charging fees for use of water and operation and maintenance are not enforced, and alternatively, voluntary contributions by way of labour, in attending to O&M activities have been encouraged, through the establishment of the Farmer Organizations.

Accordingly, a consolidation of the existing water-related laws will have to be carried out, with due recognition of the need for new legislation. An FAO project has already become operational to review the existing water related legislation and develop a " Water Code" under the guidance of the Water Resources Council.

3. Improving the management information system

The data on water sector are available in scattered form in various state agencies engaged in the development and management of water resources. Many organizations are engaged in water quality measurement, while research on water balance studies are hardly ever carried out, except for studies on hydrology and soil characteristics by the Irrigation Department. Some data are available in raw form and have not been translated into useful management information bases. Access to some of the water-related technical data are non-existent, while others have to be processed after considerable effort. Data on strengths and weaknesses of the organizations in providing the services to the public in terms of efficiency and effectiveness, have not been adequately documented. An inventory and a mechanism to assess the technical capabilities in terms of training requirements and manpower planning for future development and management of the water resources are yet to be

installed. Most of the water-related information is used for project formulation and monitoring purposes, and not for decision making on policy issues. A continuous approach to collection and analysis of reliable data relating to the demand and supply of water is an immediate need. It has therefore become important to establish a well coordinated reliable data base and more accurate processing methods which are useful for decision making in project formulation and policy reviews. It has been considered useful to adopt integrated approaches for data management and information services in the water sector.

4. Strengthening the water sector institutions through management reviews focusing on the policies to achieve financial sustainability

There are 20 principle state agencies involved in the water sector operating at the national level. The water related functions of these agencies are as follows:

Meteorology Department
(collection and dissemination of weather and climatic data and information)

Irrigation Department (ID)
(provision of irrigation infrastructure, flood control systems and salt water exclusion schemes)

National Water Supply and Drainage Board (NWS & DB)
(provision of piped water and safe drinking water schemes using surface and groundwater resources, development and management of sewerage systems)

Ceylon Electricity Board (CEB)
(provision of hydro-power and thermal power for electricity generation)

Water Resources Board (WRB)
(conducting scientific investigations on groundwater resources and commercial drilling of tube wells)

Mahaweli Authority of Sri Lanka (MASL)
(construction and management of irrigation and hydro-power infrastructure and settlements, promoting irrigated agriculture, upper watershed management and water allocation among competing users).

Irrigation Management Division (IMD) of the Ministry of Irrigation, Power and Energy.

(promoting participatory management in irrigation management of selected number (37) of major irrigation settlement schemes)

Water Resources Development (WRD) Division of MIPE

(policy reviews, coordination and monitoring of activities related to standing committees such as CCCIM and selected foreign funded projects on irrigated agriculture and watershed management)

Natural Resources Management Centre (NRMC) of the Department of Agriculture (DOA)

(promoting agricultural production through conservation measures for soil erosion and watershed management)

Agrarian Services Department (ASD)

(provision of agricultural inputs and enforcement of Agrarian laws on Farmer Organizations, administration of irrigation management procedures)

National Planning Department (NPD)

(planning of water resources projects and programs at national level and advise on resource allocations among the projects)

Central Environmental Authority (CEA)

(implementation of the Environmental Laws relating to relevant regulations while conducting environmental awareness programmes and enforcement of the provisions in the National Environmental Act)

National Aquatic Resources Agency (NARA)

(conducting research and development work in aquatic resources such as inland and marine fish resources, limnological studies in water bodies and water quality measurements etc.)

Natural Resources Energy & Science Authority (NARESA)

(administration of research grants for science and energy, publication and dissemination of research results carried out by independent researchers)

National Building Research Organization (NBRO)

(measuring water quality for state agencies and developing water quality standards)

Ceylon Institute of Scientific and Industrial Research (CISIR)

(conducts research on industrial pollution control, water quality measurements, liquid waste management etc.)

Health Department

(administration of quality of water supply and sanitation programs including prevention of water borne diseases)

Coast Conservation Department (CCD)

(administers Coast Conservation Act covering EIA regulations in coastal development projects and implementation of the master Plan of coastal zone management)

Sri Lanka Land reclamation and Development Board (SLR & DC)

(development of low-lying marsh lands, drainage improvement projects and canal maintenance)

Land Commissioner's Department

(administration of Land Ordinances, where most of the water-related legislation have been incorporated)

In addition there are provincial, divisional and local authorities such as Municipal Councils, Urban Councils and Pradeshlya Sabhas, that have been entrusted with management responsibilities.

Functions of some of the agencies are devolved, while others remain centrally managed. However, it is worthwhile to mention that even before the 13th Amendment to the Constitution for devolution, the supply of drinking water was a devolved subject in Sri Lanka. In certain instances there are over-lapping mandates of the agencies and target clientele, limited coordinating mechanisms between agencies and those that could be implemented at decentralized units. Considering the new policies that are being adopted, there needs to be a revision of the roles, responsibilities and functions of the above agencies with respect to water-related functions. Hence a management review of the existing structures calling for a re-organization programme would be needed to strengthen the institutions which will have to respond to the current development and management changes taking place in the water sector.

5. Comprehensive planning in selected watersheds

The planning processes in the water sector include individual efforts within the sub-sectors, without cross reference to total water availability and needs of other sub-sectors. The current planning practices are biased towards development of the water resources for different sub-sectoral uses with less consideration on overall management needs. There is no holistic approach for planning for water sector development and management thus creating an imbalance within the sector. Hence, there is a need for comprehensive planning approach covering the entire watershed area with due recognition of the needs of the sub-sectors, with cross reference to other sectors of the economy. The planning at watershed/river basin level should be carried out with particular emphasis on water balance, demand and supply parameters, management issues and potential for development etc. The current development planning processes are confined to the needs covered under the administrative boundaries of divisions, districts and provinces which do not coincide with the boundaries of the river basins. Planning at river basin levels would resolve some of the key issues arising from project planning by individual sectors and agencies, while optimizing the resource allocations among the projects.

D. National sector coordination programme for water supply and sanitation sector funded by the UNDP

The Government of Sri Lanka, through the Ministry of Housing, Construction and Public Utilities, and with the support of the United Nations Development Programme has embarked on a National Sector Coordination for Water Supply and Sanitation. The programme was started in 1995 and will be concluded in early 1997.

1. Rationale

To meet the demand for water of all citizens in Sri Lanka, in rural, urban and peri-urban areas in a sustainable manner, concerted action through sector coordination is urgently needed. The diversity of actions in the sectors and the lack of coordinated policies means that full government-sponsored and community- funded projects are being built next to each other. In addition, the use of water resources for drinking, agriculture and other economic purposes,

requires sharing of water and increasingly, monitoring of water quality. The multiplicity of agencies involved in basin management makes coordination and agreement on resources-sharing a complex matter. Plans for priority investment in rural and peri-urban water supply and sanitation are urgently required to offer the economic and health opportunities of improved water supply and sanitation to the under-served. Application of low-cost and affordable water supply and sanitation, for which consumers can and will pay, is necessary to ensure that operation and maintenance is effective and services are reliable.

2. Purpose

The Sector Coordination Programme initiated in the beginning of 1995 carries the promise of a better understanding of national water and sanitation issues, leading to improved coordination among sector agencies, prioritization of sector investment, and agreement on sector policies. A National Sector Coordination Committee has been established, representing all government agencies, institutions and NGOs that have a task in, or bearing on, the water supply and sanitation sector. By instruction of the cabinet, the National Sector Coordination Committee has been mandated to undertake policy review and coordination; liaison and inter-agency coordination; and advice and guidance on sector issues as well as to develop recommendations pertaining to finance, policy and strategy. All this work should be done in the formulation of a Comprehensive Sector Development Plan, including a Framework for Sector Investment.

3. Future strategy for effective coordination

The formulation of a comprehensive sector development plan covering all resource considerations and needs of the citizens of Sri Lanka is essential. The National Sector Coordination Programme is a well timed effort to do just that, by mobilizing the capacities of all governmental, semi-governmental, NGO and private sector agencies, for a concerted drive towards a sustainable, consumer-led, development plan for water supply and sanitation. In such a plan, the needs in water and sanitation of the rural and urban poor can be also spelled out as a powerful instrument in battling poverty, and offering these sectors of a society better quality of life, through better health and greater economic opportunities.

E. Application of Dublin principles in strategies and projects

The four Dublin Principles on water resources which could be applied in water resources development and management are described below.

1. Freshwater is a finite and vulnerable resources, essential for life, development and the environment

The government has recognized the need for comprehensive water resources development and management, in view of the increasing pressure on the resource by way of competing demands. The in-stream values of water for bio-diversity and sustenance of fauna and flora have been recognized under the environmental concerns, and actions are being taken for its sustainable use, while maintaining equity among users. Management measures for conservation of the resource have been initiated through participatory forestry projects and soil conservation programmes, while maintenance of water quality has been addressed through environmental pollution licensing programmes and introduction of water quality standards. Public awareness campaigns on environmental pollution prevention programmes have been raised by the NGOs, while some NGOs and the private sector have been responsible for the introduction of pollution control equipment and other pollution prevention measures.

2. Water resources development and management should be carried out on a participatory approach involving users, planners and policy makers

The government has adopted the participatory management policy for operation and maintenance of irrigation and water supply projects and programmes through the formation of Farmer Organizations and Water User Associations. Strengthening of these organizations are required to ensure sustainability in water resource management. Their involvement in project design, implementation and monitoring would enable the government to meet water requirements and improve the recovery of costs. The policy-makers and planners have been active in the introduction of participatory management concepts and implementation of the policy, with a wider focus on O&M and overall economic development of the irrigation water users. Formation and operation of the water user associations have been promoted by the water supply, sub-sectoral agencies, including NGOs, in order to provide them with technical know-how of repair and maintenance, fee collection and account-keeping, while involving them in project identification, implementation etc.

3. Water has an economic value in all its uses and should be recognized as an economic good

The water supply sub-sector has made arrangements to recover the O&M costs by charging for potable water supplied through networks. However, economic value has not been considered in respect of vulnerable groups among the beneficiaries. The private sector initiatives in the water supply sub-sector have not been developed, as water has not yet been considered as an economic good. The possibility of granting tradable water rights among the groups of water users is also being explored.

4. Women play a central role in providing, safeguarding and managing water

Women in Sri Lanka play a key role in water resources management, and are also becoming professionals in the fields of engineering, public and business administration, medicine, accounting and planning services. They also play a key role in water user associations and in agricultural production. Women have been considered a driving force in providing water for family sustenance by collecting water in remote villages, where water is scarce.

XVII. CURRENT STATUS AND FUTURE TRENDS OF WATER AND SUSTAINABLE DEVELOPMENT IN VIET NAM

Le Duc Nam
Chief of Bureau for Management of Water Resources Planning
Department of Water Resources and Hydraulic Works Management
Ministry of Agriculture and Rural Development

Abstract

Viet Nam has abundant water resources which are unevenly distributed in both space and time. At present, these resources are subjected to deterioration in terms of both quantity and quality because of indiscrimate industrialization brought about by rapid expansion of economic activities including foreign investment. Therefore, appropriate institutional arrangements, guidelines and regulations to better manage increasing water demands, coordinate sector investments, and improve the operational and financial performance of water service entities, has become necessary to achieve the sustainable development and use of water resources in the country.

A. Sustainable development of water resources

1. Environment sustainability

(a) *Water resources potential*

Viet Nam has 2,360 rivers with length over 10 km, nine of the major rivers of which have catchment areas exceeding 10,000 km^2. These are the Mekong, the Dong-nai, the Ky-cung Bang-giang, the Thai-binh, the Ma, the Ca, the Thu-bon, the Ba and the Red rivers. The total discharge of all the rivers in the country is estimated at 27,100 m^3/s. Approximately 37 per cent of the discharge is generated in Viet Nam. The total groundwater potential of the country is estimated   at   1,513   m^3/s.   The   exploitable   or rechargeable groundwater potential consists of 1-2 million m^3/day that can be immediately exploited and 2-7 million m^3/day that have been recently investigated.

(b) *Institutional arrangement*

The   country's   Central   and   provincial governments approve water development programmes and supervise their execution. The 1992 Constitution set forth the goals and policies for managing water resources and organizing government structures. Also, it described the roles, rights and powers of state entities, private enterprises and individuals.

At present, the country's regulatory structure is fragmented, weak or nonexistent. Because of conflicting interests as well as unclear and overlapping responsibilities, laws and regulations have been poorly enforced. Previously, the Ministry of Water Resources (MWR) was responsible for licensing surface waters and its mandate was expanded to include groundwater, which was under the Ministry of Heavy Industry (MOHI). It was also responsible for dam safety and flood mitigation. The regulation of water quality was carried out jointly by the Ministry of Health (MOH), MOHI and MWR.

The country is divided into 61 provinces and five municipalities (Hanoi, Haiphong, Hue. Da Nang, and Ho Chi Minh city.   At the central level, three ministries that deal with water resources: Ministry of Agriculture and Rural Development (MARD), Ministry of Construction and Urban Development (MOC), Ministry of Planning and Investment (MPI) were recently enlarged to take on additional responsibilities.

According to the Government decree 73/CP dated the first of November 1996 the Ministry of Agriculture and Rural Development was organized. The Ministry was restructured into three main branches (administration, special management, and centres of science research and training) of 21 departments.

The Decision of the Prime Minister No 354 concerning missions, responsibilities, authorities and organizations of the Department for Management of Water Resources and Hydraulic Works (DMWHRW) under MARD. The Department is to assist the Minister in implementing the State management of water resources (excluding, mineral water and geothermal water) including, rural domestic water, management of hydraulic works, management of exploitation and integrated development of rivers throughout the country.

(c)   Legal instruments for water resources management

A 1993 law on environmental protection provides broad guidelines for (a) assignment of responsibilities among the ministries, provinces and people's organizations, (b) conducting environmental impact assessments and (c) carrying out inspections and enforcing standards.

Land laws which determines land zoning and the ownership of land indirectly define the demands for water for various types of land and the acceptable levels of pollution. Under this law owner ship of land remains public but land use rights are granted to government agencies, private companies and individuals.

The former MWR (currently MARD) supported by an inter-ministerial committee drafted the new water law, which would provide a comprehensive foundation for the agencies managing the nation's water.   It recognizes the river basin as the basic geographic and administrative unit for water management   and identifies the important links between lands and water use, surface water and groundwater management, as well as water quality and quantity.

A marine law was enacted in 1990, and Ordinances have been formulated for protection and development of marine water resources.

2. Financial sustainability of water development

With the rapid growth of economy and the accompanying increase in water demand there has been a serious deterioration of water resources both in quality and quantity. Most investments in water resources development and management are made by the State. From 1991-1995 it was about US$1.08 billion, and the amount projected for 1996-2000 is about US$4.5 billion mainly for the construction of 75 medium to large scale irrigation systems; over 1,000 big irrigation and drainage sluices, over 2,000 pumping stations; 5,000 km of river dykes and 1,800 km of sea dykes. The country's proposed investment in water resources for period 1996-2000 is shown in table 30.

Table 30. Public investment in water resources development in Viet Nam

Development sector	1991-1995	1996-2000	% of PIP* for 1996-2000
Hydropower	400	1,940	43
Urban water supply	280	872	19
Irrigation, drainage and flood control	400	563	15
Inland waterways	-	116	3
Rural water supply	-	30	1
Total	1,080	1,501	100

* PIP Public Investment Programme.

B. Sustainable use of water resources

(a)   Domestic and municipal water supply

Domestic and municipal water uses (in both urban and rural areas) in Vietnam is rather low compared to other uses. The amount used in 1980 was 1.32 km^3 (or 3.48 per cent of the total 37.86 km^3 water use). In 1990 it reached 2.01 km^3 and in 2000 it is estimated to reach 2.91 km^3.

(b)   Water use in agriculture

At present, cultivated land accounts for 20 per cent of the total land area. The irrigation system in the country can provide water for 5.8 million hectares of rices and 560,000 hectares of other crops. Agriculture water use amounted to 40.6 km3 in 1985 and 47 km3 in 1990. The water use in this sector in 2000 is estimated at 60.5 km^3.

(c)   Water use in industry

Although the industrial sector in Viet Nam is not yet developed, water use for industrial purposes has increased drastically. In 1980 the amount of water use was 1.5 km^3 and in 1995 it was 2.86 km^3. A rough estimation for 2000 is 16.3 km^3.

(d)   *Water use in aquaculture*

Viet Nam has one million hectares of freshwater surface, 0.4 million hectares of brackish water surface and 1.47 billion hectares of river surface. The fish production was 285,000 tons in 1989 and 310,000 tons in 1990. Earnings fishery from export was US$170 million 1989 and US$205 million in 1990.

(e)   *Water use for hydro-power*

The country has more than 500 small hydro-power stations with a total installed capacity of 4 billion kw. Four large hydro-power plants have been constructed recently, namely, Thac-ba (108 MW), Da-nhim (160 MW), Tri-an (420 MW), and Hoa-bin (1,920 MW). The total hydro-power production at present is 11 billion kwh per year amounting to about 50 per cent of the country's total electricity production.

(f)   *Water use in navigation*

Viet Nam has 40,000 km of the navigable stretch of rivers and canals, of which 4,000 km is deeper than 2 m, 2,700 km with a depth of 1.5-2 m, 2,800 km with a depth of 1.2-1.5 m, 11,700 km with a depth of 0.9-1.2 m, and 18,000 km less than 0.9 m. Currently a total of 13,000 km of rivers is used for navigation: 6,000 km in the North, 6,500 km in the South and 500 km in Central Viet Nam.

(g)   *Water use versus water availability*

The total water use by all sectors of economy by the year 2000 is expected to be under 80 km^3, while the annual water availability is estimated at 853 km^3. However, water shortages are being experienced at certain sites and are expected to get worse in the near future. Already, in the dry season (February through May), there has been considerable competition for fresh water, particularly in the coastal towns where there is saline intrusion.

C. Status of water pollution

At present there are only a few waste water treatment plants in the country to treat industrial and domestic effluents before they are discharged into the receiving water bodies. Consequently, lakes, rivers and canals in the country are highly polluted. For example, in Hanoi 300,000 m^3 of wastewater are discharged without treatment into rivers and canals every day; in Ho Chi Minh city, the figure is 500,000 m^3/day; and in Viet-tri industrial centre it is 170,000 m^3/day. Due to over-exploitation of groundwater, the water table in the wells have been lowered by up to ten metres. This accelerated salinity intrusion and sometimes caused landslides.

Viet Nam has already undertaken certain measures to protect its water against pollution. More than 5,000 km of river dykes, 1,800 km of sea dykes and hundreds of other salinity intrusion prevention as well as flood protection works have been constructed. Laws and regulations aimed at protection of water resources have been promulgated.

D. Conclusions and recommendations

Considering that by the end of this century the population of Viet Nam is expected to reach 80 million, the country is expected to face water shortage. Therefore, for sustainable development and use of water resources water demand should be used particularly in the agriculture sector that uses most of the country's water resources.

Human activities and water works have serious impacts on sustainable development of water resources. Watershed management, water pollution control reduction of water related disasters are urgent problems to be solved in the country.

In view of the above, national water strategies and policies should be formulated; an inventory of water resources and water uses should be carried out; programmes for conservation and protection of water resources should be formulated; establishment of effective legal instruments and institutions should be carried out; and integration of water resources development and management into overall national socio-economic plans should be planned and implemented to achieve sustainable water resources development in Viet Nam.

XVIII. WATER RESOURCES ISSUES IN SMALL ISLANDS
OF ASIA AND THE PACIFIC*

A. The small island setting

Because of their size, geology, topography and climatic conditions, small islands have very serious problems related to availability of water. Due to their smallness, total volume of rainfall on such islands is small, and most of it is lost to evapotranspiration and run-off. On high rise islands (mostly volcanic), even those having high rainfall, there are seldom good water storage sites. Flash flooding is frequently a problem, and water discharges rapidly into the sea without having been beneficially used. On limestone islands, which are mostly flat and low lying, there are no possibilities for large-scale surface storage.

Volcanic rocks of the high rise islands do not in many cases form good aquifers. In the limited cases where suitable porous rocks do occur, deep drilling is needed to reach groundwater. Close to the shorelines where groundwater can be found at shallow depths, there is a considerable risk of intrusion of sea water. On flat limestone islands, groundwater may be present in thin lens-shaped bodies which are found in a very delicate equilibrium with saline sea water that can easily be destroyed by improper extraction, droughts or tidal waves. In addition, being so close to the ground surface, such water is very easily contaminated by human and industrial wastes. Not having opportunities for surface storage and very limited groundwater reserves, small islands suffer much more from the effects of droughts than larger countries.

Because of the factors listed above, there are many difficulties in small islands associated with providing a dependable supply of water to meet domestic, commercial, agricultural and industrial requirements. In many atolls there is insufficient water to meet even the most basic human needs.

Whereas in larger continental land masses, a single water resource type will suffice to satisfy most demands, to solve water supply problems in small islands, it is necessary to develop several types of water

---

* Prepared by the ESCAP secretariat.

---

resources. Marshall Islands use rain water collected from the international airport runway, as well as groundwater and desalination of sea water. Solomon Islands use rivers, springs and drilled wells for water supply to Honiara.

To investigate and assess the water resources potential for each island, to plan a rational exploitation of the resources, and to design, construct and operate water supply systems requires a substantial number of trained professionals and technicians. None of the small island countries has individually the capacity, funds or resources necessary for the exploration, assessment, planning and development that is required to solve its water supply problems.

In a number of islands demand for water already exceeds availability. Decisions have to be made regarding the allocation of water among the various sectors, at least in the medium term, with periodic adjustments envisaged. Some island countries, such as Singapore, have developed sophisticated water plans. Other island countries may also need to develop detailed plans for the supply and use of water.

B. Water use on islands

In most island countries, characterized by rapid population growth and economic development, water demand has increased in all economic sectors. Competition for the limited water resources available has developed among urban communities, rural communities, tourism, newly established agro-based or mining industries and subsistence agriculture.

Water use in most Pacific island nations is dominated by domestic consumption and tourism; these sectors will probably continue to account for a large proportion of total water use on many small islands. The other water use categories are relatively minor in most situations, as there is generally no large scale commercial, institutional or industrial development on small islands.

As for agricultural use, much of the natural vegetation occurring on small islands in the tropical regions of the world receives adequate rainfall for growth. The natural vegetation consists of a variety of trees, particularly coconut trees, and a range of bushes and grasses. These do not require irrigation, as they have adapted to local climatic conditions. Some of the natural vegetation is remarkably salt tolerant and can grow in brackish water with relatively high salinity levels. The coconut tree is one such example, as it has been observed to live and produce coconuts of good size and taste in brackish waters with salinity levels of up to at least one-third that of sea water.

Irrigation schemes on small islands, where they exist, tend to be relatively small. At the low water usage end, root and tuber crops, such as aroids, yams, cassava and sweet potato, are cultivated in the Pacific islands. One important example is swamp taro, one of the aroids, which is cultivated on some coral atolls such as in the Republic of Kiribati, in natural depressions or large pits excavated to the water table.

At the higher water usage end, cash crops such as sugar cane are commercially grown using irrigated water supplies on some islands. Apart from the Hawaiian Islands, there is no large scale irrigation carried out in the small islands of the Pacific Ocean. It is not expected that this situation will change, owing to the shortage of suitable land and soil conditions, high capital cost and lack of farming experience.

In most cases, industrial and commercial usage of water is a small proportion of total usage on small islands, mainly because of the limited development of such enterprises on small islands.

A broad distinction can be made between potable and non-potable uses. At the consumer level, potable water is generally used for drinking, cooking, bathing and washing. Particularly in water-short areas, however, the quality of water required for various purposes needs to be assessed. Potable water is required for human consumption, and specific guidelines have been published for this purpose (for example by WHO).

Non-potable water can be used, however, for many purposes including toilet flushing, fire-fighting, bathing and washing, recreation (i.e., sea water swimming pools), cooling in industrial plants, electric power generation and freezing, and irrigating non-edible crops. Typically, non-potable water is derived from sea water or brackish groundwater, treated waste water or "grey" water. Brackish

groundwater is sometimes used on very small islands such as coral atolls, for all purposes except drinking and cooking. Sea water is sometimes used for bathing. Treated sewage effluent, another source of non-potable water, is sometimes used for purposes such as watering of gardens and lawns. The quantity of water used or required to meet different demands varies according to local conditions.

C. Development of water resources on small islands

Of all the problems in the water supply field, one of the most interesting is that of obtaining fresh water on small islands surrounded by sea water. The islands are generally permeable, consisting of sand, lava coral or limestone, so that sea water is everywhere present at some depth below ground surface.

Thus, in addition to the conventional surface and groundwater systems, on small islands a variety of water development techniques not used widely in other settings can be found: infiltration galleries and tunnels for "skimming" water; rain-water catchments for potable purposes; use of lower quality or brackish water for many applications; barging of water between islands; and desalination.

The choice of technologies depends on technical feasibility and economics. Planning is necessary to make sure the water requirements of the population are met, and other demands are also fulfilled.

D. Management of water resources

The first priority of any water management policy is to ensure that the population has an adequate and safe water supply, which means that water is available in sufficient quantities for basic needs such as drinking, cooking and personal hygiene and that water is free of harmful concentrations of chemical, bacteriological and biological substances.

In many island countries a water authority is given responsibility for ensuring the adequacy and safety of water supplies. In a number of less developed and sparsely populated islands, however, there may be no authority to take on this responsibility. In such circumstances, adequacy and safety of water supplies are very much left to the control of local communities or individual households.

Because of the limited quantities of reliable water resources available on most small islands, potable water is vulnerable to various contaminants and to competition among users. It is therefore desirable to have a single organization involved in the planning and development of water resources. To allow for the expansion of the activities of a public utility into a wider management framework, the guidance of a Water Resources Board with representatives of Health, Public Works and other government departments may be helpful.

Water management at the central level involves interaction among a number of government bodies and the livelihood of the whole community. It includes legislation, administration and strategies for dealing with a wide range of water-related activities. Even on islands which are politically attached to governments on larger land masses, there is a need for many aspects to be dealt with locally, including operation, maintenance, training, and administration, sometimes by a local island council or similar body.

At the village level, water management might be partially entrusted to an individual or group of individuals. This is generally to relieve water authorities of minor maintenance matters and to allow community participation in the operation of facilities. This might include some supervision of communal tanks or public standposts to ensure an equitable distribution of supplies and to ensure that wastage is minimized. Village level management is often appropriate in the case of island groups where a central authority might exist on a more urbanized and populated island, and where there are insufficient resources to provide for the continual presence of water supply personnel on the outer islands.

In situations where individuals commonly provide their own supplies through roof catchments and water tanks, it may be possible to establish a system of state support for community investments such as large storages. Water quality would be under the supervision of the water agency or utility.

The protection and conservation of existing fresh-water resources are particularly important in island settings. Conservation of water cannot be achieved without considering the social and cultural values and habits of the people. In traditional societies there may be ways of conserving or preserving the resource that have not been incorporated into modern

laws. On the other hand, some population groups may have no traditional attitudes regarding storage and conservation of water. They have been accustomed to utilizing water in its natural condition and to allow it to flow freely from a gutter, tank, spring or faucet. It is therefore necessary that the concept of water conservation be assimilated by the population together with basic concepts of health and hygiene.

The usefulness of computer models and modelling in the management of groundwater resources has been proved in many continental and island situations. In some cases, however, other simpler and cheaper methods may be more appropriate for effective water resources management.

In order for a computer model to be effective, adequate data must be collected and the model must be physically realistic, properly calibrated and then later verified. There must also be, staff sufficiently trained to use such a model. Often there are either insufficient data or expertise to warrant the use of a computer model for management purposes.

1. Demand management

In many small islands, with limited water resources, it has become necessary to control the demand for water (which can be equated to consumption of water for present purposes). In order to reduce demand for and wastage of potable water, a number of measures can be introduced, including:

(a) Use of non-potable water for some applications including flushing, garden watering and fire fighting;

(b) Restrictions on water supply (and interrupted supplies at certain times);

(c) Effective maintenance, including leak detection and repair;

(d) Consumer education regarding rational use and conservation;

(e) Reduction in supply pressures;

(f) Regulations for use of water-saving appliances;

(g) Increasing the cost of water to consumers.

Restrictions on and rationing of water supply in times of drought may be necessary to conserve available potable water supplies. It is indicative of inadequate water supply systems, however, if interrupted supplies or restrictions on use are required on a regular basis. Other policy measures to encourage more rational use are obviously preferable.

Pricing can serve as an important instrument of policy to further a number of government objectives and allocate scarce resources efficiently. Recovery of project costs, especially for funds that are borrowed, is the primary and immediate objective. Projects which contain mechanisms for cost recovery and which promise to be self-supporting are most likely to attract the necessary finance. Such mechanisms may include direct collection of fees, revolving funds or cross-subsidization. The other objective of pricing policies is to improve efficiency in use. Users will have an incentive to use only the amount of water they need, when additional quantities entail higher costs per unit.

Pricing structures must be appropriate to the goals and needs of the water utility and the population served. In areas where water is plentiful and easy to obtain, low income families might be required to pay only a fee to cover operation and maintenance costs. In water-short islands, high progressive tariffs may be required, with low fees for basic consumption, rising sharply with greater use. In such cases a cross subsidy situation may exist, where high-income consumers such as hotels will subsidize the costs of distribution to low income families. Such policies require full scale metering, especially if progressive rates are charged.

In rural and some peri-urban areas, it is often not practical to expect consumers to pay for water on a volumetric basis. It may, however, be appropriate to levy a fixed charge per household for covering costs of communal systems, based on size of household, size of property or distance from water source.

A water Committee or Water Users' Organization must generally take responsibility for the collection of fees, as well as for operation and management of a water facility, if it is to function properly. Only if the community has a stake in the project and can perceive a benefit from it, will it willingly pay the costs of operation and maintenance.

2. Water quality

Water quality problems on small islands are extensive and varied. In many cases these are similar to problems experienced on larger islands and continental land masses but are often far more severe, owing to more limited opportunities for water supply development.

On many small islands, groundwater quality has deteriorated or could potentially deteriorate as a result of several factors. Overpumping of fresh-water lenses has often led to sea-water intrusion and an increase in salinity. In addition to pollution problems, there are other water quality problems associated with naturally-occurring water on some islands. These include: high hardness levels and occasional problems associated with elevated hydrogen sulphide levels. The latter are noticeable in areas where vegetation such as taro has been allowed to grow at the level of the water table on coral atolls.

The fresh groundwater resources of coral atolls and low-lying limestone islands are, in general, particularly susceptible to pollution owing to relatively thin and highly permeable unsaturated soil zones. As a result, normally accepted minimum distances from excreta disposal units, such as pit latrines, to groundwater extraction points are often inadequate in these situations.

Surface water quality can also deteriorate as a result of pollutants such as petroleum products and general urban litter. Surface waters are particularly vulnerable to pollution from toxic or other chemical spills. Toxic chemicals from timber treatment industries have caused spillages and fish kills on some islands, and chemicals from the mining industry are an actual and potential threat to surface waters on a number of small islands in Papua New Guinea.

Untreated or partially treated sewage is a source of biological pollution to surface waters on a number of small islands. This problem is widespread on small islands where there are significant concentrations of people.

Drinking water on small islands, as elsewhere, should satisfy recognized standards for physical, chemical, microbiological, biological and radiological water quality. In some cases national criteria have been produced, but in most cases the World Health Organization guidelines for drinking water quality (WHO, 1996) will be appropriate for small island water supplies.

The WHO guidelines give detailed listings of various water quality standards, with important information and advice on related water quality matters, such as planning for surveillance and control, inspection, methods of collection and testing, preventive and remedial measures, and community education and involvement.

3. Manpower development

The total number of personnel required to staff a water authority or similar organization in a small island setting is dependent largely on the extent, location and complexity of the water facilities.

The type of personnel required can be separated into professional, technical and administrative staff under the leadership of a general manager or administrator.

Out of a total population of approximately 1.3 million in eight small island countries (Cook Islands,

Western Samoa, Tonga, Fiji, Vanuatu, Solomon Islands, Tuvalu and Kiribati), each year there are between 200 to 250 potential graduates of institutes of higher education in all subjects. With such a small number of nationals available for advanced education, it has become practical to establish regional training institutes in specialized disciplines in the larger countries such as Fiji, Papua New Guinea and Western Samoa. Few Pacific Island countries have sufficient technical staff. With the possible exception of Fiji, nearly all the others have only one or two indigenous people in senior technical positions.

A regional training centre could be useful for advanced or technical courses. The most frequently requested activities for the region are the Water Resources Management Certificate, the Laboratory Technician's Refresher course, the Instrumentation Maintenance and Repair course and the Pre-employment Science Workshop.

XIX. CONCLUSIONS AND RECOMMENDATIONS

The following conclusions and recommendations are based on the study and analysis of information provided by countries concerning the status of sustainable development of water resources which are considered applicable to countries in Asia and the Pacific.

A. General

As the world is entering a period in which there is increasing competition for fixed water supplies, growing risk of water pollution, and increasing economic, social and environmental costs of development, a new look at water policy, particularly in developing countries, becomes necessary.

To ensure that development is sustainable, environmental and developmental activities must be fully integrated and, as an entity, more closely coordinated. For example, development activities such as cutting trees for fuel or lumber from the watersheds upstream from reservoirs has led to accelerated erosion and siltation that shortened the useful life of reservoirs, over-exploitation of groundwater has resulted in saline intrusion, lowering of groundwater levels and sometimes ground subsidence. Such development is not considered sustainable as environmental considerations has not been taken into account. Too often, the economic and social benefits of projects are emphasized and their negative environmental impacts are not given adequate consideration. With regard to storage reservoirs, these adverse impacts include silt entrapment, loss of water by evaporation, shoreline erosion, salinity and waterlogging in irrigation schemes, spread of waterborne diseases, degradation of landscapes and other amenities, destruction of wetlands and floodplain fisheries, etc.

Water resources come from systems which include rivers, lakes, wetlands and aquifers. Their planning and management must therefore be considered in association with their functions in the hydrologic cycle and their interactions with physical, chemical, and biological processes in terrestrial ecosystems. Developmental activities related to water are growing in number but their interrelated adverse environmental impacts are not always fully considered during the planning period. Withdrawals of water upstream may limit downstream supplies and agricultural, industrial, domestic and recreational uses may cause pollution incompatible with downstream uses. Each activity must therefore be planned to take account of the different values of freshwater systems including those associated with meeting domestic, industrial and agricultural needs as well as aesthetic and recreational values.

To meet the requirements of environmentally sound, sustainable development and management of water resources, the water policy should promote a multi-sectoral and multidisciplinary approach to integrated water resources planning and management that optimizes the interests of environmental protection and sustainable socio-economic development. By multisectoral, it is meant that all the water use sectors, namely, water supply for drinking and domestic use, irrigation, industrial use, navigation, etc., should be considered altogether in planning. Attempts to isolate any one of the sectors in the planning process, for example, water supply and sanitation sector, will adversely affect the objectives of environmentally sound, sustainable development and management of water resources. The requirement for multidisciplinary approach is based on the fact that sustainable development and management of water resources encompasses many disciplines such as engineering, economic, social, health, environment, legal, political, and other disciplines related to water development and management.

Integrated water planning and management endeavour to reconcile the conflicting demands of people to use water for different purposes in different places and on different time-scales with the environmental concerns that reflect all the functions of freshwater systems. It is therefore an approach to be strongly encouraged.

Because of the significant link between water resources and agriculture, forestry, terrestrial and aquatic ecosystems and urban development, degrading water quality and the misuse of available water resources impose a major threat to the health and development possibilities of the population in the region, even in areas with abundant water resources. Present lifestyle changes and aspirations, including significant increases in the standard of living and per capita income, continued rapid population growth, industrial development, agricultural trends and increased urbanization - all demand higher water consumption in the decades to come. This requires close attention to water-management issues and to adopt sustainable production and consumption patterns.

B. Principles and approaches

Water in rivers, lakes and underground is in permanent contact with other environmental compartments and, even more important, with a variety of socio-economic activities. Some of socio-economic sectors of importance are agriculture, forestry, energy, urbanization, industry, atmosphere, health impacts (drinking water supply). The protection and sustainable management of freshwater resources require an ecosystemic approach and an adequate knowledge and appraisal of linkages with environmental and socio-economic issues. First, there is a need to understand the nature and biogeographical implications of freshwater resources at the global, regional and local levels. Second, there is a need to recognize the cause-effect relationship between the environmental issues and the development of water resources for socio-economic development.

Integrated water planning and management, based on a comprehensive ecosystem assessment, taking full account of the use of water in human activities should therefore be the main principle behind the environmentally sound, sustainable development and management of water resources. Human use of the environment is an essential part of every day life and is an essential component in development. Integrated planning and management of water resources must therefore take full consideration of the use and potential benefits of environmental processes in human activities and must manage activities and resources with due consideration of environmental protection for sustainable development.

In developing countries, this is usually achieved through the setting-up of a national master water plan, which provides a framework for the planning of individual water development schemes and ensuring the optimization economic and social benefits while minimizing adverse environmental impacts as a result of thorough analysis and study of trade-offs between economic and social benefits as well as environmental impacts.

The use of systems analysis techniques in setting-up national master water plans helps to find solutions that can achieve optimum social and economic benefits while observing a series of conditions and limitation required for achieving environmental protection and sustainable development.

A commitment to integrated management must usually arise through legislation, planning or regulation to be put into effect action. Integrated water resources planning and management may be achieved through close cooperation between existing institutions or a new institution may be established to perform basin-wide integrated management. In any event, integration will require the best use of the resource compatible with development objectives, harmonization of methodologies and analysis, good communication and intersectoral cooperation.

The main components for the establishment of integrated water resources planning and management are: First, political credibility and commitment must exist, producing a basis for policy harmonization, administrative authority and conflict resolution. Second, organizational structures must be established with defined boundaries of responsibility, compatible objectives and the capacity for flexibility and change in the light of evaluation of progress. Third, processes and mechanisms for integrated management are needed, covering planning, pollution control, economic evaluation and enforcement. Last, organizational culture and participant attitudes must support integrated management, ranging from ministerial support, through interagency communication to staff training and recruitment policies.

The concept of water as a free common good must be reassessed and given a proper economic value, safeguarding the needs of the poor. Such an approach requires the establishment of a balance between economic, social, technical, organizational, managerial and legal measures and skills. Institutional frameworks should be decentralized in support of self-sustaining and socially relevant programmes, which include community involvement, with emphasis on the role of women. A participatory process, leading towards integrated water management must be enhanced and encouraged. To achieve this, a high priority must be given to human resource development and institution-building and strengthening. The new emphasis on human resource development should be expanded to train users with community-planned, developed and operated schemes, taking into account social, cultural or economic groups in water use, particularly women groups.

Far-reaching measures must also be taken to preserve the quality of water bodies and the physical integrity of aquatic ecosystems. New approaches, such as integrated pollution control, involving air, land and water, should be developed as a matter of urgency. Rational management of transboundary freshwater resources is another imperative, requiring increased cooperation among countries sharing international river basins in the region. Agreements should apply to rivers, lakes or groundwater, and should include the protection of the quality of receiving marine waters. Protection of the aquatic environment is of paramount importance for preserving life on earth.

C. National water policies

The essential elements of a national water policy may be grouped under two broad categories as preservation of the integrity of the natural water resources system and provision of water and water-related services to people in an economically efficient, equitable, environmentally sound and sustainable manner, using an integrated approach to water resources planning and management.

The natural water resources system consists of the components of the hydrologic cycle such as precipitation, evaporation, surface run-off, and groundwater flows, as well as other related components such as water bodies, soil, biota and atmosphere. Some of the major elements necessary for the preservation of the natural water resources system include:

(i) Establishing and maintaining an effective national hydrologic data system; coordinating this system with other specialized public and private data systems; establishing open access to these databank systems; participating in a national geographic information system combining data series on land, water and other resources; and promoting the highest scientific standards in all of these activities;

(ii) Sustained support for research on understanding the natural water resources system and its linkages with other natural resources and human activities;

(iii) Adopting appropriate spatial units for water resources assessment and planning such as the river basin or groundwater aquifer, so as to incorporate major land-water-ecosystem interactions;

(iv) Adopting conjunctive management of quantity and quality of surface water and groundwater to maintain the integrity of the hydrologic system and achieve efficient use of these water resources;

(v) Managing water resources for multiple purposes in order to capture complementaries and to reduce competition and identify trade-offs among uses in the natural water resources system;

(vi) Integrating environmental impact assessment into water planning, including the effects of development on aquatic and terrestrial ecosystems, on humans, and on the environment.

The requirements for provision of water and water-related services to people in an economically efficient, environmentally sound and sustainable manner can be grouped under three sub-headings: demand management, reduction of pollution from human activities, and establishment of appropriate mechanisms and institutions.

(a)   Demand management

(i) Adopting demand management as an integral part of water management, including formulating and evaluating demand reduction methods and strategies as complements to and substitutes for supply augmentation projects, in order to bring projected demands for and supplies of water into balance;

(ii) Using prices as a tool for demand management including volumetric pricing of supply or wastewater on the basis of marginal supply or disposal costs, along with increasing block rates. Where appropriate, seasonal pricing and temporary drought surcharges would be imposed;

(iii) Using efficient technical means to reduce urban water use and transmission losses in the supply system. This includes changes in plumbing codes to require water-saving plumbing fixtures, programmes of leak detection and control, and sustained operation and maintenance;

(iv) Recycling and other technical means to reduce withdrawal rates for water for industry, especially for cooling;

(v) Using technical means for reducing irrigation water use, including drip irrigation, sprinkler irrigation, land levelling, canal lining, along with institutional means such as modifying water rights systems to encourage efficient use of irrigation water;

(vi) Use of lower-grade water for certain domestic, commercial, industrial and agricultural purposes. The use of brackish water and treated wastewater for non-potable purposes often involves installation of dual water supply systems.

(b)   Reduction of pollution from human activities

(i) Reducing generation of pollutants at the source, through changes in production processes, by-product recovery, and wastewater reuse, making use of technical advice, regulation and enforcement, pricing policy, and tax incentives;

(ii) Adopting a polluter pays policy including the levy of effluent charges adequate to achieve desired reduction of pollutants, and earmarked to finance the clean-up costs of residual pollution;

(iii) Installing basic sanitation facilities in rural and low-income urban areas, including community involvement in planning and installing and maintaining low-cost facilities meeting minimum standards;

(iv) Reducing water pollution from agricultural, grazing and forestry activities, by lowering sedimentation from soil erosion, cutting discharges of pesticides and fertilizers, and reducing the saline content of irrigation return flow. Tools which may be used are subsidies (where appropriate), removal of perverse subsidies, changes in property rights, tighter regulation of forestry activities, and enforceable stipulations on types and methods of application of agricultural chemicals.

(c)   Establishment of appropriate mechanisms and institutions

(i) Establishing a national water code, which may involve private ownership of surface water and groundwater rights (riparian or prior appropriation), full

government ownership, with rights to use (including limitations) granted by government, or mixed public-private rights to water use which recognize water as a collective good. The code should include a water rights system which recognizes the hydrological realities of surface water, groundwater and return flow linkages, and the stochastic nature of precipitation and stream flows;

(ii) Approach to recognization for water resources management, including integration of activities of different agencies at the planning and implementation stages, spatial integration by river basin, water resources demand region, or political jurisdiction, and division of responsibilities for water resources management among national, provincial, local public, and private sectors. The activities involve water allocation, regulation of use and abuse, development, preservation, and operation of water supply and treatment facilities;

(iii) Establishing unified national objectives and priorities for water resources management, including setting guidelines for resolving the conflicts between national economic growth and self-sufficiency, regional development, equitable income distribution and social impacts, environment quality, and sustainability of the resource base;

(iv) Developing constructive international agreements on water management, involving equitable sharing of benefits and costs of development/ management of international river basins, and clear definition of rights and responsibilities of affected nations;

(v) Guiding national investments in water resources development by means of capital investment budgets and programmes, national-local cost-sharing, international or bilateral grants and/or loans, cost-sharing by provincial, local and private agencies, and private investment;

(vi) Adopting project formulation and evaluation criteria involving benefit-cost analysis, risk-assessment analysis, and multiple objective (including environmental impact) analysis, to be used for project and programme feasibility studies and monitoring and evaluation of performance;

(vii) Establishing a better balance between the creation of new projects, such as dams and irrigation systems development and management focusing on more efficient use of existing facilities;

(viii) Planning for involuntary resettlement from development projects, such as storage reservoirs, so as to minimize economic and social dislocation, promote development opportunities, and mitigate adverse effects in an equitable manner;

(ix) Adopting workable approaches to deal with water conflicts that emphasize negotiation and mediation rather than confrontation;

(x) Approaches for allocation of water and waste assimilation capacity that take account of interdependency of water uses and the role of pricing policy. Alternative approaches that may be considered include allocation through water markets with clear property rights, allocation through planning, and a combination of these two;

(xi) Approach towards centralization versus decentralization of water planning and implementation; for example, reliance on a highly-centralized national irrigation or power agency versus regional or local irrigation agencies, depending on a particular situation;

(xii) Promoting public involvement/local participation in project planning and implementation, especially for irrigation, upstream watershed management and rural and urban water supply and sanitation projects;

(xiii) Providing for adequate funding of project operation and maintenance, for example, from user charges, especially for projects to be turned over to local water users for operation and maintenance;

(xiv) Planning for effective monitoring and ex-post evaluation of projects.

The establishment of appropriate institutions is an important factor for achieving effective integrated water planning and management. In reviewing the progress made during the International Drinking Water Supply and Sanitation Decade, it was observed that progress in the formulation and implementation of national policies and objectives was hampered by the fragmentation of governmental authorities concerned with water development at either the urban or rural sector.

D. Effective techniques for integrated planning and management

Effective integrated water resources planning and management should provide optimal benefits to the society, that is, it should contribute as much as possible to the alleviation of the basic problems of poverty in developing countries, while avoiding serious damages to ecological populations and environmental quality.

It should be noted, however, that a single framework for effective integrated water resources planning is not possible for all countries and regions, given a wide diversity of their natural resources, population distribution and styles of living, economies, political, institutional, and legal structures, and other characteristics. However, some overall principles of planning may be identified based upon experiences with planning in many developing countries and the tools that are available for assessment and analysis.

Integrated water resources planning should have two principal goals: (I) to plan environmentally sound programmes and projects that are economically efficient and socially desirable, and (ii) to execute projects that will be sustainable over a long period of time, irrespective of the continued availability of external financial or technical assistance.

Appropriate administrative organization and good leadership within these organizations are very important in water resources planning and management. Adequate manpower, manpower training, organizational power, and removal of legal impediments, are needed for effective exertion of leadership. Mechanisms must be developed for proper coordination of the national, sectoral, and project organizations involved in planning, and for other organizations and individuals involved in or interested in water resources planning.

To be effective, integrated water resources planning and management should give proper attention to:

(i) Legal, institutional, budgetary and other constraints;

(ii) Planning objectives at national, regional and local levels;

(iii) Physical interrelationships among the units of a water resources plan;

(iv) Supporting infrastructure that is needed to secure the products and services of a plan, their distribution to beneficiaries, and the benefits and costs of the plan;

(v) Identification of all appropriate alternatives for development, preservation and enhancement with different contributions to planning objectives and different amounts of products and services;

(vi) Possible trade-offs among objectives, purposes, and effects of a plan;

(vii) Externalities of the plan;

(viii) All effects of the plan including those of engineering, economic, environmental, social, legal and institutional nature;

(ix) Contributions by engineers, economists, biologists, and other disciplines related to the plan;

(x) Contributions by agencies representing all economic sectors affecting or affected by the plan;

(xi) Involvement of groups or individuals affected by or interested in the plan, particularly women's groups;

(xii) Method of presenting the features and expected results of the plan so that it can be commented upon by all interested parties and assessed and acted upon by decision makers.

E. Minimization of adverse environmental impacts

The debate on conflicting interest between environmental protection and development has been going on over the years. Recently, there has been a wider acceptance of the fact that the development desired by countries should be compatible with the environment, sustained, and economically feasible.

Some of the useful methods to minimize adverse environmental impacts from water resources development projects are: economic cost-benefit analysis of environmental change, economic incentives and regulations to protect the environment, environmental subsidies, tax credits, and effluent fees.

The cost-benefit analysis (CBA) is a technique designed to measure the economic feasibility of a water project or activity over time. By including the economic value of some environmental benefits and costs in the CBA analysis, it is possible to assess projects from the economic and environmental points of view. CBA, however, has been applied to the environment with only relative success as it incorporates only those impacts to which a monetary value can be readily assigned.

Economic incentives and regulations to protect the environment include: establishment of government regulations (environmental laws, pollution standards), creation of formal procedures and mechanisms to obtain licenses and registration, promotion of economic mechanisms to improve environmental protection and to discourage pollution and resource depletion. These approaches are found to be successful in industrialized countries. However, they might not be equally successful in developing countries since their effectiveness depends on the existence of appropriate monitoring programmes, institutional support and specialized staff. In this connection, it should be emphasized that establishment of a water quality monitoring system is a prerequisite for effective water quality management.

Environmental subsidies are a simple form of economic incentive to abate pollution, by which governments can make substantial grants to local waste treatment plants and some industrial operations.

Tax credits are special provisions of income tax systems which grant tax exemptions in order to achieve various social or economic objectives. As the use of tax credits for environmental protection has both advantages and disadvantages depending on a particular situation, this mechanism should be used only when there is definite advantage over direct environmental protection grants or comparable alternatives.

Environmental deterioration can be reduced by imposing significant environmental fees. Effluent fees are the least expensive method of producing pollution abatement. First, the fee induces the polluter to develop more efficient abatement techniques, or to install pollution control equipment. Second, polluters will locate in areas where their damage to the environment is the least.

One of the promising methods of augmenting water supplies without environmental implications is desalination. It has found wide application in oil importing countries in desert areas and also in other higher income areas with deficient rainfall and/or storage capabilities.

Adverse impacts of water resources development can be prevented or mitigated by reducing the scale of the projects or by the use of management techniques and other non-structural alternatives. The reduction of demand for water from existing projects by more efficient use of water or by recycling, has also been found to be effective.

Most developing countries do not yet have sewerage systems to collect used water, that may be considered for reuse or recycling. It is therefore unlikely that this approach will be feasible for domestic uses in the developing countries in the foreseeable future for reasons of cost and health implications. It may however find increased application for agriculture and industry.

In areas of intensive agriculture, return flows represent an important source of water supply. However, the use of return flows can produce adverse environmental impacts as they have higher salinity compared to the surface or groundwater from original source.

As regards groundwater planning and management, it should be emphasized that the evaluation and forecasting of the quantity and quality of available groundwater have not only economic importance, but also ecologic and sanitary significance as the safe yield of an aquifer is usually limited by the natural replenishment rate, water quality constraints, environmental and other factors.

Many years of research on cloud seeding and reducing evaporation of reservoirs to enhance water supplies, so far has not yielded encouraging results for general application.

Efforts to minimize adverse environmental impacts must take into consideration gender issues. Women, who are the providers of basic family needs including water, food and fuel, are often more susceptible to deteriorating environment conditions. Women have a great potential for contributing towards environmental protection and resource enhancement and should therefore be provided with appropriate opportunities for full participation in the process of water development planning, decision-making, and environmental protection.

F. Towards ensuring financial sustainability

A set of indicators which can be used to assess the sustainability of water resources projects are identified by the World Bank as follows:

1. Continued delivery of services and production of benefits

(a) Comparison of actual and intended benefits and services and their stability over time;

(b) Efficiency of service delivery;

(c) Quality of services (benefits);

(d) Satisfaction of beneficiaries;

(e) Distribution of benefits among different economic and social groups.

2. Maintenance of physical infrastructure

(a) Condition of physical infrastructure;

(b) Condition of plant and equipment;

(c) Adequacy of maintenance procedures;

(d) Efficiency of cost-recovery and adequacy of operating budget;

(e) Beneficiary involvement in maintenance procedures.

3. Long-term institutional capacity

(a) Capacity and mandate of the principal operating agencies;

(b) Stability of staff and budget of operational agency;

(c) Adequacy of interagency coordination;

(d) Adequacy of coordination with community organizations and beneficiaries;

(e) Flexibility and capacity to adapt project design and operation to changing circumstances.

4. Political support

(a) Strength and stability of support from international agencies;

(b) Strength and stability of support from the national government;

(c) Strength and stability of support from provincial and local government agencies;

(d) Strength and stability of support at the community level;

(e) Extent to which the project has been able to build broad base of support and to avoid becoming politically controversial.

To provide a checklist for measuring current projects and a guide to the design and implementation of future projects, the Food and Agriculture Organization of the United Nations (FAO) has suggested the principles of sustainable development as follows:

1. Consult with villagers, farmers and all other participants. Reach agreement on both problems and solutions before taking action;

2. Plan small-scale, flexible projects. A plan should be a blueprint, not a prison. It should be able to incorporate new information that emerges during the project;

3. Let the people benefiting from the project make the decisions. The experts' job is to share their knowledge, not impose it;

4. Look for solutions that can be duplicated in other areas for the greatest impact on development. But the solutions must still be tailored to fit local needs;

5. Provide education and training, particularly for young people and women, who remain the most effective agents of change because they are bound to the realities of the family's survival;

6. Keep external inputs to a minimum to reduce dependency and increase stability. Subsidies, supplements and inappropriate technology are unsustainable;

7. Build on what people are doing right. New ideas will be adopted only if they do not run contrary to local practice. New technologies must support existing ones, not replace them;

8. Assess impacts of proposed changes. A multidisciplinary team, ideally including specialists from the same culture, should look at economic, social, cultural and environmental aspects;

9. Consider both inputs and outcomes. The failure of projects focusing on a single outcome, such as agricultural productivity, has proved that more is not always better;

10. Maintain or improve the participants' standard of living. Long-term environmental improvements are unsustainable unless they also address the problems which the poor are facing today.

G. Techniques for water conservation and wastage prevention

Conservation of freshwater resources is an important factor for the achievement of a sustainable development process.

Future sector development should be environmentally sustainable and viewed in the broader context of water resources. Water demand management techniques involving appropriate legislation, pricing policies and enforcement mechanisms have recently been recognized as the best approach to achieve water conservation and protection. In many cases, the cost of saving water is significantly lower than the cost of incremental supplies.

Some of technical and regulatory measures for water conservation include: use of non-potable water for some applications including flushing, garden watering and fire fighting; restrictions on water supply (restrictions on certain uses and on pumping); effective maintenance, including leak detection and repair, and rehabilitation of existing systems; consumer education regarding rational use and conservation; reduction in supply pressures and interrupted supplies at certain times; regulations for use of water-saving appliances; and increasing the cost of water to consumers.

The amount of water lost through leaks in the distribution network of water supply service can be substantial. Wastage can be prevented or minimized through the reduction of leaks and unaccounted-for water in the distribution network. Water is also lost through infiltration when it is transported in open canals to farms and agricultural areas, or when the reservoirs overflow after heavy rains. This problem has been solved in Israel by lining the canals and by pumping the reservoir overflow into the aquifer.

For locating lakes and reducing unaccounted-for water, utilities can place meters on the main pipe on each block to measure how much water is being used in that particular area or lost through leaks, either in the system or inside homes. In Brazil, government authorities have launched a multi-pronged effort to reduce unaccounted-for water that include: installing meters in private houses as well as on water mains; detecting leaks; updating cadastres (to learn which houses had legal connections, and thus, determine which had illegal ones); improving maintenance and renovating ageing installations.

When forced to save, agriculture and industrial sectors will start looking at the whole production process to use what measures can be taken. For example, farmers tend to use large quantities of water inefficiently. However, when prices rise, they install sprinkles, line the irrigation canals to prevent seepage, or grow crops that use less water. Similarly, industry use has numerous ways to conserve water through minimizing wastage.

The water rates paid by agriculture and industry should be high enough to force them to conserve, since they can do this more easily than the domestic sector. Further, their waste is unnecessary and environmentally harmful, since by using excess water, they produce excess waste that had to be discharged into the environment and causes contamination.

H. Application of appropriate watershed management practices

Environmental degradation of water catchment area is a threat to a reliable and acceptable water supply. Deforestation by lumber industries, charcoal merchants, agriculturalists and land speculators reduces rainfall in water catchment areas and changes clear streams, rivers and estuaries into carriers of the upper layers of fertile topsoil. As a result, water availability for both domestic and productive purposes is seriously reduced and water quality and the potential for low-cost treatments such as slow sand filtration, are adversely affected.

Watershed management has increasingly been realized to be an essential component of sustainable development. Its main purpose is to ensure that hydrological, soil and biotic regimes, on the basis of which water development projects have been planned, are properly maintained or even enhanced.

The two main problems that can be solved by proper watershed management are reservoir sedimentation and changing patterns of streamflow.

Sedimentation is a normal and unavoidable process in all reservoirs. However, application of proper watershed management methods can reduce the rate of sedimentation and prolong the useful life of the reservoirs. The main purpose of watershed management should be to reduce sediment generation in the catchment area so that storage losses of reservoirs can be kept to an acceptable level. Some of the main watershed management techniques that can be used to achieve this include increasing forest cover in the upper catchment areas, developing and implementing appropriate land use policies and preventing overgrazing. It should be noted that the results of watershed management take time to be visible. For example, of afforestation is practised, some improvement may be noted in about a decade or so. Because of the long interval needed between the beginning of an afforestation process and some observable impacts, afforestation should be initiated during the planning phase of a project.

Changing patterns of streamflow are caused by erosion of stream channels. After the sediment loads carried by a river are deposited in a reservoir, the discharge of clear water from reservoirs may create erosion problems downstream and cause channel erosion. Thus, erosion and sediment problems are interrelated.

Watershed management practices to solve erosion and sedimentation problems may be classified into two categories: structural and non-structural.

Structural measures may be defined as any measure to change or improve the surface configuration of the earth by structural protection works or to construct permanent structures of earth or masonry to protect soil from erosion by water and also to conserve water. These include interception by diversion channels, drains and waterways, conservation tillage practices, terraces, gully control structures and check dams.

The non-structural measures for erosion and sediment control may be further divided into two groups: technical and non-technical. Technical measures include providing cover crops, crop residues and mulch farming, planting forests and grass barriers.

These measures normally provide the best overall means of providing permanent erosion control on wildlands. Long-term conservation work usually involves biological measures, such as afforestation or range improvement, which may be done complementary to structural measures.

Non-technical measures, which are no less important than technical measures, are particularly concerned with giving motivation to the people directly involved in the application of technical solutions in the field. Non-technical measures may include planning, education, legal, social, political and economic.

I. Integration of women in planning and management

Development must improve the quality of life for men and women equally. Recently, there has been an increasing awareness of the specific role that women play in the process of promoting social and economic development, and in the management of natural resources. Women, who are the providers of basic family needs including water, food and fuel, are the first to resent the burden of inappropriate environmental management resulting in problems of water quality, food scarcity, and deteriorating living conditions. Women's reproductive role is an additional aspect which specifically links women and the environment.

The General Assembly by Resolution 45/181, endorses the four guiding principles, as enunciated in the New Delhi Statement (adopted at the Global Consultation held in New Delhi, 10-14 September 1990), pertaining to the need to protect environment and health, the need for institutional reforms, including the full participation of women, the need to promote community management and the need to adopt sound financial practices and appropriate technologies.

Women are often more perceptible to deteriorating environmental conditions and tend to be among those primarily affected by the deterioration of quality of ground and surface water for drinking and other purposes as a result of improper water and wastewater disposal, treatment and recycling facilities. Reduced rainfall and increased erosion from deforestation have also decreased the availability of water and soil for family food production, which is an important task of women in most rural areas. Consequently, preservation of water sources and of the

environment is increasingly an area in which development objectives and women's concern should go hand in hand.

Women should be considered not only as beneficiary or target groups, but also as active agents who can contribute to generating ideas in policy, mobilizing labour, providing resources, and disseminating and implementing innovations. For example, by involving women in the planning and management (including operation and maintenance) of water and sanitation projects, the sustainability of these projects can be enhanced.

Women represent a noteworthy potential for environmental management and resource enhancement. In spite of the importance of women's involvement in environmental protection and development, they are not yet provided with appropriate opportunities to fully participate in the process of planning and management of water resources. This indicates an urgent need to modify development strategies and activities in order to include the participation of women in water development planning and environmental and resource management. For women to be involved, it is necessary for governments and cooperating external agencies to adopt a policy of commitment to the involvement of women in development activities, particularly water supply and sanitation activities.

It should be noted that there is no single rule or model for integrating women into planning and management of water projects, which is suitable for all situations. Different approaches need to be developed for involving women according to different situations. namely, a society where women are actively involved in economic production, a society where men's and women's tasks differ and areas of responsibilities and contacts are strictly divided, a society where women have no immediately visible role in decision-making, and a society where there is large number of female-headed households. Besides the type of society to which to adapt the forms and means of women's participation, the type of projects also makes a difference. Three factors which play an important role are the size of the project, nature of the intervention and level of participation.

As regards involvement of women in management planning, women are usually elected to mixed management committees in integrated societies except when formal barriers impede their election. In societies with segregation of men's and women's work, it would be advisable to establish separate women's committees for management.

J. Trends and practices outside ESCAP region

Due to the advanced nature of their economic and technological achievements, countries of the Economic Commission for Europe (ECE) region are leading in the application of ecosystems approach to planning and management of water resources.

This approach requires integrated management because of the need to control water resources in the context of the whole environment that encompasses both the natural environment and human activities. The ecosystems approach covers the whole range of interdisciplinary and integrated activities for water basin protection, pollution control, water supply, treatment and planning for future needs. The availability of reliable and adequate information and effective communication are central to the success of this integrated management where monitoring, environmental assessment, modelling and forecasting are essential. Management of freshwater resources is now being integrated with management of marine water quality in many countries of the ECE region.

K. Action to be taken at both national and international levels

1. Integrated water resources management

Information should be made available to national governments and institutions by international agencies and donor bodies on the benefits and urgent need for integrated management. National governments should draw up policy plans and feasibility statements for integrated management, detailing changes to existing frameworks, financial implications, operational elements, monitoring, planning and management structures. Reference should be made to development plans, social and economic implications, sustainable use and to the time framework within which integrated management would be implemented.

As part of an integrated management plan, an integrated pollution control policy should be planned and implemented. This should be a low and non-waste policy, aiming to control pollution sources through land use policy, recycling and recovery, clean technology

and substitution of hazardous substances and techniques. A cradle-to-grave management policy for hazardous substances should be planned, with clear identification of responsibility. Economic tools should be developed for all pollution control. Emergency pollution plans should be developed and regularly tested.

International and national bodies should continued to research and test appropriate techniques for pollution reduction and control, particularly with reference to diffused sources such as agriculture and domestic wastewater. International agencies should produce concrete proposals for technology transfer for pollution control.

2. Monitoring and assessment of freshwater resources

Plans for water quality monitoring networks should be drawn up, where they do not already exist, by national governments for measuring both quantity and quality of surface and groundwaters. These plans should be consistent with national priorities for water use and pollution law enforcement, and aimed at environmental assessment and protection.

Existing national monitoring networks should be modified to meet the needs of integrated management requiring cooperation between existing institutions. Governments should encourage cooperation and adoption of standard methods for data collection, analysis, reporting and interpretation. Regional agencies should encourage harmonization in monitoring and water quality assessment and cooperative procedures for monitoring on a regional scale of large-scale processes.

International agencies should provide information, advice and case studies on the setting-up of water quality standards or effluent standards, drawing attention to information requirements, regulatory procedures and suitability for different situations. National governments should draw up plans for the setting and enforcement of such measures in the context of integrated management plans.

National laboratories should work within an integrated network, including standard procedures and equipment, data handling, reporting and interpretation. Cooperation and communication should occur at all levels between national agencies and should be encouraged through organizational structure and policy. Quality control and quality assurance should be a standard procedure, the results of which should be readily available.

Impartial advice should be made available on equipment procurement as to which techniques and instruments are suitable for which purposes, how to gain access to regional service centres and continuing technical support, what are the approximate unit costs and minimum staff knowledge requirements. International agencies must encourage parties to bilateral aid agreements to consider such issues.

Human resources development should include technical education on quality control, standard methods, good laboratory practice and management. Personnel policies should encourage the retention of expertise and the development of indigenous capacities for development of monitoring and assessment.

Research is required in almost every subject. Of particular urgency is the application of temperate techniques to tropical countries as such methods normally require verification and research. Biological monitoring is particularly prominent in this respect. Research is required for model verification in tropical conditions and development of groundwater quality models is particularly urgent.

3. Integration of environmental and developmental factors

The central concept of human activity occurring within and relying upon the environment should become central to water resources management and development. Awareness of the role of the environment in human uses of water should be vigorously promoted at all levels of organization, ranging from politicians and managers to the general public. Its potential role in sustainable development should be stressed.

The collection of information on the characteristics of the environment and the degree of exploitation should be integrated into plans for development. Such information should be collected as data, maps and qualitative material and should be viewed as a prerequisite of detailed planning, in order that limits of sustainable development can be accurately predicted at an early stage. Continuing monitoring and

assessment of environmental quality are essential to management evaluation of meeting objectives.

Management objectives and planning must be defined in term of human activity within the environment and must fully recognize the importance of the environment in sustainable use and future development. International agencies and national governments should produce case study material of the integration of environment and human activity in management plans, drawing attention to strengths and weaknesses. Management workshops or study material should encourage environmental analysis and decision-making.

Preservation of certain water resources should be regarded as a natural extension of intersectoral management of natural resources. Detailed information, data and management plans are essential for effective conservation, taking account of the likely effects of development in other areas in terms of environmental quality and human movements. Suitable legal provisions must be made and effective regulation designed. In some cases it may be possible to unite preservation interests with controlled tourism, groundwater protection, erosion control or socio-cultural policies.

4. Supply of adequate quantity and quality of fresh water

Freshwater availability on an equitable and adequate basis can only be achieved if this vital resources is no longer considered a free common good or a social service. Its economic value has to be taken into account when reallocating the spare resource among competing users. To this end, a judicious balance of technical, organizational, managerial and legal measures is required, including administration regulations and effective enforcement mechanisms.

Water conservation and saving programmes, for example, high-efficiency irrigation techniques, require an appropriate pricing policy and tariff structure. Technical improvements alone have not been sufficient. Similarly, the quality of freshwater resources has to be protected through water pollution control programmes which make the polluter pay for the necessary treatment and clean-up measures.

The Global Consultation on Safe Water and Sanitation for the 1990s, held in New Delhi, September

1990, also recognized that drinking water supply is not simply a technical issue, but also a crucial component of social and economic development. To this end, the Consultation recommended the following four Guiding Principles:

(i) protection of the environment and safeguarding of health through the integrated management of water resources and liquid and solid wastes;

(ii) institutional reforms promoting an integrated approach and including changes in procedures, attitudes and behaviour, and the full participation of women at all levels in sector institutions;

(iii) community management of services, backed by measures to strengthen local institutions in implementing and sustaining water and sanitation programmes;

(iv) sound financial practices, achieved through better management of existing assets, and widespread use of appropriate technologies.

These principles should guide developing countries in preparing specific national strategies for the use of freshwater resources.

5. Human resources development (HRD) for freshwater management

The requirements of HRD for freshwater resources should be assessed on a national basis, taking account of existing and required personnel and skills.

Awareness of the potential for HRD should be promoted at all levels, and it should be implemented at all levels. from politicians and managers to field workers and users. The value of non-governmental organizations for HRD should be further explored. Education and publicity should be viewed as important factors in public awareness and HRD.

For sustainable development, decentralization of management and devolution of responsibility will increase reliability when coupled with suitable training and mobile technical support. Explicit strategies for water resources management should be produced with reference to HRD at all levels, including needs

assessment, planning, design, implementation and evaluation of progress.

Training plans should be task-oriented and should become a permanent part of the management and personnel structure. Technical and managerial skills must be a priority but local training courses for field workers and community-operated schemes must be developed. Development of suitable training materials should continue.

Regional training centres should be considered where expertise is sparse and exchange programmes for technicians instituted. International construction projects should include training in operation and maintenance for local staff.

HRD should be adapted to specific socio-cultural and linguistic groups. Special attention must be given to the role of women. The momentum and experience gained by governments and UN agencies in the last decade must be maintained and developed.

International agencies should promote the importance of HRD in their programmes and institute regular communication on strategies and techniques, identifying areas of common interest and possible cooperation.

6. Strengthening of institutional capacities

International agencies should address the need for development of management and financial capabilities for water resources through the publication of reviews of specific issues in management and finance, such as economic tools and tariffs, cost control, planning and capital investment. Research with specific reference to developing countries for management and finance should be encouraged and information disseminated through publicity material and workshops. Guidelines for the setting of standards for supply, treatment, discharge and environmental quality should be produced. Sustainable and rational use of resources should be promoted.

Advice in preparing and implementing legislation and regulations should be made available to national governments, especially where the future effectiveness of institutions is concerned and where multisectoral and integrated management of water resources is planned. Comparative studies of legislation should be prepared by international agencies, covering such subjects as water supply and sewerage and cultural influences on legislation for water use.

Detailed guidelines for the assessment of institutional, financial and legal feasibility should be produced for use in individual projects and as part of the routine management of water resources. Recommendations have been made to international agencies that they should establish sections dealing specifically with institutional development (capacity-building) and that national governments should be helped to draw up plans for such development.

Technical improvements must be planned with consideration of social and cultural issues. The concept

of appropriate technology should be integral to the management of water resources to encourage sustainable methods in financial and technical terms. Tied aid should be avoided and national institutions should cooperate in efforts to standardize equipment.

Information exchange and availability must be expanded at all levels through publicity, seminars and education. Users should be made aware of the value of information, of what is available and how to gain access to it. National and international information suppliers should address real needs and provide suitable information in the required format and language. International agencies should cooperate on database operations and encourage some uniformity in the ways in which information is made available by and through national organizations.

T

Sophie
Sandi - mom
Cindy - mom